PENGUIN

1971

Major General Ian Cardozo was commissioned at the Indian Military Academy into the 1st Battalion of the 5th Gorkha Rifles (Frontier Force), where he received his basic grounding as a young officer. Thereafter, he took part in the Sino–Indian war of 1962, the Indo–Pak war of 1965 and the Indo–Pak war of 1971.

Wounded in the battle of Sylhet in Bangladesh, he overcame the disability of losing a leg and became the first disabled officer of the Indian Army to be approved for command of an infantry battalion and brigade. He thereafter commanded an infantry division and retired as Chief of Staff of a corps in the north-east. On retirement, he worked in the area of disability with an NGO and as vice president of the War Wounded Foundation, before being appointed by the Government of India as chairman of the Rehabilitation Council of India, where he worked for nine years.

He is a military historian, author and war poet. His books and poems have been widely acclaimed. His poems have been set to music and feature worldwide on leading music platforms. He is also working with an illustrator on graphic novels about the courage and competence of the Indian soldier, of which twelve have been published so far.

ADVANCE PRAISE FOR THE BOOK

'This is a unique compilation. Never have I learnt about a war through such vivid, personalized and humane stories. One comprehends not just the planning and execution of the war but most importantly the psyche and conduct of the soldiers in battlefields; their courage, dedication, honour and sacrifice. The story "And Then There Was One" left me with goosebumps. Ian Cardozo, himself wounded in this war, has produced a masterly account in this racy (like this war) and unputdownable book'—General V.P. Malik, PVSM, AVSM, ADC, former Chief of the Army Staff

'A splendid anthology of wartime tales from the inspired pen of an iconic soldier and war hero who brings alive, in these pages, India's finest hour, in all its fascinating dimensions and often through the enemy's eyes. These compelling stories of sacrifice and valour of our soldiers, sailors and airmen are a "must-read" for every Indian—especially the Gen X and millennials'—Admiral Arun Prakash, PVSM, AVSM, VrC, VSM, former Chief of the Naval Staff

'Ian Cardozo's collection of short stories on the 1971 war is crucial for understanding why the "two-nation theory" behind the partition of British India in 1947 was decisively rejected after the independence of Bangladesh. Written with humanism and pride in the professionalism of India's armed forces, this book highlights the importance of treasuring our soldiers' acts of valour and sacrifice, which have for more than a century provided the foundation for India's proactive role in international relations'—Asoke Mukerji, former Ambassador of India to the United Nations

'This book is a delightful bouquet of short stories with the backdrop of the 1971 Indo–Pak war, encompassing all three defence services and both the theatres. Each story is gripping and holds one's attention from start to finish. Reading through these stories, one gets a flavour of how operations are conducted in combat and the human elements involved in them. Written in an easy style, the book is a must-read and leaves you yearning for more'—Major General A.J.S. Sandhu, VSM (retd), author and military historian

'The author, an iconic soldier, has skilfully put together the personal experiences of soldiers, sailors and airmen in a book that tells the stories of what really happens in war. His own first-hand experience of the wars of 1962, 1965 and 1971 makes each story come alive with the drama of life and death. The stories include views of the other side of the hill and bring out rare insights into the human side of the protagonists. The book is a complete package of true, gripping and inspiring sagas; a must-read for all well-wishers of India'—Major General Gopal Gurung, AVSM, SM (retd), second-generation soldier of the 5th Gorkha Rifles (FF)

'Reading General Ian Cardozo's *1971* is like going on a historical walk with a guide who knows every nook and corner of the warzone, and is willing to show it all to you. He holds your hand and takes you through tales of incredible bravery, but also pain and loss, bringing you so close to his characters that you almost feel their breath upon your face. Seeped in history, peppered with fascinating anecdotes, these stories are told with great flair, sometimes making you laugh, sometimes bringing a tear to the eye. And to his credit, despite having been in the war himself, he shows you both sides of the conflict, often taking you inside the borders of Pakistan and into the minds of the decision-makers on the enemy side as well, paying odes to the courage of both armies. There would be very few people now living who know more about the 1971 war than General Cardozo; after all, he fought it himself. But for me, the most endearing quality of the book was that he wears that distinction so lightly, narrating his own stories with delightful wit and self-effacing charm. He features in a few of the narratives but walks in and out of these with such reticence that you recognize him only if you look closely enough. Often, he does not even mention himself by name. General Ian Cardozo's *1971* is a book that I shall keep at my bedside for a long time. No one else could have written it'—Rachna Bisht Rawat, author

'The Indian armed forces have served the nation with honour and fidelity in numerous conflicts since Independence and before it. Their tales of valour and devotion to duty are legends. Yet these have been largely confined to the domain of the officers' mess or the unit langar or narrated around campfires in remote border outposts. These true stories—woven together by a master storyteller and one of India's most distinguished soldiers—bring to life intrepid deeds of our nation's soldiers, sailors and airmen during India's finest hour—the 1971 Indo–Pak conflict'—Squadron Leader Rana T.S. Chhina, MBE (retd), Secretary, USI Centre for Military History and Conflict Studies

'*1971*—authored by the Hero of Heroes, General Ian Cardozo—is a first-hand account of a war hero for whom it was always "do or die" in the line of duty for his country. Many men can make history, but only great men can write it. General Cardozo is one of those who can do both. His book is about the Liberation War of Bangladesh of 1971, the sacrifices and birth of a nation through a tidal wave of blood. This war was fought for the cause of humanity, which makes it a just war. His book reflects the tremendous cooperation between the Indian forces, Mukti Bahini and the common people of Bangladesh. It reflects the brotherhood of men at arms who chose to fight on their feet rather than die on their knees. Let history say that they together brought to Bangladesh the winds of freedom and justice. I had the honour to see this brave commander being almost blown apart in the battlefield of Mirapara near Sylhet, and I dare say that despite the severe pain he had to endure, he refused to receive transfusion of blood of Pakistani soldiers. To me, this book revives my memory of that day when he bled almost to death under the shadow of the sword. These stories appear to me more of a ballad of blood and sacrifice than a record of history. His blood has mingled with the muddy soil of Bangladesh, and victory was achieved by sacrifices such as his. The author has told us tales few can tell. As such, his indomitable spirit is reflected in his writings in this book'—Lt Col (retd) Quazi Sajjad Ali Zahir, Bir Protik, Swadhinata Padak, Padma Shri

'Breath-holding suspense and drama of a race against time galvanize the epic sweep of action over land, seas and skies in Ian Cardozo's wartime stories. The psychological depth of his deft, finely nuanced character delineation and his vigilant eye for situational ironies and philosophical inferences are striking. The stories highlight the remarkable leadership, ingenuity and exemplary heroism of our troops in the face of heavy odds and casualties suffered during a thirteen-day war that effectively stopped a barbaric genocide in India's neighbourhood'—Vanita Singh, folk singer, composer and writer

'General Cardozo has done yeoman service by compiling this labour of love that describes important episodes of the Indian Army during the India–Pakistan war, where our soldiers and officers proved their tenacity in battles and found innovative ways (jugaad, as we call them) for overcoming both physical and mental obstacles, and succeeded. The book is much more than history; it is about the actions of gallant officers and men of the Indian Army, their indomitable spirit, their unmatched bravery and, above all, their sacrifice for the nation, which in many cases snatched victory from near-hopeless situations. There could not be a better author to compile and pen these heart-warming stories than General Cardozo, who not only fought in many battles but was also disabled, losing a leg in one of the fiercest battles of the 1971 war. This engrossing book is for the youth of the nation, nay, for all citizens; it will rekindle the interest of all who wear military uniforms or have donned them in the past'—Lieutenant General Vijay Oberoi, PVSM, AVSM, VSM, former Vice Chief of the Army Staff

1971

STORIES OF GRIT AND GLORY FROM THE INDO–PAK WAR

IAN CARDOZO

PENGUIN
VEER
An imprint of Penguin Random House

PENGUIN VEER

USA | Canada | UK | Ireland | Australia
New Zealand | India | South Africa | China

Penguin Veer is part of the Penguin Random House group of companies
whose addresses can be found at global.penguinrandomhouse.com

Published by Penguin Random House India Pvt. Ltd
4th Floor, Capital Tower 1, MG Road,
Gurugram 122 002, Haryana, India

Penguin
Random House
India

First published in Ebury Press by Penguin Random House India 2021
Published in Penguin Veer 2022

10 9 8 7 6 5

The views and opinions expressed in this book are the author's own and the facts are as reported by him which have been verified to the extent possible, and the publishers are not in any way liable for the same.

All sketches/diagrams in the book are the perception of the author specifically created to explain his views in this book, and the use thereof shall remain limited to interpreting/inferring the author's views in this book.

ISBN 9780143454557

Typeset in Adobe Garamond Pro by Manipal Technologies Limited, Manipal
Printed at Thomson Press India Ltd, New Delhi

www.penguin.co.in

MIX
Paper
FSC FSC® C010615

To
the men and women of the Indian armed forces,
the Mukti Bahini
and the peoples of India and Bangladesh,
who stood together in this moment of trial
and ultimately savoured victory in war,
the liberation of East Pakistan
and
the birth of Bangladesh

Contents

Foreword

This publication is a very well-timed one as we are celebrating the twin historic occasions of the golden jubilee of our independence and the birth centenary of our Father of the Nation, Bangabandhu Sheikh Mujibur Rahman. I thank the author for dedicating the book to, among others, the valiant people of Bangladesh and the Mukti Bahini, who demonstrated the highest degree of gallantry under Bangabandhu's supreme leadership during our War of Liberation in 1971.

This book gracefully features the root of historic ties of special friendship between Bangladesh and India, anchored in shared values of justice, freedom and human dignity. We are forever indebted to the government and people of India, who generously stood by us in helping us realize our long-cherished dream of independent Bangladesh. I like to refer to this special relationship as a 'bond of blood'.

The book is also a great source for us to learn about the tremendous personal travail, sacrifice and loss that the author experienced during our Liberation War. I salute the bravery, dedication and heroism Gen. Cardozo exhibited as a true warrior.

He was a dutiful son of his country in the face of death. His writings will reinforce and challenge readers, in both the countries, in their understanding of history and help them define our heritage and cultural identities. He marched to the valley of death in 1971, and surely he is in the best position to write about that period. Let history say that he participated to liberate our beloved motherland and helped bring the wind of freedom.

I am equally proud to learn that he mostly fought in the greater Sylhet district, where I hail from. His evocative battlefield stories also reminded me of the pains, perils and sufferings that my family and I personally went through, and the sacrifices that we had to make in 1971.

On 3 April 1971, when the Pakistan Army tried to disarm the EPR (East Pakistan Rifles), many of them, instead of surrendering, took shelter in private houses. Around 12–14 took shelter in our house. Our house was well located.

On 4 April, when the Pakistan Army came near our house, the EPR jawans opened fire and the battle continued for around four hours. We were inside the house but did not die, although a part of our house was badly damaged due to mortar attacks by the Pak Army. On the following day, when Pakistani bombers started bombing, we left the place for Fulbari, around 10 miles away from the city.

On 20 April, the Pak Army came to our area, and there was three hours of shooting. That battle is known as 'Boitikarer Juddha'. When the battle was over, the Pak Army detained me and inflicted injuries while torturing me. During the next eight months, we were fugitives, and on 4 December 1971, when Prime Minister Indira Gandhi of India responded to Pak bombing of Indian airports, we were delighted. On 12 December, the Indian Army, led by a Colonel, came to our empty house; it was full of Pakistani weapons and leftovers, and they cleaned it. Since I was working with the civilian regional coordinator, Dewan Farid Ghazi, MNA, I had the privilege of meeting many Indian Army officers, and they were very nice to us. We developed a good rapport with them during our difficult days.

I wish the author all the very best for this book. I am confident that our present and next generations will immensely benefit from this treasure trove of glorious history.

A.K. Abdul Momen,
MP, Foreign Minister, Government of
the People's Republic of Bangladesh

Preface

'The greatest love a person can have for his friends is to give his life for them.'

—Gospel of John, 15: 9–17

The year 2021 marks fifty years since the 1971 war was fought between India and Pakistan. Probably, very few people today would remember that war. Besides, a new generation has grown up that has no memory of it at all. The fiftieth anniversary of that war is therefore an opportune moment for the people of India to know how the war started, was conducted and brought to a close.

An official history of the war has been written and published by the Government of India, but history makes heavy reading, and perhaps the time has arrived for every citizen of India to have access to what happened during those turbulent days in the form of stories. Everyone loves a good story, and I hope these true stories from the battlefield will reach a wider audience and open a window to the man in the street as to what happens during a war in the life of a nation, and in the lives of the officers and the men they lead into battle.

Leading men into battle is a privilege given to very few. It is an awesome responsibility because of the underlying understanding in the minds of the combatants that they may never come back alive. Leadership, therefore, has necessarily to be of the highest order. The officers of the Indian Army lead from the front and the exhortation is 'Follow me!' Therefore, percentage-wise, the casualty rate of officers of the Indian Army is very high. In my own battalion, the 4th Battalion of the 5th Gorkha Rifles (FF), we entered the 1971 war with eighteen officers, and at the end of a thirteen-day war, four were killed and seven badly wounded. Only seven were left unscathed or with minor wounds.

The Indian soldier is among the best in the world. He follows his officers unquestioningly and with great courage, and undergoes great discomfort in unbelievably difficult circumstances. Together, the officer and the men he leads are a formidable combination.

The accounts that follow are true stories based on the personal experiences of participants, on oral and written narratives, and on historical fact and recorded interviews of officers and soldiers of both sides, conducted after the war was concluded. However, some of the dialogues of the Pakistani military hierarchy have been reconstructed on the basis of the information available at that time, and are probably very close to what took place. On the Indian side, those who are part of these stories would recognize themselves; and then there are others who were part of these events but may not have known the whole story.

I have tried to make these stories reader-friendly. Detailed descriptions of operations have been avoided to ensure that the reader does not find it difficult to follow the flow of events, and the accounts have been shorn of military terminology.

Footnotes give the meaning of military terms that could not be avoided. A bibliography is also available at the end of the book for those who would like to refer to books that give more details of the war.

The preamble that precedes the stories paints an overall picture of the war. It is important that the reader reads it first, as it will facilitate an understanding of the stories that follow.

Each story has a message, and it is up to the reader to look for it and examine whether it could add meaning to his or her life.

Men and women of the armed forces are brought up on the credo of 'country first and self last'. This has become a way of life for us. Courage, honour, duty, discipline and sacrifice are values that are held in high esteem and are parameters by which we judge ourselves. War becomes a testing ground for the conduct of service personnel, and it is the manner in which we live and behave in peace that determines how we will fight and die in war.

I hope these stories will give the reader a reasonable insight into life in the armed forces—a profession that has no equal.

Preamble

'India wants to avoid a war at all costs but it is not a one-sided affair, you cannot shake hands with a clenched fist.'

—Indira Gandhi*

The origins of the Indo–Pak war of 1971 lay within Pakistan itself. In the spring of 1969, General Yahya Khan took charge from General Ayub Khan as President of Pakistan and announced that elections would be held in 1970. He, however, failed to anticipate the possible consequences of this election. The Pakistan National Assembly election of 17 December 1970 resulted in Sheikh Mujibur Rahman's Awami League of East Pakistan winning an overwhelming victory by securing 167 out of a total of 311 seats, which was twice the number of seats of Zulfikar Bhutto's Pakistan's People's Party. This totally upset the plans and perceptions of the Pakistani government with regard to retention of power.

Sheikh Mujibur Rahman and the people of East Pakistan were greatly elated at this landslide victory, which reflected

* *New York Times*, 20 October 1971, p. 6.

the simmering discontent that prevailed in the eastern wing of Pakistan against the dictatorial domination perpetuated by successive military dictatorships of West Pakistan. Except for religion, there was nothing common between the two wings. The clear mandate won by Mujib brought Bengali aspirations to a high point, and Mujib's 'Six Point Programme' promised to remove political and economic disparity between East and West Pakistan. The outcome also meant that the President, Prime Minister and most ministers of the Pakistani cabinet would be Bengalis from East Pakistan.

To the people of East Pakistan, this victory could not have been sweeter because ever since the creation of Pakistan in 1947, the western province had relentlessly usurped the authority and resources of her eastern partner. Most galling was the attempt to force the Bengalis to adopt Urdu as the national language. All that would now be a thing of the past, and East Pakistan would emerge as 'Sonar Bangla'* in her own right and with her old cultural traditions intact.

Sheikh Mujib, however, did not reckon with the predatory predilection of the politicians and the military junta of West Pakistan. Dismayed by this unexpected result, Zulfikar Ali Bhutto, who had no intention of letting power slip from his hands, threatened to plunge Pakistan into a civil war if Mujib was allowed to form the government. Yahya Khan also could not accept the prospect of power shifting to East Pakistan and of giving up military rule.

On 21 February 1971, President Yahya Khan dissolved his cabinet, imposed martial law on the country and, on March 1, announced an indefinite postponement of the promised

---

* Sonar Bangla: Golden Bengal.

National Assembly session. This infuriated the Bengalis, and the burning discontent of decades of oppression broke loose. All government and semi-government offices, central and provincial, shut down and agitated crowds took to the streets.

Curfew was imposed in Dhaka to quell the protests, but by 3 March 1971, Mujib's writ ran wide in East Pakistan. He called for a non-violent non-cooperation movement, but even he could not control the mobs. The Pakistan Army was deployed to suppress the agitation, and a large number of Bengalis were killed. Mujib demanded withdrawal of troops to the barracks, failing which he would intensify the agitation. Lieutenant General Sahibzada Yakub Khan, the Lieutenant Governor and Martial Law Administrator of Pakistan, a mature and balanced officer who had served with the Indian armoured corps before Partition, agreed to Mujib's demand, and the troops were pulled back. This was taken as a great victory by the Bengalis, and Mujib became the virtual ruler of East Pakistan.

Yahya Khan and the military viewed these developments with disquiet. On 6 March 1971, Yahya Khan announced that the National Assembly would meet in Dhaka on 25 March 1971. Simultaneously, a massive airlift of troops to East Pakistan commenced.

It was evident that the proposed date for the National Assembly meeting on 25 March was just a ruse to play for time, and all discussion during this period was a sham. On 7 March 1971, Mujib addressed over a million people at a public meeting and made four demands for participating in the National Assembly. These were: withdrawal of martial law, withdrawal of troops, inquiry into the killings by the army, and transfer of power to the elected representatives of the people.

Yahya Khan removed Lieutenant General Sahibzada Yakub Khan and replaced him with Lieutenant General Tikka Khan, who was soon to be known as the 'Butcher of Bangladesh'. Tikka Khan let loose a reign of terror and destruction, the likes of which have few parallels in history. In what became infamous as 'Operation Searchlight', the Pakistan Army used machine guns, tanks and rocket launchers against unarmed Bengali citizens. Men were slaughtered and women and young girls raped in an unprecedented orgy of violence by the military, which will forever be a blot on the officers and soldiers of the Pakistan Army. More than one million people were killed and thousands of women and girls raped by debauched Pakistani soldiers led by their depraved officers. The killings and rapes triggered off a mass exodus of men, women and children from East Pakistan to safety in India. Their number gradually swelled till they totalled over ten million. Their shelter, food, medical, hygiene and sanitation needs became the responsibility of the Government of India. The burden of refugee relief was estimated at over $700 million.

The tragic irony of this horrific holocaust is that it failed to ignite international condemnation by the Western world, which had stifled its conscience at the altar of political expediency. The United States of America declined to acknowledge the insanity of the situation and failed to raise its voice against this mass slaughter by her protégé, whom she had always patronized. This blot on the reputation of the American government can never be forgotten.

Sheikh Mujibur Rahman was imprisoned and spirited away to West Pakistan, and no one knew where he was held captive or even if he was alive.

India's protests went unheeded by Pakistan and the rest of the world. Besides the intolerable economic burden, it created grave security problems for India. These consequences—economic, political, social and military—were becoming unsustainable.

President Yahya Khan of Pakistan had, in the meanwhile, agreed to broker a meeting between President Richard Nixon of the United States of America and his Secretary of State, Henry Kissinger, with Chairman Mao of the Republic of China and his Premier, Zhou Enlai. President Nixon was deeply gratified and greatly indebted to President Yahya Khan for his offer to facilitate this meeting, and thereafter Pakistan could do no wrong. India was effectively isolated by a Pakistani–Chinese–American nexus.

When repeated attempts to find a reasonable solution with Pakistan failed, India sought the assistance of the international community to persuade Pakistan to see reason. Indira Gandhi, the Prime Minister of India, visited all the capitals of the major powers of the Western world to request them to use their good offices to persuade Pakistan to stop their genocide. However, the West, led by the United States, was indifferent to the holocaust in East Pakistan and the Indian dilemma, and they turned a blind eye to the mass murder being perpetrated by Pakistan against its own citizens. Western countries, following the lead of the United States, accepted that this was an internal problem of Pakistan and therefore did not warrant their intervention. The refugee problem, they stated, was India's problem and a solution had to be found bilaterally between India and Pakistan. The West and the United Nations had killed its conscience, equating Pakistan, the aggressor, with India, the aggrieved.

Pushed to the wall, Prime Minister Indira Gandhi decided to get into an 'Agreement of Friendship' with the USSR to counter the unholy alliance between America, China and Pakistan.

It was an agreement that was to stand India in good stead throughout the war.

An agitated Indian public began to demand immediate military action against Pakistan, and pressure continued to build up on the government to do so without delay.

Towards the end of April 1971, Prime Minister Indira Gandhi summoned the Army Chief to a cabinet meeting* and asked him to march into East Pakistan as the situation had become intolerable. General Manekshaw, however, informed the Prime Minister that the army was not ready. He stated that his continued requests to the Defence Ministry to make up the shortfall of arms, ammunition and equipment had been persistently ignored and that unless these were made up, the army was not in a state to go to war. He also informed the Prime Minister that the time was not ripe. There were valid reasons against early intervention—political, military, economic and climatic—that demanded a self-imposed delay. This, however, encouraged Pakistan to continue with her orgy of violence in East Pakistan.

It is to the credit of the Prime Minister and her government that they could withstand public pressure, in deference to the needs and reasons projected by the Indian military. It is also to the credit of the Indian Army Chief that he could stand up to the pressures of the government and an agitating public.

A review was carried out that took into account India's state of arms and ammunition, equipment, training, commerce and industry, road and rail communication, climate, weather, morale, international opinion and enemy options. All these

* Brigadier Behram M. Pantakhi and Zenobia Pantakhi, *Field Marshal Sam Manekshaw: The Man and His Times* (New Delhi: Niyogi Books, 2014), pp. 108-10.

factors pointed to a particular timetable for war that would suit India best. Sam Manekshaw emphasized that if war was inevitable and victory was the objective, then the war had to be fought on India's terms. Indian leaders accepted his advice and adhered to his programme, and the armed forces used the intervening period to gear up to meet the expected Pakistani offensive.

Each of the three Service Chiefs had their own points to prove in the 1971 War.* In the past, Sam Manekshaw had not been given the opportunity to command an infantry battalion. After Partition, although he was on the strength of the 5th Gorkha Rifles (FF) since Partition and subsequently posted to its 3rd Battalion, he was recalled from the New Delhi railway station, while he was on his way to join the battalion, and told that he had to accompany V.P. Menon to Srinagar in connection with Maharaja Hari Singh's request for military help against the marauding raiders from Pakistan. Sam spent the war in Military Operations (MO) Directorate. Prior to the Sino–Indian war of 1962, Sam had crossed swords with Defence Minister Krishna Menon, who wanted Sam to criticize the Army Chief, General Thimayya. Sam refused, and he was consequently effectively sidelined by Menon. An inquiry on frivolous charges was ordered and his promotion held up for eighteen months.

It was only when Menon was sacked after the debacle of the 1962 war that Sam's career was resurrected. During the 1965 war, Sam was commanding Eastern Command, which played no part in that war. Now that a war with Pakistan appeared to be unfolding in 1971, Sam was grateful that he was being given

---

* Air Vice Marshal Arjun Subramaniam, *India's Wars: A Military History 1947-1971* (Noida: HarperCollins, 2016), pp. 359– 60.

a chance to do something worthwhile for his country. He was determined to make sure that India won a resounding victory.

The Naval Chief, Admiral S.M. Nanda, also had a chip on his shoulder. During the 1965 Indo–Pak war, the navy had been kept out by an order of the defence ministry that the Indian Navy must not launch offensive operations against Pakistan on the west coast, as the government did not want to escalate the war. This, the navy felt, was a blow to its self-respect. When questions were asked, the government failed to state that the navy was left out of the war on its orders. Nanda, who subsequently was FOC-in-C West, stated that given a chance, he would set Karachi on fire. He put together a plan to defeat Pakistan in the Arabian Sea and the Bay of Bengal.

The Air Force Chief, Air Marshal P.C. Lal, had a different point to prove. His services were terminated in September 1962 by Krishna Menon after a disagreement on the replacement of the aging Dakota aircraft when Lal was Chairman of Indian Airlines Corporation. He, too, was reinstated only after Menon was sacked. As the Air Chief, he made sure that the Indian Air Force was fit in every respect as and when we went to war with Pakistan.

The sequence of these events ensured that the country had the best team of Service Chiefs to lead it into a war that seemed unavoidable.

Pakistan, as expected, launched her offensive with a pre-emptive air strike against India on 3 December 1971. By that time, the nation and the armed forces were well prepared, and counteroffensives launched almost immediately on the night of 3–4 December 1971.

India's strategy was based on 'an offensive in the east and offensive defence in the south, west and in the north. The east meant East Pakistan; the west meant the plains of Punjab and the deserts of Rajasthan; and the north meant the plains, hills and mountains of Jammu and Kashmir and Ladakh.

The period from April 1971 to December 1971 was used profitably by the government and the armed forces to review all possible options to achieve the country's national objectives. The first was the avoidance of war, if that was at all possible. Every possible diplomatic effort had been undertaken to avoid a war that seemed imminent. However, if war was forced upon India, then militarily, the armed forces needed to make up their deficiencies in arms, ammunition and equipment, and to train hard for a war that could take place at any time. Communications were improved, supply bases were created, bridging equipment was moved up and administrative plans were streamlined.

The morale of the Indian Army was unprecedentedly high because of wholehearted support by the government and little or no interference by the politicians and the bureaucracy. The country was also fortunate that it had at the helm of the armed forces Chiefs of formidable stature. All officers and men rallied to the call of their Chiefs to wrap up the war as quickly as possible, before the Americans, the Chinese and the Middle East countries could come to the aid of Pakistan. Imbued with this realization, the troops used whatever was available to cross rivers, minefields and obstacles, and to get to their objectives as quickly as possible. Improvisation and innovation were the order of the day, and immediate results were obtained in surmounting 'impossible' obstacles.

Whereas the initial aim in the Eastern sector was to capture as much territory as possible, so as to be able to be able to send the refugees back home, so quick were the successes obtained that the aim was changed. Dhaka was the 'centre of gravity' of

General Niazi's defence strategy, and the capture of Dhaka now became the new aim. So, the race for Dhaka commenced.

The Mukti Bahini,* or the Mukti Fauj, contributed much to the success of the operations of the Indian Army. They were trained rigorously by Brigadier Sant Singh and Brigadier Shabeg Singh to become the eyes and ears of the Indian Army, to be the interface between the army and the civil populace, and to conduct guerrilla operations against the Pakistani forces in East Pakistan. Their role depended on their background. Those who were ex-soldiers of the East Pakistani regiments and East Bengal Rifles conducted guerrilla operations against the Pakistani forces. There were others with no military background, and they served as guides and interpreters. Senior Majors of the East Bengal Rifles and East Pakistan regiments assumed the role of Sector Commanders and served alongside the army. A few of them, like 'Tiger' Siddiqui, Ziaur Rahman and Abu Taher, became known names within the Indian Army.

Officers and men of the navy of East Pakistan operated as 'frogmen' in the riverine areas of Chittagong, Khulna and Chalna, and inflicted heavy damage on Pakistan's merchant navy by mining water channels and using limpet mines to destroy Pakistani merchant naval ships. The naval element of the Mukti Bahini was later called Force Alpha and integrated with the Indian Navy.†

The strategy of General Niazi, the GOC-in-C of all Pakistani forces in East Pakistan, was based on what he called the 'Fortress Concept'. He had built his defences on strong points called 'fortresses', which he built on river obstacles and extensive

---

* Mukti Bahini/Mukti Fauj: army of freedom fighters.

† Arjun Subramaniam, *India's Wars: A Military History 1947–1971*, p. 357.

minefields. He believed that the Indian Army would attack these defences 'head on' and get bogged down in trying to overcome them, allowing time for the Americans and the Chinese and the Middle East countries to come to his rescue and for the UN to intervene. Indian forces, however, refrained from falling into this trap; they bypassed these defences and went for the rear of these defended areas, facilitating the speed of operations.

The Indian Air Force not only supported the army admirably but was also successful in interdicting Pakistani troop movements on land and on the rivers. Total air superiority established by the IAF in East Pakistan early in the war allowed the army to move on land and on water with impunity, and heliborne assaults, paradropping operations, air supply, casualty evacuation, amphibious operations and pamphlet dropping could be carried out by our troops unhindered. The only problem was that Indian aircraft did not have night-flying capability.

The amazing success of the Indian Navy needs recognition. In the Arabian Sea, the Western Flotilla launched an attack on Karachi. Missile boats of the Indian Navy demolished a destroyer, a minesweeper, two ammunition ships and badly damaged an oil tanker. They set the Kiamari oil refinery on fire, and Karachi burned for seven days and nights. The Pakistan Navy scooted into Karachi harbour and refused to fight. A naval blockade was established outside Karachi without the presence of Indian naval warships, and no foreign merchant ship was able to access the Pakistani port of Karachi without permission from Delhi—so great was the dominance established by the Indian Navy!

On the eastern seaboard, the Indian Navy was successful in intercepting all movement in or out of the riverine ports of Comilla, Chittagong, Khulna and Chalna. Frogmen of the Indian Navy and Force Alpha of the naval wing of the Mukti Bahini caused considerable damage to the merchant ships of Pakistan by carrying out underwater destruction of Pakistani merchant marine ships and rivercraft. The Indian Navy also carried out joint operations with the Indian Army in the amphibious landings at Cox's Bazar, and destruction and interdiction of targets with its aircraft operating from INS *Vikrant*. The brilliant conduct of the operations of the 'Silent Service' on the western and eastern seaboards needs to be better recognized.

Top leadership in all the three services was at its best. The main factor for success was 'timing' of the Indian offensive, and the timing was perfect. When Pakistan attacked India on 3 December 1971, India was ready—counteroffensives on land, sea and in the air were launched almost immediately. This was also a war where the armed forces, the bureaucracy and the politicians worked in perfect harmony. P.N. Haksar, the Principal Private Secretary to the Prime Minister, and D.P. Dhar, Head of the Foreign Policy Planning Committee, were the ideal interface between the armed forces and the government. The synergy between the government and the armed forces was excellent.

If the army had marched into East Pakistan in April, as was initially desired by the government, the result would have been disastrous. The state of the Indian Army's arms, ammunition and equipment was deplorable. The troops would have been caught by the monsoon—when rivers turn into seas and the ground gets swampy—and Indian armour would have got bogged down. The troops untrained for warfare in the marshes and bogs of East Pakistan would have performed inadequately. The higher military leadership, however, had the moral gumption to stand up to the government and convince them that victory needed a particular timetable when all these limitations were removed.

When it became clear that Pakistan was going to lose the war, the Americans and the Pakistanis did their utmost in the United Nations to stop the war and ensure a ceasefire. It was then that President Nixon ordered the US Seventh Fleet to move to the Bay of Bengal to rescue his beleaguered ally.

The Seventh Fleet was a strong naval force of eleven warships, consisting of the nuclear-powered air carrier USS *Enterprise*, destroyers, missile frigates, amphibious assault ships and a helicopter carrier. In a cable to President Nixon, the US Ambassador to India, Kenneth Keating, expressed disapproval of the move, stating that deployment of the Carrier Task Force was an escalation of the war by the United States.*

However, within the first ten days of battle, the Indian Army had broken the 'crust' of the Pakistani defences, and Indian forces were within striking distance of Dhaka. The paradrop close to Dhaka at Tangail, the artillery bombardment of Dhaka close to the headquarters of Pakistani's Eastern Command, and the air raid on Governor's House unnerved the Pakistani civil and military hierarchy, and Dhaka began to wobble. By the time the American Seventh Fleet reached the Bay of Bengal, the die was cast—the war had been wrapped up and Bangladesh was born.

The fighting in the Western sector was, however, not as conclusive, but that was in accordance with India's planned strategy. Although Pakistan attacked India in the Western sector, Indian strategy was defensive in nature, with a few offensive operations to improve the defensive profile. The Pakistan

---

* Ibid., p. 391.

Army was pushed back and several areas were captured. On the surrender of the Pakistan Army in East Pakistan, some of our troops were moved to the Western Front. The United States, which was monitoring the movement of India's armed forces, was alarmed and raised an outcry. However, the unilateral declaration of a ceasefire in the West by Prime Minister Indira Gandhi scotched world criticism of India being an expansionist country wanting to demolish Pakistan in its entirety.

The planning and conduct of this war by India makes for a fascinating narrative, which will unfold in the stories that follow. Suffice it to say at this stage that Indian planners pushed through an excellent strategy that was ably executed by well-trained and highly motivated officers, and by the troops they led into battle. The rest is history.

The Hunt for the *Vikrant*

'He, who has command of the sea, has command over everything.'

—Themistocles

Karachi, 8 November 1971

Commander Zafar Mohammad Khan, Captain of PNS *Ghazi,* had just teed off at the Karachi Golf Club* with his foursome when he received a message that he was wanted immediately at Naval Headquarters. Zafar was vexed and wondered what could be so urgent to interrupt his game of golf so early on a Sunday morning!

The Karachi Golf Club was located on Drigh Road, and the headquarters of the Pakistan Navy was located at Liaquat Barracks,† sector E-8, Karachi. It being a Sunday, there would

* The Chief of the Pakistan Navy was the patron-in-chief of the Karachi Golf Club and the Senior Naval Commander in Karachi its President. Naval officers posted to Karachi therefore felt encouraged and motivated to play golf.

† Pakistan's Naval Headquarters, which was established in 1947 at Karachi, moved to Islamabad only on 15 March 1975.

US Navy submarine USS *Diablo* moving towards Karachi for induction into the Pakistan Navy as PNS *Ghazi*.

be less traffic on the roads; however, it would still take him twenty minutes to reach the Naval Headquarters. Zafar hurried to the car park, and his driver came running when he saw Zafar approaching. Zafar jumped through the door that the driver held open for him and said, 'Naval Headquarters.' The driver, sensing the urgency, stepped on the accelerator and sped off. A warrant officer who was waiting for him at Reception took Zafar to the office of the Director Naval Warfare and Operation Plans.

The Director Naval Warfare and Operation Plans, Captain Bhombal, who was a few years senior to Zafar, was on the telephone talking to someone from the Submarine Directorate, but the conversation did not seem to involve anything operational. A cup of coffee lay untouched on his desk along with the *Karachi Times* open at the sports page. The situation seemed relaxed and peaceful. Zafar wondered what was the great immediacy that had made Bhombal interrupt his game of golf.

Bhombal smiled, waved Zafar to the chair in front of his desk and when he had finished his telephonic conversation said, 'I heard that you were on the golf course, Zafar. Sorry for interrupting your game, but this is urgent and important. However, first have a cup of coffee and then listen to what is in store for you.'

Over coffee, Bhombal informed Zafar that a war against India was likely to take place very soon and he would be playing a very important part in it. He paused for a while, let his words sink in and said, 'The Naval Chief has tasked you to destroy INS *Vikrant*, the flagship of the Indian Navy'.

Having made this dramatic pronouncement, Captain Bhombal walked over to a metal cupboard marked with a white diagonal cross, which indicated that it contained secret documents. He took out a folder and handed it to Zafar, saying, 'All that you need to know about the *Vikrant* is in this folder.'

The folder had photographs and all the relevant details of the *Vikrant*—its draught, deadweight, freeboard, displacement, the thickness of its steel plates, the location of its ammunition magazine and fuel tanks, its length (192 metres), beam-wise breadth (24.4 metres), the number and type of aircraft that she carried, details of its engines and boilers, and a mass of other technical details. He was also informed that the speed of the *Vikrant* had been reduced due to a crack in one of its boilers.

The Director informed Zafar that he had received all this information from the Pakistani Naval Intelligence and that the latest update was that the *Vikrant* was in Chennai, and that he needed to study the approaches to, and details of, Chennai harbour from naval charts available with the Hydrographic Section. Finally, he was told to immediately recall all personnel of the *Ghazi* who were not on board and to be prepared to leave within the next ten days to carry out his task.

'Zafar Bhai, it will be a tremendous achievement if Pakistan could commence the war with the sinking of the *Vikrant*, and great honour awaits you on the successful completion of your task. The Chief rang me an hour ago. He said, "Brief Zafar immediately, because he will need time to prepare for this most important mission." That is why I decided to send for you without delay.'

The Story of the Pakistan Navy, published twenty years later, in 1991, states:

> The Navy ordered the submarines to slip out of the harbour quietly on various dates between 14 and 24 November. They were allocated patrol areas covering the west coast of India, while the *Ghazi* was dispatched to the Bay of Bengal with the primary objective of locating the Indian aircraft carrier, the INS *Vikrant*, which was reported to be operating in the area.

The book goes on to say:

> The strategic soundness of the decision has never been questioned. The *Ghazi* was the only ship which had the range and capability to undertake operations in the distant waters under control by the enemy. The presence of a lucrative target in the shape of the aircraft carrier *Vikrant*, the pride of the Indian fleet was known. The plan had all the ingredients of daring and surprise, which are essential for success in a situation tilted heavily in favour of the enemy. Indeed, had the *Ghazi* been able to sink or even damage the aircraft carrier, the shock effect alone would have been sufficient to upset Indian naval plans. The naval situation in the Bay of Bengal would have undergone a drastic transformation and

> carrier-supported military operations in the coastal areas would have been affected. So tempting were the prospects of a possible success, that the mission was approved despite several factors that militated against it.

The other submarines mentioned in the book were the Daphne-class submarines that were given other tasks on the western seaboard.

Orders recalling all personnel of the *Ghazi* on leave were immediately sent out and Zafar commenced making his plans for the destruction of the *Vikrant*. A day later, on 9 November 1971, he called his team of officers to the war room of the *Ghazi* and briefed them on their task and his tentative plan, explaining what he wanted done. He gave them three hours to provide the details he wanted, so that he could make his plan with specifics. He also gave directions for the *Ghazi* to be refuelled and resupplied, and for the checks to be completed for its tasks before it set out on its long journey to destroy the *Vikrant*.

Bombay, June 1970 to November 1971

A year prior to the conversation between Commander Zafar and Captain Bhombal of the Pakistan Navy, Captain Swaraj Prakash—Captain of the *Vikrant*—was looking at the report given to him by his Chief Engineer. The report stated that cracks and leaks had occurred on the water drum of the A1 boiler of the *Vikrant* and that long-term repairs were not feasible indigenously.

The report put him in a dark and sombre mood. The *Vikrant* was once again in trouble. Earlier, during the Indo–Pak war of 1965, the *Vikrant* had been unfit for war because of mechanical problems. This time, due to a crack in a boiler, the

Vikrant would now be able to work up a speed of just twelve knots, making it difficult for her aircraft to take off. Carriers need a minimum speed of 20–25 knots into the wind to allow them to put their aircraft in the air.

HMS *Hercules*, a light-attack fleet carrier, was purchased by the Government of India from Britain in 1957. She was built in 1943 but could not take part in World War II, because by the time she became fit for duty World War II had ended. HMS *Hercules* had to be overhauled and refurbished, became part of the Indian Navy in 1961 and was renamed INS *Vikrant*. Her new name meant victory and unassailability.

It didn't seem like the *Vikrant* was living up to its name. Her slow speed would also make her a vulnerable target of Pakistani submarines. Unless a solution to the problem of the errant boiler could be found, it looked as if the *Vikrant* would once again be left out of battle in any future war, and that was not a pleasant thought.

By June 1971, the possibility of a war with Pakistan had arisen. Concerned about the need for air cover for offensive operations at sea, the Indian Navy tried to work out how the *Vikrant* could best be utilized. Pakistan's Daphne-class submarines, procured from France, were far superior to the two Indian submarines of the Western Fleet—INS *Karanj* and INS *Kursura*—and the *Vikrant* in its present state would be an ideal target if she sailed in the Arabian Sea. Considering this fact, Naval Headquarters recommended that it would make more sense for the *Vikrant* to be moved to the eastern seaboard, where she would be away from the threat of the Daphne-class submarines, which did not have the necessary endurance to function that far from their base at Karachi. If, by that time, the boiler could be repaired, then the *Vikrant* could use its aircraft to conduct operations against the ports of Chittagong and Khulna off East Pakistan.

Sea trials were conducted for the *Vikrant* to see how much speed could be worked up using the other three boilers, and a speed of sixteen knots was achieved without putting too much pressure on the boilers. The Chief Engineer felt that a higher speed could be achieved for short periods with some modifications to the catapult system to launch naval aircraft into the air.

In November 1971, events now took place which revealed Pakistan's attempts to locate the *Vikrant*. Pakistani spies holed up in a hotel in Bombay that could oversee the docks continued to report to their handlers in Pakistan that the *Vikrant* was in Bombay. On 13 November, however, they were unable to locate the *Vikrant*. The *Vikrant* had disappeared!

Pakistan's Naval Intelligence started getting its act together. Some time later, it was reported that an assistant naval attaché of a Western country that was supporting Pakistan latched himself to the Aide-De-Camp (ADC) of the Flag Officer Commander-in-Chief of the Western Fleet at a diplomatic function in Bombay. This officer was particularly curious to know about the location of the *Vikrant*, and the matter was immediately reported to Indian Naval Intelligence.

One way or another, inimical agents finally found out and reported that the *Vikrant* was in Chennai.

Was it also a coincidence that an aircraft of the same Western country that was supporting Pakistan was sent to Chennai, where it inexplicably developed mechanical problems that necessitated test flights in and around Chennai harbour? And were these flights carried out to confirm that the *Vikrant* was indeed at Chennai?

Calcutta, 3 October 1971

Major General Jack Jacob, Chief of Staff of Headquarter Eastern Command, popularly known as Jakes, looked up at the huge map that had been tacked to the wall of his bedroom. The map* extended from the high ceiling of the bedroom of his old-world bungalow at Calcutta right down to the floor. It was a map of East Pakistan and the bordering Indian states. On it was marked, all in red, the dispositions of the Pakistani forces. In the Indian Army, enemy forces are always marked in red on maps and on sand models, and own forces are marked in blue, in order to distinguish one from the other. The deployment of Indian forces, however, was not marked on this map, because although General Jacob's home was reasonably secure, it was safer that this information remained unmarked. (The deployment of Indian forces was subsequently marked on the map for purposes of archival record.)

But detailed information of both sides was marked in detail on maps pinned to the sliding boards of the Operations Room of Headquarters Eastern Command, Calcutta, and was updated every day by duty officers who plotted the latest positions of the opposing forces on the relevant maps. These maps were covered with transparent talc paper so that the movement of units and formations and their latest positions could be marked, using chinagraph pencils, in red and blue arrows indicating current movement of opposing forces along with dates. The locations of Pakistani and Indian units were also marked with red and blue pins. To ensure security of

* This map is now on a wall at the library of the United Service Institution of India, New Delhi.

Sketch of the *Vikrant*.

information, the Ops Room was not accessible to anyone without the permission of General Jacob.

Placed in front of the map at his home was an easy chair and beside it were two small tables, one on either side of the chair. On one was placed dossiers on certain senior officers of the Pakistani armed forces. These dossiers contained the detailed information of the Pakistani Generals in East Pakistan and also of some senior commanders of the Pakistan Navy and Air Force. On the other side was a table that had a decanter of Napoleon cognac, a brandy goblet, his favourite pipe and a pouch of Balkan Sobranie tobacco.

General Jacob had been tasked to work out a plan for an offensive into East Pakistan. He was on a very good equation with General 'Inder' Gill, Director of Operations at MO (Military Operations) Directorate, Army Headquarters, New Delhi, and the two of them knew exactly what had to be done should Pakistan launch its offensive against India, as it had threatened to do.

It was early October 1971, and his task of formulating an offensive plan included the tying up of myriad issues, like updating the details of the riverine terrain of East Pakistan; studying the after-effects of the monsoon on the ground;

liaising with the navy and air force, and also with the Mukti Bahini headquarters-in-exile located in Calcutta; working on the movement of engineer stores; creating ammunition dumps; creating space in military and civil hospitals in anticipation of heavy casualties; deciding where workshop facilities should be positioned; liaising with civil aviation for possible contingencies; moving forward the supplies of ammunition, food and other necessities that would be required in the event of a war. All these activities had kept him extremely busy.

He would return home late in the evening and after a light dinner, sit in his bedroom and look at this huge map. A glass of cognac helped him unwind after a strenuous day, and the smoke from his favourite pipe stimulated his senses. The dossiers on his opponents gave him an insight into their minds; their qualifications in terms of military courses and past postings helped him to understand their background. He worked out in his mind what each enemy commander would do in situations that he himself would create. Topmost of the dossiers was the one on Lieutenant General A.A.K. Niazi, General Officer Commanding-in-Chief of all forces in East Pakistan. There were also dossiers on General Yahya Khan, the Army Chief of Pakistan; Vice Admiral Muzaffar Hassan, the Pakistani Naval Chief; Major General Rao Farman Ali, Military Adviser to the Governor of East Pakistan; Lieutenant General Tika Khan, Martial Law Administrator East Pakistan; Rear Admiral Mohammad Sharif, the Pakistani Flag Officer Commanding-in-Chief (FOC-in-C), East Pakistan, and some others.

A few months earlier, Pakistan had cobbled up an alliance with the United States of America and China, and the balance of power in the subcontinent had shifted clearly towards Pakistan. In order to checkmate this malevolent triumvirate, the Indian Prime Minister entered into a Treaty of Friendship with Russia, an alliance that stood India in good stead before and during the war. Richard Nixon, for some reason, had a pathological hatred for India and Prime Minister Indira Gandhi. Perhaps it was because the Indian Prime Minister refused to toe the American line. Nixon used to refer to the Indian Prime Minister as 'that woman' and other epithets that are not worth repeating. Nixon and his Secretary of State, Henry Kissinger, were up to all types of stratagems to help Pakistan in its conflict with India. Developments on this front also had to be taken cognizance of and monitored.

By early October 1971, Indian intelligence was piecing together information concerning Pakistani plans for a war that appeared imminent. It was already known that Pakistan's state-of-the-art Daphne-class submarines were, at that time, the best in the world. What was not known was how and when she intended to use these deadly underwater weapons of war.

Due to the advantage that the Pakistan Navy had in its underwater capability, it became increasingly important for India to know the plans of the Pakistan Navy, in particular as to how it would deploy its submarines.

Eastern Command, 3 October to 26 November 1971

Headquarters Eastern Command (India) had in the meantime set up a series of wireless interception stations to lock on to radio transmissions between Karachi, Lahore, Rawalpindi and Dhaka. General Jacob believed that 'being warned was being forearmed'. These wireless intercepting stations had been set up in September 1971.

All intercepted transmissions were encrypted in high-level codes, and all that the Indians had was a mass of encrypted data on the spools of their Grundig tape recorders. The encrypted information made no sense whatsoever. It was now early November, and General Jacob was desperately looking for something meaningful to link the stray bits of information that would help him to connect the pieces of the jigsaw puzzle and understand what the Pakistanis were up to.

On 8 November, Major Dharam Dev Datt, the officer commanding one of the intercepting wireless stations, was the image of concentration as he slowly turned the knobs of the Racal RA 150 radio receiver in an attempt to latch on to the messages between Karachi and Dhaka. A sudden increase in the number of messages on that day meant that there was something big in the offing, and it was crucial that India got to know what the Pakistanis were up to as early as possible. General Yahya Khan had been making statements like, 'I am going to teach India a lesson that she will never forget' and 'In a few days I shall be away fighting a war'. War with Pakistan therefore seemed a certainty, and it was necessary that India got to know when and where Pakistan would launch her offensives on land and sea, and from the air.

So far, nothing was known—just a mass of hieroglyphics that made no sense and small snatches of conversation that had no meaning.

On 9 November, however, an interesting development was about to take place.

Dharam's intuition told him that something important was on the horizon, and although twelve hours had passed, he had not gone home. Better known as 3D, he had been continuously on the radio receiver looking for the elusive breakthrough. (Dharam was called 3D because his name in official records was Dharam Dev Datt—a long name which was reduced to '3D' by a senior cadet at the National Defence Academy, and the name had stuck.) Sangeeta, his wife, had sent a towel and a change of clothes, and he had a cold bath in the toilet of his office. He was, however, once again perspiring, and this was due more to the tension rather than the weather.

Dharam was a 'go-getter'. He had lost a leg in counterterrorist operations, but that had made him even more determined to prove that he was as competent as non-disabled officers. Given a task, he would not rest till he had completed it successfully.

One more day and a night had passed with no breakthrough.

3D had by now been continuously on his radio set for the last thirty-six hours, with short breaks in between, and he was beginning to tire. Whatever messages he was intercepting, were being recorded and copied and sent across to the cryptographers. It was important that all messages were recorded and stored. The unravelling of the content of these messages would take place later. He had some of the best cryptographers in the service.

The discs of the tape recorder rotated and stopped intermittently in accordance with the length of the messages that were flying through space across the Indian landmass that separated West and East Pakistan, but the content of the messages was still a mystery.

The tape recorders were linked with an IBM mainframe computer, and the cryptographers in the adjacent room were hard at it, trying to break the codes of the cryptograms routed to them by 3D. His team had been working in shifts and there were some small successes, but the key to the code had continued to elude them.

Suddenly, on the evening of 10 November, the Pakistan Naval code was broken and everything fell into place. All the messages of the past few weeks would be decoded, scrutinized and passed on to the relevant departments of the army, navy and air force.

3D immediately rang up Major General Jacob. He had direct access to the General with orders to speak to him at any time if anything important came up. 3D gave General Jacob the code word that signified that the Pakistan Naval code had been broken.

The general was quietly elated. His intuition and anticipation had begun to pay off. He knew that with the breaking of the Pakistan Naval Code, he now had the upper hand to plan his strokes and counterstrokes.

'Good show, Dharam,' he said. 'Just make sure that no one comes to know about this. No one means no one! Neither the Pakis nor us! If this becomes known in the wrong quarters, then all our work would be in vain!'

'Yes, sir!' said Dharam and quickly passed orders forbidding anyone from babbling that the Pakistan Naval code had been broken.

The breaking of the Pakistan Naval code revealed that Pakistan was moving inexorably towards war. It was clear from the decoded messages that the primary objective of the Pakistan Navy was to destroy INS *Vikrant*, India's aircraft carrier and the prized warship of the Indian Navy. Pakistan's secondary objective was to use its state-of-the-art Daphne-class submarines—the *Hangor*, *Sushuk* and the *Mangro*—to destroy the warships of India's Western Fleet, in Bombay harbour.

Now that it was clear that the core of Pakistan's strategy was centred on the destruction of the *Vikrant* and the ships of the Western Fleet in Bombay harbour, it became imperative for the Indian Navy to evolve ways and means to checkmate Pakistani designs on the chessboard of the Arabian Sea and the Bay of Bengal. All relevant information was passed on to the relevant branches of the Army and Naval Headquarters on a minute-to-minute basis.

The decoded Pakistani messages conveyed the Pakistan Navy's assessment that the *Vikrant* was an ideal and primary target—all the more because their intelligence had found out that the carrier had a crack on one of its boilers that would slow down its speed considerably. It's sinking would be a great moral boost for Pakistan and a demoralizing blow to India. Pakistan's PNS *Ghazi* was the ideal weapon platform to destroy the *Vikrant*, irrespective of whether she was operating in the Arabian Sea or the Bay of Bengal, because the endurance capacity of the *Ghazi* permitted her to operate for long distances without refuelling.

This Tench-class submarine had been transferred by the Government of the United States of America to her protégé Pakistan in 1963, as part of its continuing military aid programme. Its original American name was USS *Diablo*. 'Diablo', a Spanish word, means the devil—a name that was by itself significant!

In 1967, the lease by the United States on the *Ghazi* had expired. This was renewed, but the state of the *Ghazi* had deteriorated, and she was due for a refit. This was done in Turkey in 1968, but by November 1971 she was again due for a refit, which could not be done due to the imminence of Pakistan's operational plans to wage war against India.

The decoded messages mentioned that it was of importance to the Pakistan Navy to track the moves of the *Vikrant,* so that she could be stalked and destroyed. The messages also revealed that the Chief of the Pakistan Navy was personally monitoring the progress of the mission given to the *Ghazi*, as he desired that the opening blow of the war against India be delivered by the Pakistan Navy.

All relevant information was further conveyed by Military Operations at Army Headquarters to those concerned—in this case, to the Indian Navy's 'Ops and Plans', and the Indian Naval and Air Force Chiefs.

At Sea: Western and Eastern Seaboards, November 1971

The *Ghazi* moved out of Karachi harbour on 14 November for its task to destroy the *Vikrant* at Chennai harbour. Details of the harbour had been carefully studied as well as photographs taken from the air of the *Vikrant* in Chennai harbour by the aircraft of the Western country working on behalf of Pakistan. The *Ghazi* made a direct run to Sri Lanka, stopping at Trincomalee on 18 November to refuel and clean up. It was while she was preparing to head for Chennai from Trincomalee, on 20 November, that Commander Zafar Khan received a message from Karachi: the aircraft that had earlier spotted the *Vikrant* at Chennai had, on its last flight around the harbour, discovered that the *Vikrant* was no longer in Chennai and that its present location was not known.

Alarm bells started ringing! Where was the *Vikrant*? She had disappeared without a trace! Commander Zafar felt cheated. He was all set to sink the *Vikrant* in Chennai harbour and his prized target had suddenly disappeared!

A flurry of messages between Commander Zafar Khan and the Naval Headquarters in Karachi was intercepted. After forty-eight hours of uncertainty, Zafar asked the Naval Headquarters at Karachi as to his next task, now that the *Vikrant* had disappeared.

Karachi sent messages to Rear Admiral Mohammad Sharif, Pakistan's Eastern Fleet commander in Dhaka, asking them if they had any information about the *Vikrant*—whether she was in the Bay of Bengal or had moved back to the Arabian Sea. A naval maritime reconnaissance aircraft was sent by the Pakistan Navy to scour the area under its control, but the *Vikrant* had indeed disappeared into thin air!

These intercepted messages were duly deciphered and sent in code to Naval Headquarters, New Delhi, and the Western Naval Headquarters, Bombay. If Bombay and Delhi knew where the *Vikrant* was, they were keeping quiet. However, 3D, who was intercepting these messages, was perplexed. Where was the *Vikrant*?

On 23 November 1971, the problem of the location of INS *Vikrant* was resolved as suddenly as it had occurred.

If India was intercepting Pakistani signal traffic, Pakistan was also monitoring the air waves and intercepting Indian messages, and Commander Zafar Khan was informed by Pakistan's Naval Intelligence that the *Vikrant* was in Visakhapatnam! They had intercepted and deciphered messages from the *Vikrant* requesting for aircraft fuel, victuals* for its crew of over a thousand officers and sailors, and fuel for the *Vikrant* itself. They obtained a fix from these messages which revealed that the *Vikrant* was in Visakhapatnam and that it was waiting to be refuelled and resupplied.

* Victuals: naval term for food supplies, pronounced as 'vittles'.

Captain Zafar Khan realized that he had to move fast. He also wanted to know to which port the *Vikrant* would be heading towards. This information was needed in the event that the *Vikrant* moved out before he could get the *Ghazi* there. The Pakistan Navy, however, did not know, because the intercepted messages did not indicate where the *Vikrant* would go next. But it was likely that she would head out to sea only after being refuelled and resupplied, and the intercepted messages indicated that this would take a few days.

The Pakistan Naval Headquarters as well as the Captain of the *Ghazi*, both realized that the best opportunity to destroy the *Vikrant* was to attack her while she was still in Visakhapatnam. As and when the *Vikrant* left Visakhapatnam harbour, she would be escorted by destroyers, minesweepers and frigates, and then it would be more difficult to attack, sink her and get away. Sinking the *Vikrant* within the Visakhapatnam harbour also posed fewer risks.

3D was very upset. It appeared to him that if the Pakistan Navy had given away its intentions through its messages, the Indian Navy was no better! He reported his observations to Army Signal Intelligence with an advisory that the location of the *Vikrant* had been compromised and remedial action needed to be taken, because the *Ghazi* was in Trincomalee, refuelled and ready to take off to destroy the *Vikrant* in Visakhapatnam harbour. 3D, however, got no reply from Naval Headquarters to address his concerns. He wondered why?

Meanwhile, Pakistan's Naval Headquarters in Karachi sent out a clutch of signals directing the Captain of the *Ghazi* to sink the *Vikrant* at Visakhapatnam harbour, before she put out to sea. War was soon to be declared, and the Pakistan Navy, as mentioned before, wanted the destruction of the *Vikrant* to be the opening blow of the war with India.

Visakhapatnam, 1–3 December 1971

The *Ghazi*, already resupplied and refuelled, moved out of Trincomalee harbour on the evening of 23 November 1971.[5] She was off Chennai from 25–27 November and then headed for Visakhapatnam. She approached Visakhapatnam harbour at 2200 hours on the night of 29 November and entered the navigational channel at 2345 hours on the night of 1 December.*

Commander Zafar examined his options. Firstly, he could lay mines in the navigation channel of Visakhapatnam harbour and hope that the *Vikrant* would pass over these mines, detonate them and be destroyed. However, it was a moot point as to whether the mines would destroy the *Vikrant*. And what if the mines did not detonate?

The second option would be to lie in wait for the *Vikrant* to move out of the harbour and to torpedo her as she came out. However, it was not known as to when the *Vikrant* would sail out of the harbour, and therefore there was no guarantee that the sinking of the *Vikrant* would follow close on the heels of the declaration of war. Also, she would be closely protected by Indian naval destroyers and frigates.

The third option was for the *Ghazi* to enter Visakhapatnam harbour, and to target and destroy the *Vikrant* with her torpedoes at the outset of the war. This appeared to be the

---

* Dates of departure of the *Ghazi* from Trincomalee, till its arrival in the navigational channel of Visakhapatnam, are approximations. Exact dates are not available.

best option. The only problem was how long could the Ghazi remain undiscovered in a harbour where a lot of activity took place every day. Also, the depth of the navigational channel did not allow her to go closer than 2.1 nautical miles from the south breakwater of the harbour. She could not go further into the harbour because the minimum submergible depth for a submarine was fifteen metres, and the margin was too small for a big submarine like the *Ghazi*. So Commander Zafar decided to let the *Ghazi* stay where she was and to destroy the *Vikrant* from her present position.

All the issues that factored into making the right decision had devolved on to the shoulders of the Captain of the *Ghazi*—i.e., the timing of the attack, the method to be used and the location from where she would destroy the *Vikrant.*

Commander Zafar Khan decided to exercise the third option. He called his officers to work out the details of the plan that he had envisaged. The meeting was held in the wardroom, and it was a tight fit. The assembled officers included only those who would be required to carry out the task. The radar officer confirmed that the large blip on the radar was the *Vikrant*; the torpedo and gunnery officer confirmed that all drills had been rehearsed, the torpedoes were ready for firing and all that he needed was the orders to fire; but the medical officer declared that obnoxious fumes had polluted the air in the submarine to dangerous levels, posing a threat not only to the health of the crew but also to the submarine. The hydrogen content was far above accepted levels due to the batteries being old and decrepit. He recommended that the *Ghazi* surface at night to take in fresh air. This would also be an opportunity to charge the batteries.

Commander Khan was in a quandary. He realized that it was essential for the *Ghazi* to surface not only for the health of his crew but also for the health of the submarine. If the hydrogen content of the submarine reached levels above the laid-down safety level, then there was imminent danger of the *Ghazi* self-destructing.

It was now the morning of 3 December 1971. The Pakistani advisories to mercantile shipping and civil air traffic, which had been made two days earlier, made it clear that Pakistan was on the cusp of going to war and that evening, at 5.45 p.m., the Pakistan Air Force would attack Indian airfields. The moment to sink the *Vikrant* had therefore arrived, but Zafar did not know this!

Otherwise, all was quiet. The Indian Army was training and getting ready for future operations. Admiral Nanda, the Indian Naval Chief, aware of the plans of the Pakistan Navy, had been to Bombay to give orders to FOC-in-C West to move the Western Fleet out of Bombay harbour. Prime Minister Indira Gandhi was in Calcutta attending a political meeting. The Defence Minister, Babu Jagjivan Ram, was also away from the capital.

Meanwhile, Zafar realized that notwithstanding the issue of the polluted air within the *Ghazi*, there was no question of the *Ghazi* surfacing in broad daylight. Visibility at sea extended over many miles, and the *Ghazi* was a big submarine and therefore could be easily spotted even from the shore. The earliest that the *Ghazi* could surface was after dark, when hopefully there would be no fishermen around. He decided to wait until dark.

At 1700 hours, the executive officer and the medical officer reported to Captain Zafar that the air within the submarine in the engine room had got really bad and had crossed danger level, and that one of the sailors had been knocked unconscious. He suggested that the *Ghazi* surface as early as possible and to not wait till darkness set in. Zafar thought about it and decided that he would surface around dusk. In fading light there would be fewer chances of the *Ghazi* being spotted. In the meanwhile, tensions within the crew of the *Ghazi* were on the rise. The air was getting fetid. Many were coughing, and their eyes were getting affected. At around 1800 hours, Captain Zafar Khan gave orders for the *Ghazi* to surface to periscope* level and decided to survey the area around before contemplating any further action.

The *Ghazi* was brought up from the deep to twenty-seven feet below the surface of the sea for an assessment of the scene. Zafar had planned to charge the batteries and bring in fresh air nine metres below the surface, with the snorkel pipe raised to suck in air to run the diesel engines, charge the batteries and rejuvenate the air inside the boat.

Orders were given by the Officer of the Watch for water to be pumped out of the ballast tanks. As the water got pumped out, the boat† would become lighter and would gradually make its way to the surface. The tanks on both sides of the *Ghazi*—port and starboard—had to empty simultaneously so that the *Ghazi* could surface on an even keel. The *Ghazi* was fifteen fathoms‡ beneath the sea, and the Officer of the Watch was giving the countdown as the *Ghazi* gradually moved to the surface: 'Fifteen fathoms, fourteen fathoms, thirteen fathoms, twelve fathoms, eleven fathoms!' The Officer of the Watch stopped when the

* Periscope: an apparatus consisting of a tube within which are placed a series of prisms and mirrors by which an observer in a submerged submarine can see things above the sea that would be otherwise not be visible.

† Boat: an informal term for a submarine.

‡ Fathom: a unit of length equal to six feet, used mainly to measure/specify marine depths.

periscope broke through the surface of the sea nine metres below the surface, at 1.5 fathoms. Zafar was looking through the eyepiece of the periscope—what he saw gave him a start!

Hardly a kilometre away was a large Indian naval patrol vessel heading in their direction. The V-shaped white plume from the bows of the craft spreading high on both sides indicated that she was moving fast. There was no time to lose. He immediately gave orders for the *Ghaz*i to dive.

'Dive the boat!' Zafar shouted to the Officer of the Watch, and the latter immediately repeated the order. The *Ghazi* closed up at 'Action Stations'* in less than a minute.

The Control Room watchkeeper shouted over the PA system, 'Dive! Dive! Dive!' The pumps of the ballast tanks began to take in water urgently, and the boat began to descend. The klaxon sounded the alarm to inform all that there was an emergency situation on hand. All ballast tanks got flooded in less than thirty seconds, and the *Ghazi* went down underwater within one minute and thirty seconds from Zafar's order to dive the boat.

The *Ghazi* descended slowly—too slowly for Commander Khan, but she managed to get below just in the nick of time. Minutes later, the patrol vessel passed over the *Ghazi*, and the wash† from its passage rocked the *Ghazi*, indicating that it was a biggish vessel and that it was moving at a very fast speed. Zafar had heard that the Indian Navy had gone in for missile boats from Russia, which were designed for the defence of ports, and also Petya boats, which were patrol boats but much larger. It could have been either of those.

---

* Action Stations: the posts to be occupied by personnel of a ship during active operations.

† Wash: surge or rush of water due to movement by an extraneous force.

Captain Khan wondered whether anyone on the patrol vessel had seen the periscope. If yes, there would be more passes by the same vessel or by others. Either way, it was too risky to surface just yet. The *Ghazi* went down to fifteen fathoms and waited in a state of suspended animation.

Captain Khan decided to 'lie doggo'* for some more time. The medical officer, however, came once again to say that the situation was very bad and that it was imperative that the boat surface as early as possible. Zafar informed him of the danger of being discovered and destroyed, and said that the earliest it would be safe to surface would be around midnight.

They would get approximately four hours to charge the batteries, have the air pumped out of the submarine and fresh air inducted. They would have to finish all their tasks by four in the morning—as that was the time when fishermen put out to sea—and would have to dive down before that.

And so, it was decided that the *Ghazi* would surface around the midnight of 3–4 December 1971 and, having carried out its maintenance tasks, go down once again at 0400 hours on 4 December to position itself to destroy the *Vikrant*. Zafar then instructed his officers to tell the crew to write letters to their families and said that the letters would be posted from the Fleet Mail Office at Trincomalee on the way back home.

Unbeknown to Zafar, at 1745 hours on 3 December 1971, the Pakistan Air Force attacked Indian airfields in Ambala, Uttarlai, Jodhpur, Pathankot, Srinagar and Avantipur, and so India and Pakistan were already at war! Zafar was already late!

Vice Admiral Muzzaffar Hassan, the Pakistani Naval Chief, was pacing up and down in his office in Karachi, waiting for

---

* Lie doggo: to keep out of sight/stay hidden.

news from Zafar that he had destroyed the *Vikrant*, but there was no communication from the *Ghazi* on the success of its task—only silence! The moment for the *Ghazi* to destroy the *Vikrant* had arrived, and he had no news whatsoever from the *Ghazi*.

Calcutta–Lucknow–Delhi, 3 December 1971

Prime Minister Indira Gandhi, the Defence Minister, Jagjivan Ram, and the External Affairs Minister, Swaran Singh, were away from Delhi when Pakistan struck the first blow of the 1971 Indo–Pak war. The timing of the air attacks was such that it appeared that Pakistan knew that Indian political leadership would be away from the capital on 3 December and that this was the right time to strike.

Mrs Gandhi was in Calcutta on 3 December, and she finished her engagements late in the evening. The attack by Pakistan on Indian airfields took place at 5.45 p.m. and the PM's aircraft had got airborne for Delhi at around 6.30 p.m. Her aircraft was an Indian Air force VIP Squadron transport aircraft, a TU-124, and it was in grave danger of being shot down by Pakistani Sabre jets. Air Headquarters got in touch with the pilot of the PM's aircraft, briefed him about what had happened and directed the pilot to divert the aircraft to Lucknow, as the Pakistani air strikes were still on and a large lumbering transport aircraft of the VIP Squadron would be an attractive target for a Pakistani fighter jet. The Prime Minister's party included D.P. Dhar, Secretary to the Prime Minister's Office and adviser to the Prime Minister for Bangladesh; J.N. Dixit, Director, Special Division, East Pakistan; and Peter Sinai, officer from the Ministry of External Affairs, Government of India.

What happened on the aircraft and thereafter is best described by J.N. Dixit in his book *Liberation and Beyond*. He says:

> As the plane reached the airspace a little east of Lucknow, the pilot of the plane came up to DP Dhar and asked him to come to the cockpit and speak on the communication system as there was an urgent message from Delhi. Mr. Dhar spent about 3 to 4 minutes in the cockpit, came out and spoke to Mrs. Gandhi, walked back to his seat and turned to us who were sitting behind him and said: 'The fool has done exactly what one had expected.' He went on to inform us that General Yahya Khan had carried out pre-emptive air strikes on Indian airbases in north western India, in Jammu, Punjab and in Rajasthan. He added that General Yahya Khan had also launched ground attacks against Indian territory. General Manekshaw, the Chief of the Army Staff, had already commenced retaliatory action. Most of northern and north central India was under a black out in anticipation of Pakistani air strikes.

Mrs Gandhi's plane instead of flying to Delhi was diverted to Lucknow airport. Mrs Gandhi remained at the airport for nearly two hours and took off around 10 p.m., landing at Palam around 10.45 p.m. Defence Minister Jagjivan Ram was at the airport to receive Mrs Gandhi. The Prime Minister and her officials were driven directly to South Block. Mrs Gandhi, Jagjivan Ram, Swaran Singh and senior officials went straight into the Ops Room. General Manekshaw proceeded to brief Mrs Gandhi and her cabinet colleagues about the counter-offensive which India had launched in the western sector. He also asked Mrs Gandhi's permission to commence operations in the eastern sector which was immediately given. Mrs Gandhi proceeded to the Cabinet Room in the western wing of South Block to preside over an emergency meeting which she had summoned while flying into Delhi.

When Mrs Gandhi walked into the Operations Room of Army Headquarters, she expected feverish activity and some amount of tension but found total calm and no flurry of activity of any sort. The Army Chief, General Sam Manekshaw, was relaxed and awaiting the arrival of his Prime Minister. 'What's happening Sam?' she asked. 'Aren't we at war?' The Chief replied, 'Yes, Madam Prime Minister, we are at war—at last! The army is already on the move and by early morning tomorrow, the army will be hitting its objectives. This is the moment we have been waiting for and you will not find us wanting.'

The Army Chief thereafter proceeded to brief the Prime Minister about the ongoing operations and the moves that had already commenced. He informed her that the Indian Navy was also on the move and that the Indian Air Force would commence attacking their targets at daybreak.

The Prime Minister was impressed not only at the preparedness of the Armed Forces but also at the calm efficiency with which they worked. She felt assured that the conduct of the war was in safe and capable hands.

The Prime Minister left the Ops Room and went to the Cabinet which was waiting for her. She met her ministers and briefed them about the urgency of the situation and the ongoing war. Shortly before midnight, she addressed the nation and informed its citizens about Pakistan's attack on Indian airfields that evening, and that India was consequently at war with Pakistan. While the Prime Minister was in the middle of her address, there was a tremendous explosion in the waters of Visakhapatnam harbour. The explosion shattered the windowpanes of the houses that faced the harbour and passers-by witnessed a huge plume of water that reached high into the sky.

Visakhapatnam, 3–4 December 1971

In Visakhapatnam, there was general perplexity at the huge explosion that had taken place. However, it was not the *Vikrant* that had been blown up. Something else had happened! Some thought that they were being bombed by the Pakistan Air Force! No one knew what had happened, and how and why the explosion had taken place.

On the afternoon of 4 December, some fishermen brought objects from the sea that happened to be the debris of the *Ghazi*, which had surfaced from the bottom of the sea. Putting two and two together, the Commander of the naval station of Visakhapatnam came to the conclusion that the *Ghazi* had come into the harbour of Visakhapatnam and had self-destructed.

The twist in this story is that the *Vikrant* was never in Visakhapatnam. She was in fact somewhere else! INS *Rajput*, an obsolete destroyer about to be decommissioned, was performing the role of a decoy ship, simulating signal traffic for rations, fuel for the aircraft aboard the *Vikrant* and fuel for the *Vikrant* itself, conveying to 'all who were listening' that the *Vikrant* was in Visakhapatnam harbour, whereas she was in a secure harbour in the Andaman and Nicobar Islands! These messages were in low-grade cipher, allowing the Pakistanis to break the code and be deceived as to the actual situation.

The engineers on the *Vikrant*, meanwhile, managed to do a great job in getting the recalcitrant boiler into reasonable shape, allowing the *Vikrant* to work up a reasonable speed that allowed its aircraft to take off from its deck to support operations against the ports of Khulna and Chittagong. And so, the *Vikrant* redeemed itself in carrying out its legitimate role in giving air cover for naval and ground operations in the eastern theatre.

The *Ghazi* lies today in her watery grave, at the bottom of Visakhapatnam harbour. Indian naval divers, who went down to the wreck the day after the sinking, confirmed that it was in fact the *Ghazi* that lay at the bottom of the sea. They reported that the submarine had been ripped apart from the conning tower to the snub, indicating that she had self-destructed due to an internal explosion. The cause was not known, but indications were that this had happened due primarily to the detonation of combustible gas, as there had been similar instances with submarines of other navies worldwide around that time.

If, as it had earlier been reported, the *Ghazi* had been blown up on its own mines that it was laying, then the bottom of the submarine would have been ripped apart, which, according to the divers, was not the case.

The wreck of the *Ghazi* lies at 17 degrees, 41 minutes, 05.7 seconds north; and 83 degrees, 21 minutes, 04.7 seconds east; and is 2.1 nautical miles from the South Breakwater at a depth of 20.4 metres. It could not go further into the harbour because submarines need a submergible depth of at least fifteen metres, and the margin was too small for a big submarine like the *Ghazi.*

The Americans offered to recover the *Ghazi* on grounds that it was an American submarine given to Pakistan on lease and that they therefore had the right to recover it. India refused permission stating that the *Ghazi* had entered Indian territorial waters illegally and was destroyed after Pakistan had attacked India. The *Ghazi*'s presence during the war in Visakhapatnam harbour, India said, was an act of war, which made her a 'war trophy' and therefore the property of the Indian government. So, the permission to recover her could not be given. The Pakistan Navy offered to recover the *Ghazi* on the basis that it was her vessel. This request was turned down for the same reasons that were given to the Americans.

However, it was the efforts of men like General Jacob and 3D and his team, who were able to intercept and interpret the aims and intentions of Pakistan, that enabled the Indian armed forces to take countermeasures to thwart Pakistan's plans. The deception measures by the Indian Navy's Eastern Command succeeded in convincing the Pakistan Navy that the *Vikrant* was in Visakhapatnam harbour when she was elsewhere. The Pakistan Navy ordered the Ghazi to occupy 'Zone Victor' (presumably Pakistan's code word for Visakhapatnam). The message recovered from the *Ghazi* states: 'Occupy Zone Victor with all dispatch. Intelligence indicates carrier in port.'*

Unfortunately for the *Ghazi* and her crew, the percentage of hydrogen within the submarine seems to have gone well beyond the danger mark. A large number of signals sent by the *Ghazi,* as recovered from her message logbook, explicitly state that the submarine had a major problem of hydrogen building up inside.

Most probably, when the build-up of hydrogen exceeded safety limits, an explosion took place, setting up a sympathetic detonation of whatever ordnance she was carrying—mines,

* Vice Admiral G.M. Hiranandani, *Transition to Triumph: History of the Indian Navy, 1965–1975* (New Delhi: Lancer Publishers, 1999), p. 142.

torpedoes, everything went off together, blowing the submarine apart. Interestingly, just before the onset of hostilities between India and Pakistan, a BBC news item mentioned that an explosion had taken place in a British submarine while it was charging its batteries in the harbour and that the damage caused the submarine to sink.*

With hindsight, it can be presumed that at around the midnight of 3 December, as the *Ghazi* attempted to surface, a spark from one of the batteries ignited the volatile gas within the submarine, and the *Ghazi* blew up in a huge explosion. According to witnesses, a massive plume of water spewed up to a height of nearly a thousand feet and all the glass panes of buildings on the waterfront shattered.

The people of Visakhapatnam were not asleep. They were, in fact, wide awake, listening to a broadcast of Mrs Gandhi, who was informing her people that Pakistan had attacked Indian airfields, that this was an act of war and that the armed forces would give Pakistan a befitting reply. When the blast occurred, the citizens of Visakhapatnam thought that they were being attacked by Pakistan. They were quite close to the truth, but not entirely.

The plan of the Commander-in-Chief, Pakistan Navy, and Chief of Naval Staff, Vice Admiral Muzzaffar Hassan, had backfired. Instead of the Pakistan Navy striking the first blow in Pakistan's war against India, the opposite had happened when the *Ghazi* self-destructed in Visakhapatnam harbour.

All this transpired because General Jacob understood that the key to knowing the strategy and plans of Pakistan was to use his own methods to find out what Pakistan was up to.

* Ibid., pp. 150–51.

His intercepting radio stations and cryptographers gave him the answers he was looking for. The strategy and plans of the Pakistan Navy fell into his lap, enabling the Indian Navy to ensure the security of the *Vikrant* and the ships of the Western Fleet, as well as to inform the Indian Army and Air Force about the timing of Pakistan's land, sea and air operations. The success of India's strategy and plans owes much to the information provided by General Jacob's teams of interceptors and cryptographers.

Half a century has passed since the *Ghazi* went down along with her complement of officers and men. She lies there alone and abandoned. All she has today for company are the fish who swim in and out of her shell, wondering what this was all about, and nobody can tell them what really happened.

Postscript

Commander (retd) K.P. Mathew, who was instrumental in recovering equipment and documents from PNS *Ghazi,* has this to say about the self-destruction of the submarine:

> The sinking of INS *Sindhurakshak*, that took place in Mumbai harbour on 14 August 2013, has an uncanny resemblance in many respects to the sinking of PNS *Ghazi*. INS *Sindhurakshak* sank, with its eighteen crew members, when a blast ripped through its torpedo compartment. It has a great deal of similarity to the sinking of the *Ghazi*. PNS *Ghazi* was a US Navy Tench-class diesel electric submarine of World War II vintage—original name USS *Diablo*—on lease to the Pakistan Navy since 1963.
>
> The submarine rescue ship INS *Nistar* recovered equipment from the Ghazi that included logbooks, charts,

message files, spool-type recording tapes, etc. The items of intelligence value were used to analyse and reconstruct the operational deployment and activities of PNS *Ghazi*. It was clear from these recoveries that the primary wartime mission of the Ghazi was to seek and destroy INS *Vikrant*, which was operating on the east coast, and that its destruction was caused by an excessive accumulation of hydrogen from the lead acid batteries that got ignited.

This story is based on factual information gleaned from *The History of the Indian Navy, 1945 to 1971*, by Vice Admiral Hiranandani; Lieutenant General J.F.R. Jacob's books *Surrender at Dacca* and *An Odyssey of War and Peace*; long discussions with him at the United Service Institution on the 1971 war; and discussions with naval personnel involved in the recovery of equipment and documents from PNS *Ghazi*.

I am aware that two movies have been made on the sinking of the *Ghazi*. The theory that the *Ghazi* was sunk

Sketch of the *Ghazi* at the bottom of the sea at Visakhapatnam.

by an Indian Naval ship/submarine has been refuted by the Indian Navy in the history of the Indian Navy mentioned . . . above and by General Jacob in his book *Surrender at Dacca*. I have no comments to offer on either of these movies. It is up to the reader to decide on the authenticity or otherwise of their stories.

The Gates of Rattoke

'Courage is what it takes to stand up and speak. Courage is also what it takes to sit down and listen.'

—Winston Churchill

The tension in the sand model room at the Division Headquarters was palpable. The Divisional Commander was perturbed but kept his calm. The Corps Commander looked grumpy and grim. The Brigade Commander was uneasy and uncomfortable. The cause of all this discomfort was the Commanding Officer (CO) of the 1st Battalion, the 5th Gorkha Rifles (Frontier Force). He had stated that the corps plan for the capture of the Sejhra Bulge was not workable!

It was towards the end of November 1971; Pakistan had not yet declared war on India. However, in anticipation of the war, the 'nuts and bolts' for counteroffensive tasks by India in the Western Sector had been finalized a few weeks earlier. This Gorkha Battalion had to launch its counterattack, should Pakistan open the war. Intelligence inputs indicated that Pakistan would soon attack, and here was the Battalion Commander informing his superiors that the corps plan was not workable!

Landscape of Sejhra.

The overall Indian strategy for the war was a swift offensive in the east, and an offensive defence in the south, west and north. The east meant East Pakistan, the west meant the plains of Punjab, the south meant the desert region of Rajasthan and the north meant Jammu and Kashmir. With the strategy of limited offensives in the west, south and north, India aimed at defending our borders and at the same time capturing sufficient Pakistani territory, so as to be able to be in a position of strength for negotiating the exchange of ground that normally took place when such wars concluded.

In this instance, the Sejhra Bulge was the focus of attention. This bulge was like a fist that extended into Indian territory and was the outcome of the Radcliffe Line, drawn on a map by Sir Cyril Radcliffe in 1946. Radcliffe was a lawyer by profession, had never been to India and had no idea about the cultures of, and rivalries between, the two major communities of the subcontinent. He was tasked by the British government to draw the boundary line that would delineate the two emerging countries of India and Pakistan. He did just that with a thick-nibbed pen and returned to Britain unaware that his line would cause the greatest migration in human history and that millions of people would be condemned to die due to the line drawn by his pen that ran roughshod through districts, villages and homes.

The Sejhra Bulge was of great advantage to Pakistan as it facilitated ingress into Indian territory. During the Indo–Pak war of 1965, Pakistan used the Sejhra Bulge to launch its offensive on Khemkaran, and Pakistani civilians from Sejhra, backed by Pakistani Rangers, transgressed across the boundaries of the Bulge and raided and looted Indian villages. The Indian Army had decided that if war did break out this time, there would be no repetition of what happened in this area in 1965.

The 1st Battalion, the 5th Gorkha Rifles was commanded by Lieutenant Colonel Suresh Gupta. He had taken command of the battalion while it was in Naga Hills. After its field tenure, the battalion was posted to Ferozepur, and a few months later, the families joined the battalion. The CO's wife and his two young sons arrived at Ferozepur and settled down to life in a peace station after a break of three years.

While the CO was busy ensuring that the battalion settled down to its operational tasks, Mrs Gupta got the boys enrolled at the local school. One day, while she was driving the boys to school in her car, she took a sharp turn; the car door flew open and the boys tumbled out. An oncoming truck ran over the boys and both were crushed to death. Mrs Gupta and Colonel Gupta were devastated by this. Mrs Gupta felt responsible for the tragedy and was inconsolable.

The possibility of a war with Pakistan had, in the meanwhile, been gathering momentum, and the battalion had already been nominated to carry out the offensive. Now, some officers at higher headquarters questioned the wisdom of appointing a unit whose CO had yet to get over such a deep personal tragedy.

The Divisional Commander, who was from the same regiment as Colonel Gupta, put it across gently to Colonel Gupta that he could give the task to another unit if necessary. Colonel Gupta took this as an affront to his reputation, both personal and professional, as well as to his role as the Commanding Officer of a reputed battalion. He replied that his personal distress had nothing to do with his duty and commitment to the army and his country, and that he would continue to ensure that no stone was left unturned for the success of the offensive. The General Officer Commanding of the division let the matter rest. However, some officers questioned the wisdom of this decision.

The task given to the Gorkhas was the straightening of the Sejhra Bulge by the capture of Sejhra. Command Headquarters had approved the plan but left the planning and conduct of the offensive to the Corps Headquarters. Meticulous planning and detailed reconnaissance by the artillery, armoured corps, other infantry battalions, the signals, the engineers, the administrative services, the medical branch and all the formation headquarters were undertaken, and all that was now left was the launching of the counteroffensive by the Gorkhas.

However, the Commanding Officer of the Gorkhas stated that repeated front-line recces by units and formations had alerted the Pakistanis. Not only did they know that an Indian attack in this sector was in the offing, but multiple reconnaissance patrols had given away the direction of the approach for the attack to be launched by his battalion. Convinced that the Indians would attack along this approach, the Pakistanis had, within the last one month, concretized their bunkers, laid extensive minefields, strengthened their barbed wire entanglements and were presently digging a deep ditch on the home side of their minefield to deny this approach. The digging work was being done by mechanical diggers in broad daylight. The CO stated that all these developments had been intimated to higher headquarters through his daily sitreps,* but it appeared to him that no cognizance of his reports had been taken by anyone up the chain of command.

Lieutenant Colonel Suresh Gupta was quiet and soft spoken but not the type to be browbeaten by distressing circumstances or intimidating superiors. He was calm and collected even in his personal tragedy. He managed to pull his wife out of her despair by his exceptional care and compassion, while at the same time subordinating his personal grief. It was difficult, but his belief and trust in God helped him overcome his misfortune. The battalion rallied round the CO and his family, and Mrs Gupta, much like her husband in his stoic acceptance of what had happened, gradually came around.

A week prior to the sand model discussion, on a visit to the forward area, Lieutenant Colonel Gupta heard the soothing sound of the Gurbani† coming from a gurudwara close to one of his forward companies located in Rattoke. After he had finished his work, the Commanding Officer decided to visit the gurudwara.

Before entering the gurudwara, he took off his footwear and covered his head, as is done when a person enters the precincts of a holy place, and paid obeisance to the holy Guru Granth Sahib. He sat cross-legged on the floor in quiet contemplation,

* Sitrep: Situation Report that gives the latest information about terrain and activities about the enemy and own troops.

† Gurbani: Teachings of all the Sikh Gurus, compiled by the Fifth Guru, Guru Arjun Dev, who summarized the message from the Guru Granth Sahib on how to lead a good life. Contents of the Gurbani are rendered by the granthi, the Sikh priest, in the form of kirtan (hymns).

listening to the ardas[*] by the granthi. After fifteen minutes, as the CO was getting up to leave, the ragi jathas[†] commenced a kirtan. He put on his boots at the jora ghar[‡] when one of the sevadars[§] came to him and said that the granthi would like to speak with him. Chairs were brought, and the CO and the granthi met in the courtyard.

Speaking in Punjabi, the granthi said: 'Sahibji, it is a matter of great happiness that you have come to us at last. We have been waiting for you.'

'Waiting for me?' said the CO with surprise. 'Why were you waiting for me?'

'Sahibji, it has been foretold that one day a CO Sahib from a Gorkha *paltan* would come to us and bring our gates back.'

The CO was mystified. 'Gates? What gates?' He asked.

'Has nobody told you?' said the granthi. 'The gates of our gurudwara—the gurudwara of Rattoke!'

'No,' said the CO. 'Nobody has told me anything about the gates of the Rattoke Gurudwara. Where have they gone?'

This was too much for the granthi. He said, 'Sahibji, it is a long story, and if you are the one who would bring our gates back, you need to know what happened. Please have guru ka langar[¶] with us, and I will tell you the story of the gates of our gurudwara.' Without waiting for an answer, he clapped his hands and a sevadar appeared.

---

[*] Ardas: Prayer by the granthi, asking the Almighty to take care of his people.

[†] Ragi jathas: Musicians who recite the kirtan. One plays the harmonium and two are on tablas.

[‡] Jora ghar: The place where the footwear of the congregation is kept.

[§] Sevadar: One who serves. In this case, one who assists the granthi in carrying out his duties.

[¶] Guru ka langar: Food cooked in the kitchen of a gurudwara.

'Call the CO Sahib's driver inside and give him food, and also bring some for us—*kaali daal* and *garam-garam rotiyan*.'

The CO looked at his watch and felt that he needed to know the story of the gates of Rattoke, particularly since it had been ordained that he would bring the gates back. There was no other commitment that evening, so he waited to hear the story.

This is what the granthi said:

> 'I don't remember the exact date sahib, but during the 1965 war, sometime around the second week of September, villagers from Sejhra, backed by Pakistani soldiers, came across the border and raided our village and our gurudwara, and not finding anything useful, they took away our gates. We had decided to make new gates for the gurudwara, but the previous granthi, before passing away, had said no to our proposal. He had said that the original gates would come back and that they would be brought back by a Gorkha paltan, and here you are today, Sahibji, visiting us just as the old granthi had said you would come. The war will soon start, and we look forward to getting our gates back.'

Lieutenant Colonel Suresh Gupta was in a reflective mood as he drove back to his Battalion Headquarters. He felt incensed at the thought of a whole horde of villagers backed by the Pakistan Army Rangers, coming across the international border to loot the Indian village of Rattoke and, in particular, to steal the gates of a gurudwara. After listening to the granthi, he felt it would be good if he could get those gates back.

However, Sejhra had first to be captured, and the Pakistanis, by strengthening their defences, were making the

The gurudwara in Rattoke.

task increasingly impossible. Repeated reconnaissances by our own units, had given the game away. The Pakistanis now knew that Sejhra was the objective of an Indian offensive and also the approach along which the Indians would attack.

The CO was convinced that attacking according to the original plan was virtual suicide, and he was determined to prevent that from happening. He looked for alternative routes to the objective. One of the approaches that had been rejected was to the west of the Sejhra defences. It had been rejected because there was a natural obstacle in the form of a river, approximately 40 feet wide and 8–9 feet deep, that blocked this approach. But that was in the month of September, soon after the monsoon! It was now mid-November. Surely, the depth and width of the river would have reduced?

He decided to find out. He recalled how Alexander had defeated Porus at the Battle of Hydaspes by deceiving his opponent as to the place of attack. Alexander's decision to cross the monsoon-swollen river in order to catch Porus's army from a flank has been referred to as one of his 'masterpieces'. Lieutenant Colonel Suresh Gupta determined to do what history was trying to teach him. Alexander had left his campfires burning to deceive and surprise the enemy. In Colonel Gupta's case, this could be replicated by other means, i.e., by letting the Pakistanis believe that India would attack along the expected eastern approach, whereas he would be attacking from somewhere else!

Patrols were sent out to determine whether there were places along the river which could be crossed. The patrols brought back information that the depth of the river had indeed reduced to about 4–5 feet. However, even that was too deep, because the Gorkha soldier averaged five feet in height, and he would be encumbered with his arms, ammunition and equipment. Further recces found that there were more crossing places which averaged four feet. That was more than neck deep for the Gorkha soldier. Was the risk too great?

The CO decided to take the problem to his company commanders and the JCOs.

The officers and JCOs were all in favour of the river approach. They had seen the enemy preparations on the approach selected by the formation headquarters and knew that the eastern approach was suicidal. They were unanimous that the river approach was far better. The banks of the river on both sides had bushes and trees, which would give them adequate cover.

The CO decided to share his concerns with the Brigade Commander and to offer an alternative plan. The Brigade Commander saw the logic of the CO's plan, but there were many matters to consider. Firstly, the Pakistani offensive was imminent, and there was barely any time to put together a new plan based on a different approach. Secondly, what would be the reaction of the formation headquarters? After all, the plan had been approved by the division, corps and command, and that had involved meticulous planning by the artillery, armour, engineers, the administrative staff and units, including presentations and sand-model discussions. The detailed operation plan included the artillery fire plan, armour, engineer support and the signal communication system, and these had been dovetailed with the administrative requirements that included the resupply of arms, ammunition, food, water and the evacuation of casualties after Sejhra had been captured. The only thing now left was to launch the attack, as and when required.

The Brigade Commander and the CO took the issue to the Division Headquarters. The Divisional Commander, Major General Freemantle, was taken aback by this late development and said: 'What's the matter, Suresh? Why these doubts at the last minute? Getting cold feet?'

Colonel Suresh Gupta did not want to be disrespectful. Also, the Divisional Commander was from his regiment. So, all that he said was: 'Sir, we are all working for the same aim. Please look at the logic of what I am saying. This problem has not been caused by my battalion. Instead, it is due to the over insurance of the units of the division who have continued to recce the forward area, time and again, from where the attack is to be launched, despite my protests—verbally and in writing.'

'So, where do we go from here?' asked the Divisional Commander.

'Let me do it my way,' said the CO.

'And what is that?' asked General Freemantle,

'To attack from the west, across the river.'

'But that has been ruled out due to the depth and width of the river and the speed of the current,' said the Divisional Commander.

'Yes, sir, but that was in September, soon after the monsoon! I have carried out fresh recces of the river, and I have found places where we can cross. This river is rain-fed. It is now the end of November. The river has slowed down, and its width and depth have reduced.'

'Have you spoken with your officers and JCOs?'

'Yes, sir, I have. They are all for it.'

The Divisional Commander saw the merit of what the Commanding Officer of the Gorkhas was saying. The problem was that the attack had to be launched soon, and there was no time whatsoever for the supporting arms and administrative units to rework their plans at this late stage, particularly the artillery fire plan.

The Divisional Commander called for an immediate conference. He put the problem to the Commander Artillery, the supporting arm commanders and the heads of the administrative units.

As expected, there was a bedlam of protests. In fact, everyone was outraged and upset at the demand for a last-minute change by the Commanding Officer of the Gorkhas. To them, it meant that the detailed planning and reconnaissance over the last two months were now being junked. Would they be required to abandon 'Plan A' and make a new 'Plan B'? Would they be required to start all over again? Where was the time? Some of the officers, who had doubted the wisdom of giving the task of the offensive to Lieutenant Colonel Gupta because of his personal tragedy, began to say: 'See, we told you not to give this task to the Gorkhas!'

The Divisional Commander had meanwhile informed the Corps Commander that there were some hiccups over the attack by the Gorkhas, and that he was sorting things out.

The Corps Commander was surprised when he heard about what was going on and asked to be briefed. What he heard made him very angry.

As commander of a holding corps, whose main task was defensive, he had been asked to undertake just a few battalion-level offensives. He had accepted that with alacrity, and all action had been taken to ensure success. The Gorkha Battalion had been given all the support it would require. And here was this Battalion Commander saying that the plan was not workable and that too at the last minute! He felt he was justified to be annoyed and made no attempts to conceal his displeasure.

Also, his reputation was at stake! He had acquitted himself well at the battle of Walong as the Brigade Commander during the Sino–Indian war of 1962, where he undertook a fighting withdrawal against overwhelming hordes of the Chinese army. He had thereafter established the Haile Selassie Academy in Ethiopia and commanded an infantry division successfully in Ladakh.

The Divisional Commander was also disappointed at the turn of events. He was from the same regiment as the battalion selected to attack. When asked initially by the Corps Commander to select the infantry battalion to undertake the offensive, he promptly selected the 1st Battalion, the 5th Gorkha Rifles. He had told the Corps Commander that this battalion had an excellent reputation for success in war and in peace, and that it would deliver. When advised that the offensive should be given to another unit because of the personal tragedy of the Commanding Officer of the Gorkha Battalion, he had overruled them and insisted that there would be no change. His own reputation was now at stake, not only as the Divisional Commander but also as an officer of this famous regiment.

Fortunately, the Brigade Commander was from the same regiment as the Corps Commander—the Brigade of the Guards. They had served together and known each other and their families over many years and across several locations. A thorough gentleman, he accepted the reasoning of the Battalion Commander but was also aware of the problems of a last-minute change. He decided to meet the Corps Commander informally and to request him to hear out the Commanding Officer of the Gorkhas as early as possible.

The Corps Commander was displeased at this upheaval, but he grudgingly agreed to come to the Divisional Headquarters the next day to listen to what the Battalion Commander and the Heads of the Arms and Services had to say.

The discussion was held in the sand model room at the Divisional Headquarters. The attendees were invited on a 'need-to-know basis'. That meant that only those directly concerned with the offensive would attend. Even so, the number of officers attending the discussion came to a total of seventeen. Strictest secrecy was required, and no one was allowed to take notes.

The situation, in fact, had the appearance of a court-room scene, with the Battalion Commander as the defendant in the dock. The judge was the Corps Commander, and the one-man jury was the Divisional Commander. The prosecution would be led by the Commander Artillery, who would make the case, against the change of plans, on behalf of the Heads of the Arms and Services.

The Corps Commander would listen to the prosecution and the defence, and would give his decision after the Divisional Commander gave his 'summing up', having heard the arguments of both sides.

The Divisional Commander, General Freemantle, made the opening statement in a matter-of-fact manner. He stated that the corps had been tasked with a few offensives and that it was important that these offensives succeeded without a hitch. He recalled the meticulous planning at all levels by the supporting arms and services and the staff—all that was left was the offensive to be launched as planned. Whereas the other offensives posed no problems and would go according to plan, the offensive by the Gorkhas threw up issues that needed consideration. Since the desired outcome was 'success', it was important that the Battalion Commander charged with the offensive be heard.

Lieutenant Colonel Suresh Gupta stated his case in a simple yet effective manner. He gave the reasons for the change of plans, and reminded the gathering of the principle of 'surprise' in war, the need to bring flexibility into their thinking and not insist on reinforcing a plan that was not workable. He asked all concerned to apply their minds to the issue as it existed today, as opposed to what it was a few days earlier. He added that his modified plan would ensure minimum changes in the already approved plan.

The first to speak from the opposition was the Commander Artillery of the division. First of all, he thanked the Corps Commander for the artillery resources given to him by the corps and said that the artillery plan had been made in great detail to ensure the success of the offensive. He stated that all contingencies had been taken into consideration and that every phase of the offensive had been accounted for, including unforeseen enemy defences that might come alive during the assault. Forward Observation Officers accompanying the assaulting companies would take on opportunity targets during the assault and reorganization stages.* The artillery fire plan, in his opinion, left nothing to chance and was perfect. He saw no reason for 'second thoughts' and said that the assault should go ahead as planned. If there was going to be a change in the conduct of the offensive, then more time would be required to make a new plan, which would delay the offensive from whatever date it would be required to be launched.

There was some murmuring of assent among the listeners, and the Divisional Commander had to ask for silence.

The Commander Artillery then stated that it would be better that the Heads of the Arms and Services speak for themselves, and that he would intervene when required.

Next to speak was the Squadron Commander of the Armoured Regiment, in support of the assault. He stated that if there was a change in the plan, he would have to look at the ground situation and would provide whatever support possible.

However, it might not be possible to support the assaulting troops from a flank, as had originally been planned, because he did not know the alternative approach. He could, however, look at the new approach and see how the plan could be modified.

The Commander Engineers stated that his role commenced only after the objective was captured, to commence de-mining operations and make the vehicle-safe lanes,† and therefore there was no change in tasks. He was all right with a change in plans,

---

* Reorganization stage: A stage in the operation of war of defence where all action is taken to defeat the inevitable counterattack by an enemy. This includes the resupply of arms, ammunition and other supplies, and the evacuation of casualties.

† Vehicle-safe lanes: Paths cleared by the engineers through the enemy minefields to allow vehicles carrying ammunition, supplies and reorganization stores to reach the captured objective and to enable the evacuation of casualties.

provided there was no change in the location of the vehicle-safe lanes that he would have to make.

The Commander Signals also said that he would establish line communication once the objective was captured and the vehicle-safe lanes were made. However, if the communication cables to be laid were to follow the assaulting troops along a different approach, then there might be problems. However, such problems could be resolved in cooperation with the signal platoon of the battalion.

The Col Adm. (Colonel-in-Charge Administration) stated that his task to resupply the troops would commence once the objective was captured and he would ensure that the reorganization stores reached the assaulting troops as soon as the vehicle-safe lanes were made. He foresaw no difficulty if there was a change in approach as long as the safe lanes were made in time.

The ADMS (Assistant Director Medical Services) spoke next. He said that whereas the method for the evacuation of casualties had been made according to the existing plan, there would not be a change in his plans as they would follow the safe lanes. However, there could be a problem if the fighting on the objective took longer than anticipated, as that would delay the making of the safe lanes, which in turn would delay the evacuation of casualties.

It was now left to Lieutenant Colonel Suresh Gupta, the Commanding Officer, to defend his plan and state how his alternative approach would be better than the existing plan.

General Freemantle asked permission from the Corps Commander for a ten-minute tea break. Permission was granted, and the buzz of conversation that had been suppressed all this time broke out anew.

Lieutenant Colonel Gupta kept sitting where he was. General Freemantle walked up to him and said: 'Suresh, what is the matter? Are you all right?'

'Absolutely okay, sir. I am just trying to collect my thoughts before I take the stand again.'

While Lieutenant Colonel Gupta was making his notes for his answers to the issues raised, an officer whom he knew well came up to him and said: 'Suresh, I hope you know that if your offensive according to your last-minute change of plans fails, then you will most probably have to face a court martial.'

'Yes,' was Lieutenant Colonel Gupta's reply. 'And I hope you also understand that no one can court martial dead bodies, which will be the case if I am forced to attack according to the existing plan.'

After the break, once everyone had settled down, General Freemantle asked Lieutenant Colonel Gupta if he was ready to make his closing statement. He added that his defence had better be good, because during the tea break some of the officers had come up to him and said that it looked like the CO of the 5th Gorkhas had developed cold feet.

Lieutenant Colonel Gupta stood beside the sand model, took a deep breath and said: 'I will not comment on that frivolous remark regarding cold feet, except to say that it depends on the wearer of the shoe. I am the Commanding Officer of my battalion and I am aware of my responsibilities and that the reputation of the corps, of my regiment, my men and my own reputation, depends on the success of this offensive. Before stating my case and answering the observations made by the previous speakers, I would like to point out a few landmarks on the sand model, so that you would be able to follow my line of thought.'

Lieutenant Colonel Gupta then began to point out the important features on the sand model. He focused on the objective, the two possible approaches and the river that flowed in the vicinity of the western approach.

'Firstly,' he said, 'despite my objections to all concerned—and who happen to be here today—on the frequent recces made by officers and men of the supporting arms and services, those recces continued, and my objections were ignored. As a consequence, the enemy has not only got wind of the fact that we are planning an offensive in this area, but they are also quite clear of the approach that we are going to take. Alarmed by our frequent reconnaissances, they have concretized their defences, laid extensive minefields and barbed-wire entanglements, and are now in the process of digging a deep ditch forward of their defences. We are aware that the Pakistani battalions have medium machine guns as part of their companies, and I have no doubt that they would have concentrated maximum machine guns along this approach. As all of you are aware, there is no cover whatsoever on this approach.

'Secondly, with regard to artillery of both sides: intelligence reports conveyed to us indicate that the quantum of enemy artillery allotted to the sector opposite to us has greatly increased. So, whereas our own artillery will have minimum effect on their concrete bunkers, my men will be exposed to the heavy punishment of enemy fire that includes medium and heavy artillery concentrated on this approach.

'With regard to armour, since I will be attacking across a river, it might be difficult for the tanks to shoot us on to the objective. However, the squadron commander in support is on my radio net. Should I require him to destroy opportunity targets during the reorg stage, I will ask him to do so. An officer or a JCO with a radio link, who would accompany us, would be helpful even on this approach.

'With regard to the Engineers and the Signals, there is no change to the existing plans. The vehicle-safe lanes will be made by the engineers through the enemy minefields after the objective has been captured under cover of our existing artillery fire plan. And the brigade signal detachment, which is already with me, is aware of what needs to be done along the river approach. The Detachment Commander has been with me and has seen the approach I intend to use. He has arranged for the cable that would be required. In addition, the Commander Signals would, I am sure, be making duplicate arrangements through the vehicle-safe lanes.

'The Col Adm. of the division has given his views, which I concur with. And as far as the casualties are concerned, my regimental medical officer has made adequate arrangements for their evacuation. I have spoken to my officers and JCOs, and we are prepared to accept delay in the evacuation of casualties. This is based on our firm conviction that if we attack the way we want, there will be no delay as far as the task given to my battalion is concerned, and the casualties would be minimal because of the surprise factor.

'I am convinced that an unexpected approach will guarantee success. I intend to attack the enemy in the hours of darkness, and the key to the success of this offensive is the principle of surprise.

'On the objections raised with regard to artillery support, I would like to emphatically suggest that the existing fire plan must in no way be changed. The enemy must be convinced that we will be attacking along the approach that he expects us to use. He will be expending his ammunition on this approach, but we will not be there. We will be elsewhere, on an approach that he least expects.

'The principal reason why the enemy does not expect us on the approach that we have selected is that he is under the impression that the river is a formidable obstacle to an assault from that direction, due to the depth of water. However, we have found crossing places that meet our needs. This approach also has sufficient vegetation along the banks of the river to conceal our movement.

'In light of what I have said, if we attack on the original approach, there is no chance of success. You will only be confronted with a failed attack and the bodies of me and my men. However, if you let me launch the offensive the way I want, then I would like to extend an invitation to the formation commanders to have breakfast with me on the objective at eleven o'clock on the morning of the attack.'

The CO ended by saying, 'There is also the issue of the gates of Rattoke that have to be brought back.'

The GOC said, 'Suresh, what is that you said towards the end?'

'Nothing, sir.'

The GOC gave the CO a quizzical look but did not take the matter further.

It was now left to the GOC to sum up the arguments and for the Corps Commander to take a decision. In fact, there was nothing much to say. General Freemantle summed it up as follows:

> 'Firstly, I thank the Corps Commander for taking the trouble to come to the Division Headquarters and to listen to this contentious issue of the change of plans at the last minute for the capture of the Sejhra Bulge.
>
> 'Secondly, I appreciate the manner in which this discussion has been held and the manner in which this

controversial issue has been logically examined and objectively analysed by all the participants.

'Thirdly, after hearing out the Commanding Officer of the Gorkhas, I see that he has dovetailed his new plan nicely into the previous one and there will actually be no change in the plans of the supporting arms and services. There will only be a change in the direction of approach by the battalion.

'Lastly, the Battalion Commander will have to justify his request for a change in the direction of approach by succeeding in the capture of the objective within the timeline stipulated by us.

'I now request the Corps Commander to give us his views.'

The Corps Commander said, 'Well, gentlemen, we have heard the Battalion Commander's plan on how he would like to capture Sejhra. I do not like last-minute changes, but I understand and accept the Commanding Officer's line of argument, but he has to translate his arguments into action, by doing what he says he will do. I hold him and his battalion to deliver as stated. I am sure he understands that the reputation of the corps, the Indian Army and his Regiment rests on his shoulders and that of the men of his battalion. I expect the supporting arms and services to make sure his plan succeeds. In any case, I will not accept failure under any circumstance, or any shortfall by him or anyone else, in the execution of the new plan. I wish all of you the best of luck for this offensive.'

Lieutenant Colonel Gupta breathed a big sigh of relief.

The granthi of the gurudwara of the village of Rattoke was also praying for the success of the attack by the Gorkhas. He led the ardas, which continued for seven days, praying for the success of the offensive by the Gorkhas.

Pakistan attacked India on the evening of 3 December, and the Indian counteroffensive by the Brigade went ahead as planned, on the night of 5–6 December. A battalion of the Brigade, 6 Mahar, moved off after dark to establish a roadblock south-west of Sejhra to cut off the enemy's escape routes, and 9 Sikh LI commenced their operations around the same time, to capture the border posts to ensure free movement of our troops for subsequent operations. The 1st Battalion, the 5th Gorkha Rifles commenced their approach march to Sejhra at 7 p.m.

The Western Army Commander, Lieutenant General K.P. Candeth describes Sejhra, its strategical importance and the manner in which it was captured in his book *The Western Front: The Indo–Pakistan War 1971*. This is what he says:

> [Sejhra] is a Pakistani salient of about 55 square kilometres jutting into Indian territory, just north of Ferozepur and south east of Khemkaran. The responsibility of holding it was that of Pakistan's 52 Infantry Brigade. They had inside the bulge about a battalion strength of troops consisting of 25 Baluch, Sutlej Rangers and Mujahids supported by elements of their reconnaissance and support battalion and some anti-tank guns. The village of Sejhra itself was a formidable position, situated on an escarpment 20 feet high, and protected by extensive minefields on the north, east and west and in the south by a stream called the 'Snake' which was 5 feet deep.
>
> As the area provided to Pakistan a secure base from where to attack our main defences at Voltaha and from where their armour could be launched to attack and capture Harike

> bridge which was vital to us, it was decided to eliminate this bulge . . .
>
> Meanwhile 1/5 Gorkha Rifles left their assembly position at 7 p.m. and carried out a brilliant approach march and got behind the enemy without being detected even by the village dogs. However, the depth of the 'Snake' came as a surprise but holding their weapons high over their heads, the Gorkhas forded the stream and attacked the position, shouting their battle cry of AYO GORKHALI. The enemy had a network of bunkers and put up a stiff resistance but they were winkled out bunker by bunker. The position fell and by 6 a.m. on the 6th Sejhra was in our hands.

Sejhra was captured much ahead of the laid down timelines. Huge amounts of arms and ammunition were captured, including two anti-tank guns, six mortars, many medium and light machine guns, and large quantities of small arms and ammunition that filled three three-ton trucks. The American magazine *Newsweek* published an article with photographs that showed that the enemy commander had left his trousers behind, having been caught literally with his pants down! The Corps Commander, the Divisional Commander and the Brigade Commander were able to have mugs of tea on the captured objective at eleven o'clock on the morning of the attack.

The Divisional Commander and the Brigade Commander were at the rear of the Assembly Area on the night of the attack, watching as the Gorkhas moved silently to their FUP* and waiting anxiously for the success signal of the Gorkhas. In the early hours of the morning, they heard the war cry of

* FUP: Forming-up place, where troops line up to attack an objective.

the Gorkhas—'Ayo Gorkhali!'—as the attack went in. They were also witness to the colossal fire from the enemy artillery, mortars and medium machine guns on the approach that the enemy expected the Gorkhas to use and came to realize that no troops in the world could have survived the immensity of that concentrated fire. By three o'clock in the morning, the battalion had captured Sejhra and radioed their success signal.

The battalion lost one JCO and eight other ranks; there were twenty-three other ranks among the wounded. For its exceptional performance, the battalion was honoured with 'Sejhra' as a Battle Honour and 'Punjab 1971' as a Theatre Honour; it was also awarded four Vir Chakras and five Sena Medals.*

The 1st Battalion, the 5th Gorkha Rifles lived up to its reputation and was presented a silver cup by the Corps Commander for the unit that performed best in the Corps Zone during the 1971 war.

However, what especially pleased Lieutenant Colonel Suresh Gupta and the battalion was the fact that they could bring back and return the gates of the Rattoke gurudwara, fulfilling the prediction of the old granthi who had foretold that the gates would be brought back one day by a Gorkha battalion.

After the war had concluded, the Commanding Officer of the Gorkhas, his officers, JCOs and some of his men were invited to the gurudwara to celebrate the return of the gates, participate in the *path*† and partake of the guru ka langar. It was a joyous

* Vir Chakra and Sena Medal are awards given for gallantry. Vir Chakras were awarded to the Commanding Officer Lieutenant Colonel S. Gupta, two Company Commanders, Majors Sheel Puri and K.S. Gill, and a Platoon Commander, Naib Subedar Narbahadur Gurung.

† Path: Prayer.

celebration, and the Commanding Officer felt particularly happy that he was able to bring the gates back.

For many years thereafter, the gurudwara continued to mention the 1st Battalion, the 5th Gorkhas (FF) as part of its ardas, thanks to which the battalion has been blessed and continues to do exceptionally well in all its endeavours.

Postscript

Convinced that he was right, Lieutenant Colonel Suresh Gupta, VrC, did not waver in his conviction, irrespective of the outrage and opposition of all the commanders and staff in the chain of command for the last-minute change of plans. Backing his conviction was his professional competence, his ability to evaluate risks and the courage of his officers, JCOs and men who ensured an outstanding success. The stance that he took, despite the overwhelming opposition he faced, convincingly proves that moral courage is as important as physical courage, and that although flexibility in not a principle of war, it is something important to consider when a better option presents itself rather than reinforcing a plan that will not work.

The Commanding Officer also proved that there is no point in reinforcing the probability of failure when an alternative plan, even at the last minute, can succeed. And, most importantly, the element of 'surprise' in war must never be forgotten.

Finally, the granthi of the gurudwara in Rattoke was overjoyed that the gates of the gurudwara had come back, just as the old granthi had predicted, and he bestowed his blessings on the Gorkhas, who, together with the granthi, exclaim, 'Waheguruji ka khalsa! Waheguruji ki fateh!'

Mission Karachi

'From the days when humans first began to use the sea, the great lesson of history is that the nation that is confined to a land strategy is in the end defeated.'

—Anonymous

Prelude to the War of 1971

Admiral B.S. Soman, Chief of the Indian Navy, looked at the file that had just been put up to him and at the noting signed by H.C. Sarin, Secretary, Defence Production, Ministry of Defence.* The noting stated

> With reference to the notings mentioned above, the ongoing operations by the Army and Air Force and the current situation with regard to the Andaman and Nicobar Islands: the Indian Navy will not initiate any action against Pakistan at sea and will not proceed more than 200 nautical miles beyond Bombay nor

* Vice Admiral G.M. Hiranandani, *Transition to Triumph: History of the Indian Navy, 1965–1975* (New Delhi: Lancer Publishers, 1999), p. 30.

operate north of the latitude of Porbandar, except in pursuit of any Pakistan Navy offensive action.

On the morning of 6 September 1965, the Indian Army had attacked across the international border in response to Pakistan's 'Operation Grand Slam', which had been launched for the capture of Akhnur during the war of 1965. One of the options to counter Pakistan's assault on Jammu and Kashmir was the opening of a second front in Punjab. Thanks to the courage and sense of purpose of Prime Minister Lal Bahadur Shastri, the Indian Army had crossed the international border and gone on the offensive in the Lahore, Sialkot and Dera Baba Nanak sectors. The reasoning of the Prime Minister was that Pakistan needed to understand that if they attack Jammu and Kashmir, they attack India.

After a series of hard-fought battles, the Indian Army had reached the outskirts of Lahore as the Indian Air Force fought for the control of the sky. The Indian Navy, however, had been left out of battle. The galling message from the Ministry of Defence, that the Navy should not widen the war and in that context was not to proceed more than 200 nautical miles beyond Bombay, effectively prohibited the Indian Navy from launching offensive operations against Pakistan.

The Western Fleet heading for Karachi.

Admiral Soman, the Naval Chief, was indignant and extremely unhappy with this communication from the Ministry of Defence and asked for an appointment with the Defence Minister. The Naval Chief and the Indian Navy were straining at the leash to attack Pakistan across the sea, but the message from the ministry restricted them from doing so.

The next morning, the Naval Chief met Defence Minister Y.B. Chavan. The Defence Minister noticed that the Naval Chief was visibly upset. After asking the Naval Chief to sit down, he said, 'Yes, Admiral, what can I do for you?'

'Mr Chavan, I have received this communication yesterday from a Joint Secretary from your ministry,' said the Naval Chief as he slipped the file with the errant note across to the Defence Minister.* 'Why is the Navy being stopped from carrying out its legitimate operational role?'

The Defence Minister, without looking at the note, said, 'Admiral, the bulk of your Navy is already on our eastern seaboard carrying out its legitimate role of preventing Indonesia from capturing the Nicobar Islands, which, as you know, from intelligence sources, is a very real threat. So, what are you so upset about?'

'Mr Chavan, the role of the Navy encompasses the Bay of Bengal, the Arabian Sea and much of the Indian Ocean. So, if, as you say, we are carrying out our role in the Bay of Bengal, then what about the rest of the role that we are tasked to do?'

'Admiral, I must admit, that the ministry has not done enough to upgrade the Navy as we have done for the other two services after the 1962 war. However, it is an issue of available resources

---

* Conversations as reported by Admiral Soman. See *Transition to Triumph*, p. 31.

versus priorities. We are aware of this shortcoming, and I propose to address this matter soon after the present situation is resolved. Till then, you must not escalate the situation on the west coast. You do not have the resources to fight offensively on both fronts.'

'Mr Chavan, it is good news that the ministry has realized at last, that it has not met the Navy's needs. However, my officers and men are prepared to fight with whatever we have. A passive policy will set a wrong precedent. What is the purpose of having a Navy if it is not allowed to fight? Failure to fight offensively on the west coast will adversely affect the morale of the Navy and that, Minister, is not acceptable.'

'Admiral, it is my duty as the Defence Minister to listen to the Service Chiefs and to take decisions. I have listened earlier to you, as well as the other Service Chiefs, and it is my decision, in the interest of the country, that the Navy will take on a defensive role on the west coast and will not do anything that will escalate the situation.'

'Minister, if it was your decision, then why was it conveyed to me by a secretary of your ministry?'

The Minister took the offending note that was lying in front of him, initialed it and slid it across to the Naval Chief. 'Is it all right now?' he said.

'Thank you, Minister,' said the Naval Chief. 'I would, however, like to see the Prime Minister on this issue.'

The meeting was quickly processed and the next morning, the Naval Chief was ushered into the Prime Minister's office. Chavan was already there, sitting next to Lal Bahadur Shastri.

Prime Minister Shastri opened the conversation with, 'Well, Admiral Soman, I understand that you wish to see me?'

'Yes, Prime Minister. It is with regard to a direction from the Ministry of Defence, that the Indian Navy will not undertake offensive operations of any kind against Pakistan on the west coast or cross the 24th parallel, and will not do anything that might escalate the situation unless attacked.'

'Yes, that is true. We have examined the issue in detail. You are aware, I am sure, of the collusion between Indonesia and Pakistan with regard to an effort by Indonesia to take over some of our islands in the Nicobar chain, and that recently there has been increased activity in the sea around the Nicobar Islands. Ensure that nothing untoward happens there, Admiral. That is where your priority lies. As far as the Pakistan Navy is concerned, we do not perceive a threat from them as of now. We are aware of your resources and have decided that the navy will adopt a defensive posture on the west coast unless attacked. I do not want the situation on the west coast to escalate into a full-blown war. We have enough on our hands already.'

'Prime Minister, as the Naval Chief, I am aware of my tasks and my priorities, as far as the security of our seas, our island territories and the Indian Ocean is concerned. I am glad that this situation has brought to light the fact that the navy needs to have its sources upgraded, if it is to carry out its legitimate role, and we do hope that, as the Defence Minister has said, this matter will soon be addressed. I have consulted my officers and we are prepared to fight with whatever we have. Our inability to fight offensively will send the wrong message, that we are unwilling to fight. That will adversely affect the morale of the navy.'

'Admiral, your reservations have been conveyed to me by the Defence Minister. We have once more reviewed the situation, and there is no change in our decision and you need to accept it.'

'Prime Minister, I do understand your reservations. However, I need your permission to meet the President, who is the Commander-in-Chief of the Armed Forces.'

'No, Admiral. Permission is denied. Please do as you have been ordered. Thank you.'

The Prime Minister was firm, and the Naval Chief had put forward his view up to a point. After all, orders were orders, and that was that.

These orders from the government prevented the Indian Navy from undertaking any offensive operations against Pakistan, even when the Pakistan Navy bombarded Dwarka on the west coast with impunity. Although this gave Pakistan no military advantage, it gave the Pakistan Navy a boost in morale. To the Indian Navy, it was a humiliating affront. Officers and men of the Indian Navy found it difficult to understand that although it was the Defence Ministry that had issued these directions, it was the navy that had to answer questions from the public and the media as to why the Indian Navy did not react to the Pakistani raid. As a consequence, the reputation of the navy plummeted to a very low level.

After the war, an article titled '1965: Somnath and Ghaznavi' appeared in a Pakistani naval magazine, which extolled the shelling of Dwarka by the Pakistan Navy and played up the event as a great naval victory. The article likened the raid by the Pakistan Navy to the raids by Mehmud Ghaznavi on Gujarat and the destruction of the Somnath temple in the eleventh century. PNS *Khyber* was a destroyer that was part of the raiding force, and there was great excitement on board that ship, because the name of the Torpedo and Anti-Submarine Officer on board happened to be Lieutenant Commander P.N. Ghaznavi. The ship's crew was told on the intercom that they were repeating history and that they were going to do what Mehmud Ghaznavi did a thousand years earlier, except that Mehmud Ghaznavi's horses were replaced by steel warships and that they were attacking from the sea. This story was all the more irritating to the officers and men of the Indian Navy, because the Pakistan Navy was taking mileage from a non-event.

In early 1966, a debrief* of the 1965 war was held at Naval Headquarters, New Delhi. The Indian Navy's operational directive and the note sent by the Ministry of Defence were read out, and the aspect that the Indian Navy should not 'widen' the war was also narrated. There was an uncomfortable silence, till Captain K.K. Nayyar got up and spoke.

Captain Nayyar pointed out that the navy was also accountable to the people of India and to Parliament, who needed to know about the role played by the Indian Navy in the 1965 war, and that he and others wearing the naval uniform had no answer. Since it was the decision of the government to restrict the role of the navy in the 1965 war, then the least that the government could have done was to have made a public statement after the war that it had directed the navy to adopt a defensive posture on the west coast to not allow the situation to develop into a 'full-blown war'. By failing to do so, the government had let down the navy very badly.

Nayyar's plain-speaking raised the level of the debate, and his comments probably shaped the thinking of several future naval chiefs as well. Ultimately, the repercussions of this debate had a useful outcome, as this was the primary factor that motivated the navy and some senior naval officers, like Admiral Nanda, to make sure that the Indian Navy played its rightful role in the next conflict.

* A 'debrief' is an analysis and discussion on an operation/event that has taken place, to examine the conduct of the operation and to see if there are any lessons to be learnt or any corrective action needs to be taken.

Three years later, Admiral Nanda was in Bombay as Fleet Officer Commander-in-Chief, Western Naval Command, and was in line to be the next Naval Chief.

Still smarting from the humiliation of the navy not being able to take an effective part in the 1965 Indo–Pak war, he made a statement that was published in *Blitz*, a Bombay newspaper. He said that having spent his early years as a young naval officer in Karachi, he knew the layout of the harbour and its waters like the back of his hand, and that, given the opportunity, he would set Karachi on fire!

Meanwhile, being aware of Pakistan's obsession to use force to settle disputes, the Indian Navy decided to acquire missile boats for the defence of its ports and harbours. These hard-hitting, high-speed missile platforms had been designed by the Russian Navy to take on targets at great distance and with great accuracy. They were primarily designed to be used only as defensive weapons.

A team under Captain K.K. Nayyar was sent to the Soviet Union to be trained by their naval experts and get fully proficient in the understanding and handling of these sophisticated missile boats. This team consisted of specially selected, highly qualified and enthusiastic young naval officers, mostly in the rank of Lieutenant Commanders, who had expertise in navigation, gunnery, torpedo and anti-submarine operations, engineering, communication, etc. The team spent a year training in the Soviet Union and not only mastered the handling of this weapon platform but also learnt the Russian language, which was essential to understand the technology and nuances of handling these missiles and missile boats.

The training was carried out at Vladivostok, where the team weathered Arctic-like conditions during one of Russia's coldest winters. It was while they were there that Captain Nayyar tossed a question to the team as to whether they could think about the possibility of using these missile boats in an offensive role? This was an exciting proposition, which triggered a whole new line of thinking as to how missile boats, a weapon meant for defence tasks, could be used in an offensive mode.

There were a number of issues to consider. These were boats designed for speed but not for travelling long distances in the open sea. Due to the need for speed, these boats powered by modified aircraft engines guzzled great quantities of fuel and their endurance was therefore limited to less than 500 nautical miles. So, how could they go all the way to Karachi and get back? Also, due to the necessity of speed, the waterline of these boats was low and therefore not at all suitable for an ocean-going mission, as high waves could swamp the boats. All these aspects were exercising the minds of the officers. They were, however, told never to speak about the possibility of using these missile boats in an offensive role; not even in their dreams, because the mission could only succeed if the element of surprise was ensured.

At the end of the training programme, which had lasted for over a year, the Russian instructors were pleased to see the knowledge and competence of the Indian team, who had taken them far beyond the frontiers of their own specialized knowledge. The Russians admitted that they had to prepare assiduously for each training session, because of the in-depth questions that were asked by the Indian team on every aspect of the missile and the boats. The use of the missile boats in an offensive role was, however, never mentioned.

The use of these missile boats in the attack role was discussed 'in house', among a select few officers. One of the officers,

Lieutenant Commander Vijay Jerath, was asked to write a paper on how these boats could be used in the offensive role. This paper, duly vetted by Captain Nayyar, was sent by hand to Naval Ops and Plans at Naval Headquarters, New Delhi. Nothing further was heard about the paper thereafter.

The dispatch of the missile boats to India commenced in January 1971. Each missile boat, stripped to its bare essentials, weighed approximately 180 tonnes, and it was learnt that Mumbai did not have heavy-duty cranes big enough to unload the boats from the mother ship, and so the missile boats would have to be unloaded at Calcutta. The next problem was how such boats, with limited endurance and ocean-going capability, would make their way from Calcutta to the west coast. After a number of experiments, a towing gadget was designed, by Lieutenant Commander Kwatra, for each missile boat, and they were towed around the Indian peninsula, from Calcutta to Bombay. The towing gadget had to ensure there was no collision between the towing boat and the missile boat. There were eight missile boats, and an equal number of ships were required to tow them.

The rest of the Indian Navy was unaware of the characteristics and capabilities of these missile boats, as they had only just been inducted into the navy. Some senior officers were sceptical about the claims being made about the capability and accuracy of the missile boats, and a demonstration was asked for. Tests were initiated to evaluate the missiles on distant targets, and the results were spectacularly successful. A naval exercise was also held, and the officers and men of the navy, who witnessed these tests for the first time, were astonished at the radar range of the missile boats and the accurate hit-precision of their missiles.

The Indo–Pak War of 1971

Meanwhile, far away in East Pakistan, politics had taken an ugly turn. A series of events had led to a state of confrontation between India and Pakistan, and war became a real possibility.

On 3 December 1971, at 5.45 p.m., Pakistan opened the war by attacking Indian airfields in the northern and western sectors. Prime Minister Indira Gandhi, Foreign Minister Sardar Swaran Singh and Defence Minister Babu Jagjivan Ram were all away from Delhi. It appeared as though Pakistan was aware that the Prime Minister of India and her Ministers of Defence and External Affairs would be away from Delhi on that day.

The Indian Armed Forces, however, had been preparing for an offensive by Pakistan. Admiral Nanda had just returned from Bombay that morning; he had gone there to speak to the officers and men about a war that everyone felt would soon take place. Admiral Nanda had made it clear that if Pakistan did attack, he would take the war on the sea to Karachi. He also made it clear that he would not accept any shortfall in performance and that anyone having any reservations about the offensive would be free to step back. There was no one who had any reservations.

At his briefing in Bombay, on 1 December 1971, Admiral Nanda shared with his officers the information he had received that there was a strong probability of Pakistani submarines

A missile boat in action.

launching sneak attacks on ships of the Western Fleet within Bombay harbour. Concerned about such a situation, he ordered the fleet to be out of the confines of the harbour the next day and to head out to the open sea.

His premonition was correct. PNS *Hangor,* a state-of-the-art Daphne-class Pakistani submarine was lying in wait outside Bombay harbour, waiting for the war to start, so that as soon as war was declared, they could destroy ships of the Western Fleet as they emerged from Mumbai harbour. But unfortunately for the Pakistani submariners, the Western Fleet had moved out of harm's way before the start of the war, thanks to the intuition of the Naval Chief. The Pakistani submarine could therefore not take advantage of the excellent position it had placed itself in.

The ships of India's Western Fleet passed over the waiting Pakistani submariners without the Pakistanis being able to do anything about it. Within hours of the Pakistani offensive against India, the Western Fleet was on its way to Pakistani waters. Pakistan was caught off guard by the quickness of the Indian response.

Prior to the war, Admiral Nanda had outlined his vision, strategy and action plan should there be a war with Pakistan and shared them with his Commanders-in-Chief East and West. Recounting the discussions he had with Admiral Nanda, Admiral Krishnan, Flag Officer Commanding-in-Chief East, said:

> . . . We talked at length of our tasks ahead. All our discussions stemmed from one overriding thought, a firm conviction, bordering on obsession, that should war come, the Navy should throw everything it had into battle and our entire strategy from the very onset of hostilities should be one of

> bold offensive. We should scrap, erase and wipe off from our minds any ideas of a defensive posture, we must seek action, taking any risks that were necessary and destroy the enemy in his ports and at sea . . .*

The Missile Squadron, meanwhile, had already assembled south of the coast of Saurashastra by the end of November and launched its attacks against the Pakistan Navy. Three attacks by the Missile Squadron on Karachi had been planned—Operations Trident, Python and Triumph.

The first attack by the Missile Squadron was executed by the missile boats *Nipat*, *Nirghat* and *Veer*. The missile boats were escorted by two Petya-class frigates, the *Kiltan* and *Katchal*, on 4 December1971.

Ironically and in fitting retribution, the first Pakistani naval ship to be destroyed by the Missile Squadron was PNS *Khyber*, the ship that had bombed Dwarka during the 1965 Indo–Pak war and the crew of which had exulted in replicating the raids by Mehmud of Ghazni and in having a Lieutenant Commander Mohamed Ghaznavi on board.

PNS *Khyber* was patrolling the south-west approaches to Karachi. At about 2215 hours, her radar informed her that an enemy force was approaching Karachi. The enemy consisted of the missile boats escorted by the Petyas in arrowhead formation and moving at full speed towards Karachi, with INS *Nipat* in the lead and *Nirghat* and *Veer* following behind. The closing range with which the *Khyber* and the *Nirghat* were approaching each other was approximately 60 knots. At about 2240 hours, when the *Khyber* was at a distance of approximately 20 nautical miles,

* *Transition to Triumph*, p. 120.

Nirghat fired its first missile. The crew of the *Khyber* mistook the approaching missile to be an enemy aircraft and opened up with her close-range anti-aircraft guns but failed in preventing the missile from hitting her. The missile struck the *Khyber* on the starboard side. Her boiler room was hit and her speed greatly reduced. A huge flame shot up in No. 1 boiler room, and dense black smoke poured out of her funnel. The ship was plunged into darkness. The wireless operator passed on a message that the ship was under air attack. This incorrect assessment of what had hit them delayed the rescue of the survivors by almost a day.

Commander Yadav, the leader of this group who had positioned himself on INS *Nipat* and had ordered the first missile to be fired, now ordered the second missile to be fired by *Nirghat* at the *Khyber,* which was now 17 nautical miles away. After the second missile hit the *Khyber*, her speed came down to zero. The ship caught fire and dense smoke emanated from her. At 2200 hours Pakistan Standard Time, the Captain of the *Khyber* decided to abandon ship; her list to port* had become dangerous. By 2215 hours, the ship was abandoned by all who could leave. Explosions due to bursting ammunition continued to rock the ship as men jumped overboard from the sinking destroyer. The *Khyber* sank stern first at 2230 hours. On the radar screen of the Indian missile boats, the *Khyber* had first showed as a blip. After she was hit, the blip kept diminishing in size, till it disappeared altogether. The *Khyber* was no more. She sank approximately 35 nautical miles south-west of Karachi.

The second ship to be destroyed was PNS *Muhafiz,* a Pakistani minesweeper. The *Muhafiz* was on patrol and was probably sent to assist the *Khyber.* While she was heading

* List to port: When the angle of inclination of the ship is towards the left.

towards the *Khyber,* she saw a ball of light hurtling towards her and suffered a direct missile hit on the port side, towards the rear. She caught fire and disintegrated without being able to even send out a distress message. The ship's structure continued to burn till it finally sank, with the survivors floating amid the burning debris. Two more ships carrying ammunition, the *Shahjahan* and *Venus Challenger*, were also destroyed.

The orders were that maximum missiles should be fired in the first attack, as surprise was considered to be the dominant factor for overall success. So, INS *Nipat* carried on towards Karachi. *Nipat*'s radar picked up the Kiamari oil tanks, and when the range was 18 miles *Nipat* fired a missile at the oil tanks. There was an explosion on the horizon. Huge flames leapt into the sky. The explosions, caused by the destruction of the ships carrying ammunition and the burning oilfields together, resulted in a firework display that many who were watching the raid from the other Indian ships will long remember.

Operation Python, the second attack on Karachi, which was to be carried out on 6 December, had to be postponed due to bad weather and rough seas. This attack was carried out on 8 December by missile boat INS *Vinash*, escorted by two frigates, *Trishul* and *Talwar*. This single missile boat, commanded by Lieutenant Commander Vijay Jerath, not only severely damaged the Pakistani oil tanker PNS *Dacca*, but also destroyed and sank two other vessels. Its fourth missile smashed into an oil tank at the Kiamari oil farm and set it once again on fire. The huge flames shooting into the sky could be seen by ships from as far as 60 nautical miles. IAF pilots who went to bomb Karachi the next morning reported that it was the biggest bonfire in Asia. The fire raged for seven days and nights, enveloping Karachi in a pall of black smoke that shut out the sun for three days. It shocked the Pakistan Navy, which promptly recalled all its ships into the safety of the inner harbour.

The third attack, code-named Operation Triumph, had to be called off because by the time the regrouping of resources could take place, the war had come to a close.

Admiral Nanda's promise was carried out three years after he made his statement that he would set Karachi on fire! What is more, the Pakistan Navy bolted into Karachi harbour and refused to come out and fight. Unfortunately for them, the Pakistan Air Force refused to come to the aid of their sister service, and the Indian Navy and Air Force had a field day around and above Karachi. The Indian Navy was now in firm control of the Arabian Sea, and no merchant ship or aircraft of any country was allowed to enter or leave Karachi's territorial waters or airspace without the permission of the Government of India!

Russian satellites, in the meanwhile, were relaying to the Russian Naval Chief, Admiral Gorshkov, the naval battle in the North Arabian Sea. Satellite images of Indian missile boats attacking the Pakistan Navy and Karachi at first surprised the Russian Naval Chief, who could not believe what he was seeing! But surprise and consternation soon gave way to amazement and admiration at the way the Indians were using Russian missile boats. So much so that he shouted with laughter and joy and did a little jig in the Russian Naval Ops Room, to the surprise and amusement of his staff!

Pakistan had all along relied on America and China coming to its aid. The Indian armed forces, however, had wrapped up the war in thirteen days, before any intervention could take place.

President of the United States, Richard Nixon, frustrated at Pakistan's performance in the war, had ordered the American Seventh Fleet to enter the Bay of Bengal. But his orders to the American Fleet Commander were imprecise, and the American Admiral was not clear as to whether the American Navy was to intimidate the Indian Navy, or to rescue Pakistani and American officials holed up in Dacca, or to attack the Indian Navy. In any case, it was too late. By the time the US Seventh Fleet entered the Bay of Bengal, the Indian armed forces had wrapped up the war, East Pakistan had been liberated, and Bangladesh, a new nation, had been born.

Soon after the war, Admiral Gorshkov of the Russian Navy arrived at Mumbai harbour with part of his fleet. He expressed his amazement and delight at the manner in which the Indian Navy had used the Russian missile boats in an offensive role, when they had been created and designed only for the defence of ports and harbours. He told the Indian Naval Chief, Admiral Nanda, that he would like to meet the intrepid officers of the Missile Squadron who had used his Russian missile boats to such devastating effect. The occasion was a celebratory dinner aboard INS *Vikrant,* the Indian aircraft carrier. All invitees, Indian and Russian were in their ceremonial mess dress. The missile boat commanders were, however, still in their combat dress. The Russian Admiral was informed that the missile boat commanders would not be able to attend the dinner as they were inappropriately dressed. But the Russian Admiral requested Admiral Nanda to let them come for the dinner, and his request was acceded to.

Admiral Gorshkov met the commanders of the missile boats, personally congratulated them and gave each of them the characteristic Russian 'bear hug'. He told them how impressed he was with their performance. He also said something that is important but is not generally known. He said: 'You need to know that you were not alone. We were monitoring the movement of the Seventh Fleet of the US Navy and would have intervened if it became necessary. Nevertheless, you boys have used our missile boats better than we could have ever imagined, even in our wildest dreams. Well done and heartiest congratulations!'*

Postscript

This story brings out how innovative and bold use of weapons can lead to outstanding results in war, and the important part the Indian Navy plays in safeguarding our national interests. Good leaders ensure that wars do not take place, but that can only happen if we are strong. The strength of a nation is contingent not only on political and military will but also on the weapons and infrastructure made available to the armed forces to carry out their tasks.

* *Transition to Triumph*, p. 169.

The Beeb's Best Broadcast

'Battles are won or lost in the minds of men, before they are won or lost on the ground.'

—Brigadier Desmond Hayde, MVC

Lieutenant Colonel Arun Bhimrao Harolikar, Commanding Officer of the 4th Battalion, 5th Gorkha Rifles (FF), was in a reflective mood. The battalion had fought two fierce battles at Atgram and Gazipur, and had come out on top. At Atgram, it had decimated 'B' company of Pakistan's 31 Punjab, and had ravaged 22 Baluch at the battle of Gazipur. The *khukri** had struck terror in the hearts and minds of the Pakistani soldiers as the Gorkhas slashed and severed heads with abandon. Pakistani soldiers who survived passed on the fear of cold steel to the other soldiers of those units. Those who had survived the glint of the khukri, on those moonlit nights, would probably never forget

* Khukri: A knife used by Gorkhas. It has a curved blade, about 14 inches long, thicker on the top and tapering towards the cutting edge, which is very sharp. The handle is made of bone or wood or metal. The blade has a small notch on the cutting edge close to the handle, to prevent blood flowing on to the handle and making it slippery.

the blood-curdling cry of '*Ayo Gorkhali*' as the Gorkhas went about their business of war.

The heliborne attack: Battle of Sylhet.

The morale of the battalion was sky high, but it had paid a heavy price for those victories. Hawa Singh and Johri, two of the young officers whom Harolikar had groomed and trained, were no more. Kelkar, his Second-in-Command and college mate, had also been killed. Four more—Yeshwant Rawat, Virender Rawat, Young Bharat* and Rajesh Sherawat—had been wounded. The battalion had entered the war with eighteen officers, and in one week three had been killed and four wounded. Only eleven officers were left to execute future tasks. These two gruesome battles had cost his battalion the lives of three officers, one JCO and nineteen other ranks, with four officers and seventy-four other ranks wounded. Leave parties from Nepal had not yet fetched up with the battalion, and the strength of the Rifle Companies ranged from fifty-three to sixty-two, against an

* Named Young Bharat by his grandfather because he was born on 15 August 1947.

authorized strength of 114. He had asked for a replacement of his Second-in-Command, but there was no news as to who this would be and when he would arrive.

The rifle companies had to be reorganized, Company Commanders replaced, men had to fill in the places of those who had been killed or wounded, and the new incumbents briefed and trained in their new roles. During training, Harolikar had emphasized that every individual should be able to take on more than one role, and he had to now make it work. The reality of war was so different! The battalion had been blooded, but it had also been bloodied. It was not easy to forget that some of the youngsters who, just a few days earlier, had been so keen to get to grips with the enemy were no more! It was not fair that they should have died so young.

Doing well in battle has a price, which is that you are given more and more difficult tasks. That was what happened after the success at Atgram. Another battalion had attacked and failed to capture a strongly entrenched enemy in Gazipur, and the Corps Commander, General Sagat Singh, had said: 'Send in the Gorkhas.' And so, they went in and captured Gazipur, but at great cost.

Colonel Harolikar had to write to the next of kin, and that was a daunting task. Army Headquarters would send an impersonal telegram, starting with the words, 'Regret to inform you that . . .', a message that every army wife or mother dreaded to receive. It was better to have no news than to receive that message. However, as the head of the family of the 4th Battalion, he had to write a more personal letter telling the wife or mother how well her husband/son had done in battle. He also had to write the citations for those who had been extraordinarily brave and courageous. He felt that he needed a few days' break before he could carry out the next task that would inevitably be allotted to his battalion.

He had messaged Brigade Commander Bunty Quinn that his battalion needed a few days to rest and reorganize. The Brigade Commander had readily acquiesced, and Harolikar had been given a break of four days to reorganize for their next task.

The battalion had commenced moving to the rear areas, and the Quartermaster and his party had left to find a suitable forest grove where shade and water would be available. The men had not had the opportunity to bathe for six days, nor had they had hot food during this period. A break, therefore, was welcome. The cremations of the deceased compatriots had been done, but a lot of paperwork had to follow. A few days were also needed to clean the weapons, replenish ammunition, wash clothes, send letters to families and lay down telecommunication lines to the Brigade Headquarters.

The men had just finished bathing in a jungle stream. Their clothes were being dried while the men waited for their first hot meal after what seemed an eternity. But then, there was a telephone call for the Commanding Officer from the Brigade Headquarters.

The Commanding Officer took the call. He was told that his battalion was given yet another task and that they needed to move immediately.

Colonel Harolikar protested that his men needed a break. They had not slept for four days. What was so important that could not be done by another battalion? There was so much to be done before he could be ready for the next task. The Brigade Commander, Bunty Quinn, listened quietly and said: 'Harry, I am sure you know that I would have protested as much as you are protesting now, and that my protests have been overruled.'

That was true. Brigadier Quinn was known to be an officer who was fair and just, and would never put his troops in harm's way if he thought that it was not right. Harolikar knew that and answered: 'All right, sir, tell me: When do I have to move?'

Brigadier Quinn said: 'Harry, can't spell out the details over the phone. I am coming over to you right now.'

An hour later, Brigadier Quinn drove up to where the battalion was located and informed Colonel Harolikar that his battalion had been given the task of undertaking the Indian Army's first heliborne assault, and that the objective was Sylhet in East Pakistan.

On the morning of 6 December, the same day that the Gorkhas had moved to their rest area, the Corps Commander, Lieutenant General Sagat Singh, had met with Brigadier Quinn. Sagat Singh informed Brigadier Quinn that he had learnt Sylhet had been evacuated by the Pakistani troops. The Corps Commander felt that it was imperative that the Indian Army occupied Sylhet at the earliest. An advance on foot through enemy-held territory in the required timeframe was not possible. But Sagat had ten helicopters available in Agartala, as a corps resource. He informed Quinn that a battalion had to be airlifted to Sylhet the next day and that he wanted the Gorkhas for this task. He added that they had to move immediately to Kalaura, the place nominated as the launch pad for the heliborne operation.

Brigadier Quinn informed Lieutenant Colonel Harolikar that Sylhet was strategically important because it gave depth to Dhaka and formed part of the 'Fortress Concept'—General Niazi's strategy for the defence of East Pakistan. The early capture of Sylhet would facilitate General Sagat's intention to be the first to reach Dhaka. The mission involved the capture of an airfield, a communication centre and a road junction—a task which would normally have been given to a brigade.

The Brigade Commander informed General Sagat that he had given the Gorkhas four days to rest and reorganize after the battles in Atgram and Gazipur. The Corps Commander told Quinn to cancel his orders and said that the Gorkhas should be asked to start moving immediately. He said he knew the Gorkhas and that they were best suited for such a task. There was no time to waste.

General Sagat was relentless in the execution of his tasks. If the Gorkhas had done well in Atgram and Gazipur, then he would use them again for more difficult tasks to achieve his aim, even though they had suffered heavy casualties in officers and men.

Initial intelligence at Headquarter 4 Corps indicated that Pakistan's 202 Infantry Brigade, along with its supporting arms, was holding Sylhet. That was the equivalent of over 3000 troops. But according to the Corps Commander, the brigade had moved out, for the defence of Dhaka, and there were now only about 200 irregulars holding Sylhet.

Sagat Singh, General Officer Commanding 4 Corps, knew that speed was essential for the success of this task, but Sylhet was many miles in the interior and far ahead of his advancing forces. The only way of ensuring the speedy capture of Sylhet would be the use of faster modes of transport. Group Captain Chandan Singh, the air force officer on the staff of General Sagat's headquarters, had ten helicopters available, but they were meant only for logistical purposes; they were soft-skinned and had no protection whatsoever, even against small-arms fire.

The main problem, however, was not only that the helicopters were vulnerable to small-arms fire but also that there were no means of softening up the enemy weapons that would be aimed at the helicopters in the air and the troops on the ground. The Indian Air Force did not have attack helicopters, and their fighter aircraft did not have night-fighting capabilities. Besides, Sylhet was far beyond the range of the Indian artillery. The Gorkhas would therefore be on their own, without any fire support.

The Corps Commander and Group Captain Chandan Singh realized the risks involved, but both believed that taking risks was part of decision-making in war. So they decided to take that risk.

Immediately after speaking with the Brigade Commander on the morning of 6 December 1971, General Sagat briefed the General Officer Commanding 8 Mountain Division, General Krishna Rao, on his plan to capture Sylhet and directed him to fly out and brief the Brigade Commander and the Commanding Officer of the 4th Battalion, 5th Gorkha Rifles (FF) immediately. There was no time to lose.

The battalion moved to Kalaura, the launch pad for the heliborne operation. Major General Krishna Rao and Brigadier Bunty Quinn were waiting for them, and briefed the Commanding Officer. They told him that the plan required the entire battalion to be on the ground at Sylhet by the end of 7 December and that it would be linked up with another ground thrust coming from the north in the next forty-eight hours.

Colonel Harolikar had reservations about the information that Sylhet was undefended and also about the planned link-up happening in the forecasted timeframe of forty-eight hours. He said so to the GOC in clear terms. In fact, he stated that it would be the division and the corps who would be responsible if things did not go right due to this insistence on a plan based on unconfirmed and uncorroborated information.* As a disciplined officer, this was not easy for him to say, but he did say it, because a failed operation would impact not only on the reputation of his battalion but also on the Indian Army as a whole.

The Corps Commander was prepared to take the risk, but he was the Corps Commander—many levels removed from the man who had to actually execute the task on the ground, behind enemy lines! And that man was Colonel Harolikar, the Commanding Officer of the Gorkha Battalion, who had a more realistic appreciation of the ground risks involved.

There were many questions to which there were no answers. Had 202 Pakistani Infantry Brigade actually moved out of Sylhet? Did it make sense for the Pakistanis to move the brigade from Sylhet when it would be better to fight a defensive battle away from Dhaka rather than from within the city's boundaries? Would there only be 200–300 irregulars holding Sylhet? How would he capture his objectives without artillery support? Would the link-up with his battalion actually take place within forty-eight hours? How would casualties be evacuated? Most important, who would take over from him if he became a casualty? His Second-in-Command had been killed at Gazipur, and his replacement had not yet arrived. The remaining officers were too young and inexperienced to lead the battalion.

But the critical question was this: What was the strength of enemy defences holding Sylhet? The Corps Headquarters had repeatedly stated that Sylhet was held by approximately 200–300 *razakars*.† However, the strategy of Lieutenant General

* Confirmed by Commanding Officer 9 Guards, Lieutenant Colonel Raghubir Singh, who was present at the meeting that took place on 7 December 1971.

† Razakars: Irregular soldiers.

A.A.K. Niazi, Pakistan's General Officer Commanding-in-Chief East Pakistan, was to defend his territory by a string of strong fortresses based on river obstacles and deep minefields. Sylhet was one such fortress, and it was out of tune with his strategy to give up such a key fortress without a fight. In addition to this unanswered question, there were several issues that needed to be resolved if the operation was to succeed.

The first was that the capacity of the Indian Air Force to heli-lift troops in this operation was limited. Would it be able to lift his whole battalion in one day before last light on 7 December? The lift-off was scheduled for 2.30 p.m. and last light was at 4.30 p.m., which meant they had just two hours to complete the lift. It was known that the first one hour was crucial in holding ground against an enemy counterattack in heliborne or para-drop operations, and therefore there had to be enough troops on the ground to hold it against the inevitable counterattacks.

Secondly, the advancing friendly forces from the north were many miles away and were not part of 4 Corps. They, too, would have to fight their way against enemy opposition. Laid down principles of heliborne or para-drop operations behind enemy lines required the advancing forces to link up with the force dropped behind enemy lines within forty-eight hours. It was accepted in principle that if the link-up within this period was not achieved, the ability of the force that had been placed behind the enemy would gradually get degraded, till it would eventually disintegrate and be destroyed, due to enemy offensive action, increase in the number of casualties and lack of supplies and reinforcements.

It was not clear as to who would ensure that this force linked up with the battalion within the given timeframe of forty-eight hours. In any army, especially in war, responsibility and accountability are very important, as no one would like to take the blame for a task gone wrong.

The Commanding Officer of the Gorkhas was not convinced that Pakistan's 202 Infantry Brigade had withdrawn to Dhaka. If indeed they were still there, then the odds would be greatly in favour of the Pakistanis. However, in light of the repeated assurances that 202 Pakistani Infantry Brigade had moved away from Sylhet, he had no option but to fall in line and go ahead with his plan for its capture. In the Indian Army, you could protest up to a point. After that, orders were orders!

Considering all these uncertainties, the Commanding Officer decided to make his own plans to fight the battle at Sylhet. He consulted his officers and JCOs and suggested that they would need to take more ammunition and grenades to hold out if the link-up did not take place on time, and that this would have to be at the expense of rations, water and their big packs that contained their second pair of uniform, a blanket and other small accessories.

The officers and JCOs accepted the Commanding Officer's suggestion, but they also asked when the promised link-up would take place. To this, the Commanding Officer had no answer and he said as much. He was alive to the fact that when you lead men into battle, you need to tell them the truth. Evasive answers would not do.

By this time, it was common knowledge that Pakistan had allied itself with the United States of America and China, and that both these countries had made a commitment that they would come to the aid of Pakistan if it was attacked. The orders from Delhi, therefore, were to wrap up the liberation of East Pakistan as early as possible, before the Chinese or the Americans could intervene. In that context, the Corps Commander's plan to leapfrog and capture Sylhet, which had been denuded of its defenders, made sense.

Less than an hour after the meeting on 7 December, between General K.V.K. Rao, Brigadier Quinn and Colonel Harolikar, Group Captain Chandan Singh arrived at Kalaura in an Alouette helicopter for a reconnaissance of the Sylhet area. Brigadier Quinn and Colonel Harolikar accompanied him. Chandan Singh had been deputed to IV Corps HQ to facilitate army–air force cooperation. Sagat and Chandan Singh had developed a strong working relationship and between them planned one of the quickest heliborne operations in military history.[*] The battalion received orders for the heliborne operation at 7.30 a.m., the reconnaissance was carried out at 9.30 a.m., and the heli-lift started at 2.30 p.m.—all on the same day!

The three officers flew over Sylhet on an aerial recce and from the air itself selected a landing site near Mirapara on the northern bank of the Surma River, south-east of Sylhet, about 2 km from the railway bridge. They did not detect any Pakistani movement, nor did they encounter any ground fire. This seemingly confirmed that Sylhet was undefended.[†]

The Commanding Officer of the Gorkhas told the Division and Brigade Commanders that, given the strength of the enemy as communicated to him, he was confident of capturing his objectives. His question, however, was how long he was expected to hold on to the captured objectives without artillery support. Being a key location, the Pakistanis would most

---

* P.V.S. Jagan Mohan and Samir Chopra, *Eagles over Bangladesh: The Indian Air Force in the 1971 Liberation War* (Noida: HarperCollins India, 2013), p. 218.

† Ibid.

certainly counterattack, and he would be hard put to defend the objectives which were spread out over a large area. It was therefore critically important that the rest of the brigade linked up as quickly as possible.

The GOC reminded Colonel Harolikar that they had flown over the area, and that there was no evidence of regular troops defending Sylhet. He added that in any case, he would do his best to ensure that the link-up took place within forty-eight hours.

Colonel Harolikar knew that moving without enemy opposition would take any force more than forty-eight hours to link up. Against determined enemy opposition, it was anybody's guess as to how much time the link-up would actually take. But he kept these thoughts to himself. How much could he protest? What if the GOC and Corps Commander were right and there were no regular troops defending Sylhet?

Notwithstanding all these obvious disadvantages, the battalion prepared to move at short notice for the capture of Sylhet. At Staff College, the teaching was that heliborne operations required at least a week's joint planning between the army and the air force, and here the battalion was being tasked to conduct the Indian Army's first heliborne operation at a moment's notice!

It was a mammoth task that the battalion had been given. Considering the spread and size of the targets, the Commanding Officer would have to divide his force, and the necessity of a Second-in-Command became all that more important. What would happen if he himself became a casualty? Command and control was crucial in an operation like this. This was the Indian Army's first heliborne operation, and failure was not an option.

The Commanding Officer had been told that an officer who was doing the course at the Staff College was already on the move to join his battalion as its new Second-in-Command. They were from the same regiment but had never met. The battalion, meanwhile, was gearing up for the heliborne offensive. The battalion area was a frenzy of activity. Load tables were being made; arms, ammunition, rations and equipment were being weighed, because the helicopters could take only a limited load, and every additional load, however small, mattered. The tactical plan was being worked out and battle drills rehearsed. The officers and men were excited at their battalion being chosen for the first heliborne operation of the Indian Army, and the Section and Platoon Commanders were busy briefing their commands on their tasks. The Commanding Officer was, however, alone with his thoughts.

He got just thirty minutes to give his operational orders for the capture of Sylhet to his Company and Platoon Commanders. He briefed them on the strength of the enemy they were likely to meet, the order in which the companies would be flown in, the allotment of tasks, the likely counterattacks by the enemy and how they would be repulsed, the need to dig in and automatically take an all-round defensive position with mutual support, the allotment of a force to protect the landing ground, and the need to be offensive and aggressive in whatever they did. Before he commenced his orders, he had asked who would volunteer to be the first to fly in, and Major Mane Malik, 'C' Company Commander, had raised his hand.

The heliborne operation for Sylhet began at 2.30 p.m. as scheduled, with the first Mi-4s taking off from Kalaura, carrying the troops of the 4th Battalion of 5th Gorkha Rifles, Squadron

Leader Sandhu, CO of 105 HU (Helicopter Unit), led the first wave of seven Mi-4s. The troops of 4/5 GR had no specialized training in heliborne operations; indeed, this was the first time they had ever moved by helicopter. Heliborne operations were still a novelty for the Indian Army, and no unit had acquired any expertise or training with helicopters.[6]

Led by Major Mane Malik, the 'C' Company of 4/5 GR landed in Sylhet at approximately 3.30 p.m., along with the Commanding Officer and his Tactical Headquarters. As the first helicopters of the first wave landed, they encountered heavy fire from the Pakistanis. As the troops were jumping off the helicopters, the Pakistanis attempted to assault the landing with cries of 'Allah hu Akbar'. The Gorkhas, however, hit the ground running and charged at the enemy with the regimental war cry of 'Ayo Gorkhali'.

Describing the initial moments of the landing, the Commanding Officer stated: 'Our boys charged at the enemy straightaway on landing, and I could see the enemy running away—an unbelievable sight, because the earlier battles at Atgram and Gazipur had been fiercely contested. I then realized that these troops must be the razakars I had been told about. I was wrong! I later came to know that these were the soldiers of 31 Punjab, who had had a taste of the khukri at Atgram. The fear of the khukri had taken root and was now paying handsome dividends.'*

The enemy now resorted to plastering the landing ground with artillery, mortar and medium machine gun fire, and our casualties started mounting. The Adjutant, Major Karan Puri, was severely wounded in the abdomen and had to be evacuated.

---

* Ibid., p. 220.

He finally passed away at Guwahati Military Hospital. He and others who had been wounded in the initial landing were evacuated in the returning helicopters.

The Commanding Officer's radio set had not been loaded on this sortie, and Colonel Harolikar was not able to inform the Brigade Commander about the progress of the battle.

The second sortie came after an hour, bringing the remainder of the 'C' Company and part of the 'B' Company. The enemy increased its rate of artillery, mortar and medium machine gun fire with greater accuracy.

The third sortie brought the remainder of the 'B' Company and the CO's wireless set. Thus, by last light on 7 December, two rifle companies, the CO's Tactical Headquarters, two sections of three-inch mortars and two detachments of medium machine guns had been landed. A total strength of 254 all ranks.

By this time, within the first three hours of landing, the battalion had managed to capture the landing ground, beat back a number of counterattacks and partially dig in. In order to project a strength larger than they were, the battalion kept moving its automatic weapons peripherally while at the same time establishing a perimeter defence. The enemy was trying to establish a cordon around the troops that had landed, but their attempts were thwarted by counterattacks by the Gorkhas.

The GOC, General Krishna Rao, and the Brigade Commander, Bunty Quinn, watched the Gorkhas take off on their mission to capture Sylhet with a silent prayer. Both were aware of the risks involved, but there was nothing they could do once the mission was launched. So, they stayed there, waiting for news of the battle from the returning sorties.

In the meanwhile, the officer from Staff College, who belonged to the unit and had been posted as the Second-in-Command, was doing his best to reach his battalion as quickly as possible. He had travelled by day and night from Wellington in south India without rest and managed to reach Kalaura at around 3 a.m. on 8 December.

The Gorkha troops of his battalion were lying on the fields in tactical groups. Most were asleep. Soldiers learn to sleep anywhere and anytime, because one never knows when the next opportunity to rest would come. The JCOs and NCOs, however, were wide awake, checking on the men and equipment, and waiting for the choppers to return. They were talking in whispers. There was absolutely no need for whispers as the enemy was very far away, but the occasion seemed to demand it.

The officer who had arrived saw three persons standing on a field some distance away. He walked up to them to find out who they were. The tallest one spoke in a kind but authoritative voice. 'Who is it?' he asked.

The officer answered and informed him that he was Major Ian Cardozo, the Second-in-Command designate of the 4th Battalion, 5th Gorkha Rifles (FF), and that he was reporting for duty. The tall officer happened to be Major General K.V.K. Rao, the General Officer Commanding, 8 Infantry Division. He shook hands with the officer and welcomed him to the division. The other two were Brigade Commander, Brigadier Bunty Quinn, and the Commander Engineers Colonel, 'Billoo' Suri.

The Brigade Commander took the Major aside, informed him that most of his battalion had been heli-lifted to Sylhet, and briefed him about the operational situation and the task given to his battalion.

While he was being briefed, he could hear the hum of the returning helicopters in the stillness of the night. The NCOs started waking up the men. The choppers landed, and the pilots got down and asked for help to unload the casualties they had brought back.

For these casualties the war was over, but they would now face different and difficult challenges in their lives ahead.

After the wounded had been taken out, the pilots examined their aircraft, pointing to the bullet holes that had pierced the soft bodies of the choppers. Luckily, no fuel tank had been pierced and no fuel line damaged. While the troops embarked, the returning pilots briefed the pilots of the next wave on the enemy fire they would encounter, and the ground and air situation. The pilots were young, brave, confident and enthusiastic.

The fourth sortie took off early, at 4 a.m., on 8 December. The remainder of the battalion embarked, and the helicopters constituting the last wave rose and hovered for a while before they headed for Sylhet. This sortie carried the remainder of the Rifle Companies and battalion support weapons, the Regimental Medical Officer with his medical platoon and Major Ian Cardozo, the Second-in-Command designate.

The flight to the objective took twenty minutes. As they were in the 'run in' for the landing, the pilot announced over the intercom, 'Sit on your packs. It may help to protect you against ground fire.' Everyone would have liked to do as advised, but their big packs had been left behind! The Adjutant of the battalion had been seriously wounded by ground fire while being flown in on the second wave. One could hear the crack of the bullets as they pierced the soft aluminum bodies of the helicopters. There was nothing one could do except hope and pray that he would be spared the indignity of being shot in his bottom. The last waves of the morning of 8 December were able to land the remainder of the battalion, including the

Second-in-Command, bringing the total strength to 384 all ranks. In addition to the men, two mountain guns were lifted into the perimeter held by the Gorkhas.

Slowly, the choppers landed in a clearing among the bamboo groves. The landing area was marked by small flames called 'goose necks', which were kettle-like contraptions with a long spout at the end of which a small flame burned in the darkness, giving indication to the choppers in the sky as to the location of the landing area. The landing was met with a lot of fire from the entrenched Pakistani defenders. The crump of enemy mortar bombs, and the whine and crash of their artillery fire indicated that the enemy was determined to beat back the heliborne attack.

Artillery shells threw up huge mounds of earth and showers of shrapnel. The volume of fire reached a crescendo as the enemy tried to destroy the choppers and the disembarking troops. It was clear from the volume of fire that the enemy was in considerable strength.

By now, the formation headquarters seemed to understand the overwhelming opposition being faced by the battalion, and orders to capture the railway bridge and radio station were cancelled. The battalion was told to hold on to the landing ground and to carry out aggressive defence.

The enemy, with its overwhelming strength, was in an excellent position to destroy this under-strength battalion but failed to do so. Yet, Radio Pakistan, with its typical ability to propagate false propaganda, announced that 'the 4th Battalion of the 5th Gorkhas of the Indian Army, while attempting to land at Sylhet, were wiped out. There were no survivors.'

A resumption of the heli-lift on 8 and 9 December brought in two mountain guns as well as the Battery Commander Major

Segan, but with limited ammunition. The resumption of the heli-lift, however, created an impression in the minds of the Pakistanis that a second battalion of Gorkhas had landed.

The heliborne landings are best described in the words of P.V.S. Jagan Mohan and Samir Chopra. In their book *Eagles over Bangladesh*, they write:

> The sudden appearance of IAF helicopters and the landing of Gorkha troops unnerved the Pakistani Brigade commander at Sylhet. Contrary to the Indian assessment, Pakistan's 202 Infantry Brigade had not withdrawn from Sylhet, nor had they any intention to do so. General Sagat had felt that the Gorkhas would face minimal resistance but they were now caught in an awkward situation with a strong enemy just outside their landing area and with lines of supply restricted to aerial ones.
>
> The Pakistan Army now sent an ad-hoc force of troops to the landing zone to engage the IAF helicopters and the Gorkha Rifles with small-arms fire. The small landing force could have been easily overwhelmed had they been attacked with gumption, for in the first crucial hour Indian forces barely measured company strength. But the Pakistan Army preferred to surround the landing area and engage in small-arms fire. The Gorkhas fought back vigorously and soon established a perimeter the Pakistan Army was unable to breach. The Gorkhas were only carrying pouch ammunition and had to exercise strict fire discipline, opening fire only when sure of hitting their targets. The Pakistanis had brought in several MMGs and automatic weapons but even then, failed to carry out an infantry charge on the landing zone; a bayonet assault by the Pakistanis would have cleared the

landing area and put paid to the heliborne operation. And neither was the ad-hoc force reinforced.

When the first wave of helicopters returned to Kalaura with bullet damage, it was obvious this was no unopposed landing. As the Kilo Flight Alouette was the only one in Eastern Command rigged with two rocket pods, Flight Lieutenant C.M. Singla, with his co-pilot, Squadron Leader Sultan Ahmed, took off ahead of the second wave of Mi-4s. Arriving at the helipad, he laid down suppressive fire on Pakistani positions, diverting attention from the Mi-4s that followed him.

The second wave of Mi-4s was led by the flight commander of 105 HU and made the twenty-minute flight in receding light, carrying with them another company of 4/5 GR troops and their CO, Lieutenant Colonel Harolikar. Dusk was fast approaching. Sunset was at approximately 4.45 p.m., and it would be dark at 5.05 p.m. It was obviously too late to send the third wave of MI-4s, and Pakistan ground fire was now steadily on the increase. By the time the day's operations were called off in the evening, the helicopters had airlifted 254 personnel to the landing zone in two waves of twenty-two sorties.

Flight Lieutenant Vaid carried out the last sortie of the day, carrying an air control team (ACT) led by Flying Officer Satish Chandra Sharma. The ACT, along with their radio equipment, was dropped at the landing area at 5 p.m. in almost complete darkness. The ACT came under small-arms and mortar fire immediately on landing. Gathering his wits, S.C. Sharma assembled his men and moved them to cover. Within minutes he had moved to a vantage position from where he could observe Pakistani positions. He contacted an armed Alouette of the Kilo Flight, which did some useful work in suppressing Pakistani fire.

The strike effectively silenced the Pakistani probes on the landing area for the night.

Helicopter operations were not yet done. After the last sortie was flown out at 5 p.m., Group Captain Chandan Singh had ordered the helicopter force to stand down. This upset army commanders who wanted to send in more troops and supplies. After hectic discussion, Chandan Singh directed Flight Lieutenant Vaid to fly another sortie in the dark of the night, at 10 p.m. Dressed in the ubiquitous 'lungi', a Bengali civilian dress, Vaid and his co-pilot, Flying Officer B.L.K. Reddy, carried out three sorties to and from Kalaura, dropping supplies, troops and even evacuating a wounded soldier.

The Pakistan Army had been deceived by the number of sorties flown by the IAF helicopters and had estimated a far greater opposition. It had assumed that the heliborne force was being transported by the larger Mi-8 helicopters—which had not entered service yet—and estimates of a brigade-sized force made the rounds. The fierce opposition put up by the Gorkhas in the battle for the landing zone also distorted whatever reasonable estimates the Pakistanis may have had. One can only conjecture what the Pakistanis might have done if they had known the heliborne landing had only managed to drop 254 troops.

By now it was clear to the Gorkhas that the force holding Sylhet was certainly many times more than the 200 razakars as estimated by the corps. What was not known to them was that 202 Infantry Brigade was still at Sylhet! It had not moved to Dhaka! Not only that, Sylhet had been reinforced

> by 313 Pakistan Infantry Brigade! This brigade had reached Sylhet on 7 December, the same day that the Gorkhas had landed. By the time the battalion had consolidated its defences around its defence perimeter, enemy forces at Sylhet would have increased to nearly a division consisting of two Pakistani infantry brigades and the Sylhet Garrison, which was commanded by a brigadier. But the Gorkhas did not know this.

The Pakistanis were now in overwhelming superiority; the impossibly unequal ratio between the Gorkhas and the Pakistanis had become 1:20. Whereas the strength of the Pakistani forces would keep increasing by the day as fresh troops joined in, the strength of the Gorkhas would keep decreasing due to casualties. There was no hope of resupply because the helicopters were required to fulfil their main role, which was to provide administrative support for the advancing troops elsewhere. The strength of the Gorkhas was limited to just 384 all ranks, due firstly to the heavy casualties suffered in previous operations; secondly, because the returning leave parties had not yet caught up with the battalion; and lastly, the helicopter lift could not take a force larger than this within the specified timeframe. This meant in effect that the strength of the Gorkhas was less than half an infantry battalion.

On the first day itself, the Gorkhas found themselves fighting with their backs to the wall. Heavy medium machine gun fire, artillery and mortar concentrations caused many casualties. It was now only a matter of time before the Pakistanis would come to know about their own overwhelming superiority and be encouraged to eliminate the Gorkhas. The situation for the Gorkhas had become critical. By the afternoon of 9

December, forty-eight hours had elapsed and the promised link-up had not taken place. Casualties were mounting. They had already run out of food and water, and their ammunition was running dangerously low. IV Corps realized the predicament of the Gorkhas and organized support by IAF fighter aircraft at Kumbhigram and Agartala by day, and in the absence of helicopter support requested for air drops of supplies and ammunition.

It was at this stage, when the situation had become critically dangerous, that the British Broadcasting Corporation (BBC) came to the rescue.

In a radio broadcast, the BBC mistakenly announced that 'a brigade of Gorkhas had been heli-landed at Sylhet'. It is not known whether the BBC war correspondent who had filed his report got mixed up between the terms 'battalion' and 'brigade', and whether he knew that a brigade was three times the strength of a battalion!

The world knew that the BBC was a source of authentic news. Generally, they managed to not only get their facts right but also get their reports out ahead of everyone else. Their enterprising war correspondents were given permission by the Indian government to accompany the advancing forces and were therefore able to send back reports straight from the battlefield. Everyone therefore listened to what the BBC said and believed it to be true. By broadcasting the truth, the BBC rendered Pakistani propaganda useless, and no one believed Radio Pakistan any more. The world listened to the BBC because the BBC always told the truth. This time, however, it had made a mistake—a mistake that the Gorkhas could use to their advantage.

It took a little time for the battalion at Sylhet to understand the import of the BBC's error in reporting that a 'brigade' of Gorkhas had landed at Sylhet when in fact it was only a battalion, and that too a battalion at reduced strength, of just 384 all ranks when they were heli-landed. Now they were even fewer, owing to the attrition suffered due to those who were killed and wounded.

On the night of the BBC broadcast, officers of both armies that were facing each other at Sylhet were also listening to the news on their transistors. Colonel Harolikar of the Gorkhas said, 'Did you hear that? The BBC has just said that a brigade of Gorkhas has landed at Sylhet!'

One of the officers said, 'Yes, sir. Wonder how they got it so wrong?'

The Battalion Second-in-Command, however, said excitedly, 'They haven't got it wrong, sir. They've got it right! We must capitalize on this broadcast! The Pakistanis must also be listening! We need to simulate that we are in fact a brigade. The opposition here seems to be much more than a battalion. If we are able to bluff them that we are here in brigade-strength, it would impose caution on them.'

The answer for the Gorkhas was to bluff the Pakistanis that they were a brigade!

The Commanding Officer thought about it. Nearly three days had elapsed since the battalion had landed at Sylhet—twelve hours more than the anticipated link-up! The battalion had already suffered a number of casualties and was running low on ammunition. The rations and water that they had brought had finished, and they were managing on what little grain was available in a few abandoned huts within the perimeter of their defences. There was no water to drink, except water from dirty ponds that they had to strain through handkerchiefs.

Simulating a brigade would mean dispersing the battalion over a wider area, and such a move had several disadvantages. It opened the risk of the companies being destroyed individually, and inter-company support would not be available due to dispersion. The advancing Indian forces were still many miles away. It was not clear as to when the link-up would take place. The risk was enormous, but it was worth taking, and the Commanding Officer took it.

The Commanding Officer and the Second-in-Command relocated the companies, dispersing them over a wider area. Nests of small groups of soldiers, armed with automatic weapons, were placed in the gaps between companies to prevent Pakistani patrols from discovering that the Indian force holding Sylhet was in fact half a battalion and not a brigade.

In some cases, the companies had to fight their way to occupy new areas. In one case, a platoon was tasked to occupy a mound which, if occupied by the Pakistanis, would give them effective ability to observe and fire at the Gorkha defences. Apparently, the Pakistanis thought of occupying this mound at the same time, but the Gorkhas got there first and brought effective fire on them. Confused fighting took place, but the Gorkhas had the upper hand with the use of their khukris. The Pakistani attack failed, and they were seen carrying away their dead and wounded.

The Gorkhas extended the area of their defensive perimeter during the day, when the Indian Air Force was able to support them. Thanks to the Flight Lieutenant and his ACT (Air Control Tentacle), close air support arrived whenever the enemy was observed to be collecting in large numbers, and this was a morale booster for the Gorkha troops, who clapped their hands in glee when the IAF MiG-21s and Hunters blasted away at the

Pakistani forces assembling for their counterattacks. At night, Gorkha patrols dominated the ground forward of the companies.

On 11 December, the request to resupply the Gorkhas was routed to 33 Squadron at Guwahati. Most transport aircraft were being prepared for an upcoming para operation on the outskirts of Dhaka, but Caribous were available. Flying Officer Rudra Bishnoi was detailed to carry out the drop, with H.S. Sahni as his co-pilot. They were accompanied by a navigator and a two-man ejection crew. After loading up at Agartala and Kumbhigram, he proceeded to Sylhet to drop his load of ammunition and supplies.*

The Caribou, with Bishnoi at the controls, arrived over the drop zone at Sylhet on schedule—in near darkness, with heavy fighting underway in the battle zone. The aircrew could observe Sylhet in flames due to the Indian strikes as well as the artillery from the Pakistanis and the mountain guns with the Gorkhas.

Bishnoi circled for a while and then ejected his loads on the ground marked by the Gorkhas with parachutes which were discernable even though it was dark. As he did so, he was hit by ground fire but managed to get away.†

The Second-in-Command and a group of Gorkhas rushed into the drop zone to collect the ammunition. The Pakistani artillery zeroed in on the drop zone. Despite heavy shelling, the Gorkhas cut loose the ammunition from the parachutes with their khukris. Fortunately, there were no casualties. On examining the loads that were dropped, the Gorkhas were disappointed to find that they consisted of artillery and mortar ammunition but not what they really needed—small arms

* Ibid., pp. 279–80.

† Ibid., p. 280.

ammunition or rations. The next urgent requirement was the evacuation of the dead and wounded. This need was also met by Group Captain Chandan Singh. He sent two helicopters at night for this purpose. Goosenecks were lit to mark the helipad at night.

The evacuation of the dead and wounded was another big morale booster for the troops. The reappearance of Indian Air Force helicopters at night apparently convinced the Pakistanis that the Gorkhas continued to be reinforced, whereas in actual fact the helicopters had only come for casualty evacuation.

All these actions convinced the Pakistanis not only that the Gorkhas were in brigade-strength but also that they had been reinforced. The Gorkha Battalion's reputation for extensive use of their khukris demoralized them further and made them cautious.

The presumption on the part of the Gorkhas that the Pakistanis would have also heard the BBC broadcast was correct, but they still did not know the strength of the Pakistani force opposing them.

The Gorkhas continued their active patrolling and ambushes. Small-arms ammunition, however, was running alarmingly low. As he went around the defensive positions, the Commanding Officer found the Gorkhas sharpening their khukris. When asked why they were doing this, they answered, 'Sahib, if we run out of ammunition, we would use our most trusted weapon—our khukris.'

From 9–14 December, the Pakistanis strengthened their cordon around the Gorkhas and made futile attempts to evict them with relentless pounding by artillery fire. The Pakistanis, however, kept at a safe distance and seemed to lack the stomach to get involved in close combat with the Gorkhas at Sylhet, due to 31 Punjab and 22 Baluch having been at the receiving end of khukri attacks by the Gorkhas at the battles of Atgram and Gazipur.

The Gorkhas, on the other hand, aggressively dominated the areas around the airfield by strong patrols, well-laid ambushes and roadblocks, and cutting road communication between Sylhet and Khadimnagar. These strong patrols also carried out raids on the enemy dispositions. In one such raid, they captured the regimental colours of 31 Punjab Regiment. These regimental colours are considered sacrosanct and fought for till the last man and the last round. The 31 Punjab regimental colours are now displayed in the Museum of the Indian Military Academy, Dehradun. It speaks volumes about the tenacity, grit, determination and indomitable spirit of all ranks of the battalion that held their ground for nine days in the face of fierce opposition, nearly twenty times its own strength. Even two brigades and the Sylhet Garrison, commanded by a brigadier, with their artillery and overflowing ammunition dumps, could not wipe out a handful of determined Gorkhas.

On 11, 12 and 13 December, the Indian Army Chief, General Sam Manekshaw, issued ultimatums to General Niazi to surrender. In these ultimatums, the Army Chief reiterated that he would ensure the safety of all West Pakistanis who laid down their arms. Along with the ultimatum, General Manekshaw also issued a caveat that if they did not surrender, they alone would be accountable for the casualties they would suffer.

At 0900 hours, on 15 December 1971, two days after Sam Manekshaw's call for surrender of all Pakistani forces in East Pakistan, two Pakistani officers approached the defended area of the Gorkhas with a white flag. The account is given in *Forever in Operations* by Colonel R.D. Palsokar, MC. He states: 'In the early hours of 15th December 1971, the Pakistani Garrison Commander at Sylhet sent a team of two officers with a few men carrying a white flag to the 4/5 Gorkha Rifles defended location. The officers conveyed that their Commander wanted to surrender his troops at Sylhet to 4/5 Gorkha Rifles.'

Actually, when Major Mane Malik, Company Commander of 'C' Company, observed this small party with a white flag emerging from a wooded area some 1500 metres away, he informed the Commanding Officer and asked for instructions. Lieutenant Colonel Harolikar went forward and observed a large group of some 1000–2000 armed Pakistani soldiers gathered at the edge of the forest while a small party with a white flag was moving towards 'C' Company. There was, at this time, no information about a ceasefire or surrender in the rest of the war zone of East Pakistan from the Brigade Headquarters, nor any news on our lone transistor radio. The CO therefore became suspicious of Pakistani intentions.

The officers handed over a note saying that the Garrison Commander at Sylhet wanted to surrender the entire garrison to the Indian Brigade Commander. The Commanding Officer of the Gorkhas immediately realized that the deception carried out by his battalion to simulate a brigade-sized force had worked. However, he also realized that even at this stage, if the Pakistanis came to know that it was only half a battalion that was facing them at Sylhet, the situation could get difficult. The Indian Brigade Commander was many miles away, and it was essential that he came as soon as possible to take the surrender.

The officers were told to go back and inform their Garrison Commander to come in person to discuss the modalities of the surrender. As the two officers were on their way back and were halfway there, the battalion noticed that the large group of Pakistani soldiers had started running forward, towards our defended locality. Realizing that this could be a ploy to overcome our company with sheer strength of numbers, Major Malik ordered his light machine gun detachment to fire a couple of bursts, as a warning for the Pakistanis to not come closer. As soon as the warning bursts were fired, the Pakistani soldiers went to ground. Major Malik told them to go back. This must have been the first offer to surrender by the Pakistan Army in East Pakistan even before the ceasefire was announced later that evening. The Pakistani group returned to their defences.

A message in code, as to what had transpired that morning, was passed on to the brigade, and the Brigade Commander was asked to come over to take the surrender.

On the afternoon of 15 December 1971, Brigadier Bunty Quinn arrived by helicopter to accept the Pakistani surrender. The Pakistan Garrison Commander met Brigadier Quinn at 1500 hours, and the modalities of the surrender were discussed. On 16 December, the Sylhet Garrison surrendered, bringing an end to the battle of Sylhet.

However, there were new surprises for everyone. The Pakistanis were surprised to see the Brigade Commander come by helicopter and were astonished to learn from him, after he had landed, that the Gorkha troops holding Sylhet was only half a battalion. The Gorkhas were even more surprised to learn that it was not a battalion but two brigades and the Sylhet garrison that had faced them at Sylhet. Three brigadiers, 173 officers, 290 JCOs and nearly 8000 troops surrendered to the Commanding Officer of 4/5 Gorkha Rifles. The three Brigadiers were Brigadier Salimullah Khan, Commander, 202 Pakistani Infantry Brigade; Brigadier Iftikhar Rana, Commander, 313 Pakistani Infantry

Brigade; and Brigadier S.A. Hassan, Commander of the Sylhet Garrison.*

After the surrender, the Pakistani Garrison Commander was chivalrous enough to convey to Brigadier Quinn that, 'If this battalion was not here in Sylhet, we would have held Sylhet for another ten days.'

The troops who surrendered belonged to 31 Punjab, 91 Mujahid Battalion, 12 Azad Kashmir Rifles, 22 Baluch, 30 Frontier Force, 31 Field Regiment, 88 Independent Mortar Battery, and troops from Khyber Rifles, Thal Scouts and Tochi Scouts. The strength of the Gorkha Battalion had been reduced to just seven officers and 329 other ranks.

What came out clearly after the surrender, however, was that 4/5 Gorkha Rifles had not only captured and held on to Sylhet against a force twenty times its strength but also tied down two Pakistani Infantry Brigades and the forces of the Sylhet Garrison from 7–15 December, thereby hastening the fall of Dhaka.

With regard to the action at Sylhet, General J.F.R. Jacob, Chief of Staff of Eastern Command, Calcutta, has this to say in his book *Surrender at Dacca*:

> On 7 December, 4/5 Gorkha Rifles of 59 Mountain Brigade had been lifted by helicopters to the south-east of Sylhet across the Surma River. The Pakistanis had evacuated the civil population from Sylhet and fortified the town. The defences were held by Pakistani 202 Infantry Brigade. Pakistani 313 Infantry Brigade, ex- Maulvi Bazar, joined the Sylhet Garrison, bringing the strength up to six battalions,

* Major General Shaukat Riza, *The Pakistan Army 1966-71* (Lahore: Services Book Club, 1990).

> one regiment of 105 mm guns and one battery of 120 mm mortars. The move of the Pakistani 313 Brigade from Maulvi Bazar to Sylhet had not been anticipated by us at Command Headquarters and came as a surprise. We had expected this brigade would fall back to the Coronation Bridge on the Meghna for the defence of the Meghna crossing and Dhaka. Had they done so, IV Corps' progress across the Meghna would have been very difficult. When we got radio intercepts confirming their move to Sylhet, we were very relieved. It meant for all practical purposes, that two infantry brigades were out on a limb at Sylhet where they could be contained and their effectiveness neutralised. After the war, whilst interrogating the GOC of the division, Major General Abdul Quazi, I asked him why he had moved this brigade to Sylhet. He replied that he was determined that he would not let us capture Sylhet. Niazi's fortress strategy and the Divisional Commander's implementation of this policy speeded up the disintegration of Pakistan's defence capabilities and facilitated the capture of Dhaka.

Major General Fazal Muqeem Khan of Pakistan, in his book,* states that Pakistan's 202 Brigade was reinforced by 313 Brigade, but he gives no explanation as to how and why it happened. However, Lieutenant General A.A.K. Niazi, Army Commander, East Pakistan, in his book *The Betrayal of Dhaka*, says that Commander 313 Pakistan Brigade, which had been ordered by his GOC to fall back for the defence of Dhaka, disobeyed his orders and for unknown reasons joined 202 Brigade at Sylhet.

---

* Major General Fazal Muqeem Khan, *Pakistan's Crisis in Leadership* (Islamabad: National Book Foundation, 1973), p. 180.

The move of Pakistan's 313 Infantry Brigade to Sylhet instead of Dhaka led to the sacking of Major General Qazi Abdul Majid, General Officer Commanding 14 Infantry Division, of which this brigade was a part. The failure of this brigade to also evict 4/5 Gorkha Rifles from Sylhet must have added fuel to the fire.

However, those nine days in Sylhet extracted a heavy price in fourteen killed, including one officer, two JCOs and eleven other ranks, and thirty-nine wounded. Although he had been evacuated, Major Karan Puri passed away at the Guwahati Military Hospital. Overall, in the 1971 war, the battalion lost thirty men, including four officers and three JCOs, with 123 wounded, including seven officers. The Commanding Officer, Lieutenant Colonel Harolikar, was awarded the Maha Vir Chakra for his outstanding courage and leadership in the battles of Atgram, Gazipur and Sylhet; the Air Force Officer, Flying Officer Satish Chandra Sharma, was awarded the Vir Chakra for his courage and impressive control of the air battle over Sylhet. Captain Sengupta, the Regimental Medical Officer, Naib Subedar Tirthabahadur and Captain Rana* were awarded Sena Medals for their brave conduct at Sylhet. Some of the company commanders, like Yeshwant Rawat, Dinesh Rana, Virendra Rawat, Mane Malik and the Battery Commander Major K.D. Segan as well as many JCOs, NCOs and men ought to have been decorated for their outstanding courage and performance at the battles fought by the battalion at Atgram, Gazipur and Sylhet, but their bravery has not been recognized. If the senior

---

* Captain Rana was an officer from the Army Service Corps who came to Sylhet in one of the helicopters and voluntarily stayed behind. Due to the shortage of officers and JCOs, he was given a platoon to command, and he did an excellent job.

leaders thought that the battalion needed to be repeatedly given difficult missions, then the courage of its personnel deserved better recognition.

The success of the Gorkhas was tempered by the loss of many of their officers and men, who were not around to savour this moment of victory of the Indian armed forces in which they had undoubtedly played a memorable part. Much of the credit in facilitating the Gorkhas to capture Sylhet and to hold on to it needs to be given to the Indian Air Force, who supported them in every possible way. The Gorkhas, however, were also deeply aware of the crucial role played by the BBC in facilitating their survival.

Without doubt, the BBC's mistake in reporting that a 'brigade of Gorkhas had landed at Sylhet' helped 4/5 Gorkha Rifles substantially in working out a strategy to deal effectively with a force more than twenty times its size. It was this historic error by a media house known for its authentic reporting that helped the Gorkhas to turn the tables on a far superior force.

Postscript

Although all this happened fifty years ago, the surviving officers and men of the 4th Battalion of the 5th Gorkha Rifles (FF) take this opportunity to say 'thank you' to the British Broadcasting Corporation for their historic error. For them, it was the BBC's best broadcast, and it is never too late to say thank you.

Long Shot at Longewala

'The battlefield is a scene of inevitable chaos. The winner will be the one who controls that chaos; both his and the enemy's.'

—Napoleon Bonaparte

'Hold on my child. Joy comes in the morning
The darkest hour means dawn is just in sight.'

—Words from the song 'Joy Comes in the Morning'

Longewala, 3 December 1971

All was quiet on the southern front. Major Kuldip Singh Chandpuri, Company Commander, 'A' Company of the 23rd Battalion of the Punjab Regiment, gave an involuntary shiver as he looked across the vast expanse of the rolling sand dunes ahead of him. It was the night of 3–4 December 1971, and it was cold, as nights in the desert always are. The moon was on the wane, but it had been a full moon the previous night. It was now like a lamp in the sky, and he could see far into the distance by its soft light. The desert in front of him looked very much like

The armoured column of Pakistan being attacked by IAF Hunters.

a sea. He remembered bits and pieces of the lecture at the Indian Military Academy on 'Navigation by Stars'. The instructor had compared operations in the desert to operations at sea. Both were devoid of landmarks, and in both cases one had to rely on the stars for direction.

The border area of Rajasthan–Sind is generally desert terrain with very little road or rail communication. Indian strategists expected Pakistan to be generally on the defensive in this sector and maybe launch limited, local offensives to improve its defensive stance. They did not realize how wrong they were in their assessment.

That evening, of 3 December 1971, All India Radio had informed its listeners that Pakistan had attacked Indian airfields at 5.45 p.m., and among them were the Jodhpur and Uttarlai airfields, which fell within Southern Command. Major Chandpuri's battalion, brigade and division were also part of this command.

It was around midnight. Venus was dipping towards the horizon when he heard Prime Minister Indira Gandhi's speech informing citizens that Pakistan had attacked India, and that the nation had no option but to defend herself and fight back.

Major Kuldip Singh Chandpuri informed the Screen Position Commander, who was about three miles ahead of Longewala, that the war had begun and that he needed to be extraordinarily alert. The Screen was a strong detachment ahead of the main defences, which were his 'eyes and ears'. Its task was to give early warning of the strength and direction of enemy movement.

Major Chandpuri searched the area in front of him and on either side, but there was no movement or sound of any sort. Sound carries far in the desert because there are no buildings or trees to absorb sound waves; but at that moment, there was total silence. He went around the company-defended locality to check on the sentries and to inform the Platoon Commanders that the war had finally started. He wondered whether Pakistan had any intention to launch offensive operations in his area. His was a lone company, out on a limb, with no armour and very little artillery support. He was aware that in the desert, mobility was the answer to success in battle and that tanks were a battle-winning factor in desert warfare.

He had learnt earlier that a brigade* from his division† (12 Indian Infantry Division) was to launch an offensive across the International Border, in the area of Rahimyar Khan, and that most armour and artillery resources had been allotted for the offensive. He was many miles away from Sadhewala, the location of his Battalion Headquarters, which was his only source of support. On his request for anti-tank resources, he was told not to worry, as no threat was envisaged in his area, and that anti-tank mines would be sent to him. Major Chandpuri decided to lay the mines when they came and, in the meanwhile, he decided to stretch a single strand of barbed wire across his front to indicate a deep minefield, which in fact did not exist.

Unknown to the Indians, Pakistan General Headquarters had approved an offensive plan that had Longewala as its first objective, and 'A' Company 23 Punjab would be bang in the

---

* An infantry brigade consists of three infantry battalions. Each battalion has on its strength about a thousand soldiers. An infantry brigade group, in addition to infantry, has other arms and services, like armour, artillery, etc., grouped with it.

† An infantry division generally has three infantry brigades, an artillery brigade and units of engineers, signals, ordnance, army supply and transport, and army medical corps. It is an organization that is self-contained and capable of fighting independently.

middle of the Pakistani assault. Pakistan's 18 Infantry Division, in addition to deploying a brigade group for the defence of the Rajasthan–Sind sector, had two infantry brigade groups in reserve for offensive operations.

Major General B.M. Mustafa, GOC, Pakistan's 18 Infantry Division, had called for a conference on 16 October 1971, to explain his concept of his forthcoming offensive. Since the operation was armour-centric, he had called Lieutenant Colonel Z.A. Khan, Commanding Officer 38 Cav (Sherman tanks), and Lieutenant Colonel Akram Hussain Syed, Commanding Officer 22 Cav (T-59 tanks), to hear his plan and give comments on the feasibility of the operation. His Colonel Staff, Wajid Ali Shah, made the initial presentation.*

General Mustafa explained that the plan was to hold the front south of Rahimyar Khan and Barmer with a brigade, and to launch an offensive with two brigades supported by armour against Ramgarh along the Tanot–Longewala approach and thereafter exploit to Jaisalmer. He proposed to do this by outflanking the Indian left flank, and then seize Ramgarh and Jaisalmer. One brigade, with an armoured regiment in support, was to seize Ramgarh, and another brigade, with another armoured regiment, was to neutralize the airfield at Jaisalmer. The GOC asked for comments on the practicality of his plan from the tankman's point of view. The presentation also mentioned that GHQ required the approach march from firm base to Jaisalmer, a distance of 120 miles, to be covered

* Extracts from a January 2002 interview, by Narendar Singh, of Brigadier Z.A. Khan, who was the Commanding Officer of 38 Cavalry during the battle of what the Pakistanis call 'Loganewala': http://www.strategicfront.org/forums/threads/battle-of-longewala-dec1971-pakistani-perspective-brigadier-za-khan-pakistani-army-then-commanding-officer-38-cavalry.2495

in one day. The armoured regimental commanders said that the plan was feasible provided that: the approach march to the border and advance to Jaisalmer was made in two nights; and air cover was made available from the first day, from dawn to dusk, till Ramgarh and Jaisalmer were secured. The GOC accepted the suggestions and said that the plan was top secret and was not to be talked about at all.

This was his initial plan but changes would keep creeping in as time passed.

In the first week of November, General Abdul Hamid Khan, and the Air Force Chief, Air Marshal Rahim, came to Rahimyar Khan, where the 18 Pakistan Infantry Division plan was discussed. On being asked for confirmation that air support for the offensive would be available, Air Chief Rahim said that air support would be given.*

On 2 December 1971, Lieutenant Colonel Z.A. Khan, Commanding Officer of 38 Cav, among others, was called to the Pakistan 18 Division Headquarters and told that the move for the offensive would commence that night. He was given the details of the offensive—51 Pakistan Infantry Brigade with 22 Cavalry was tasked with capturing Ramgarh and Jaisalmer, and 206 Pakistan Infantry Brigade with capturing Longewala. 38 Cavalry was to follow 51 Pakistan Infantry Brigade up to Longewala, and after the capture of Longewala, it was to proceed to Jaisalmer to neutralize the airfield. The H-Hr† for the offensive was 2130 hours, 3 December. The launch of the offensive was later postponed by a day and changed to 0200 hours, 4 December.

* Ibid.

† H-Hr is the commencement time for an operation.

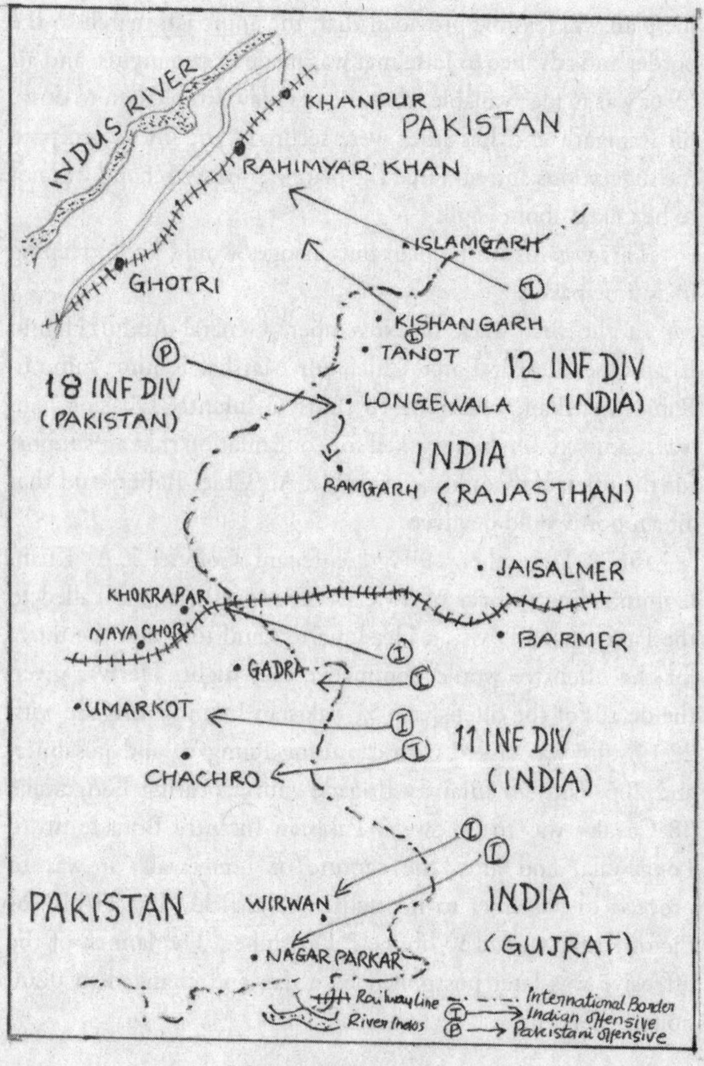

The area of operations.

On conclusion of the briefing, those assembled were asked if there were any questions. During the question-and-answer session, Lieutenant Colonel Z.A. Khan observed that there were some shortcomings in the planning of the offensive. The Indian infantry division opposing them was 12 Indian Infantry Division and not 11 Indian Infantry Division as mentioned in the briefing. The maps held by the Pakistani division and the artillery in support were blank in the areas across the border. Worst of all, there was no confirmation that air support was available. A Pakistan Air Force Wing Commander, who came for the orders, stated that the PAF would not be able to support the offensive because the Jacobabad airfield had not been activated. Commanders of 51, 55 and 206 Pakistan Infantry Brigades were taken aback and asked the GOC to cancel the offensive, because without air support the offensive was likely to fail.

The GOC telephoned General G.S. Hassan, the Chief of General Staff and discussed the viability of the offensive without air support. After some discussion, the GOC informed the 'O' Group that the offensive had to be conducted even without air support, 'in national interest'! The Brigade Commanders once again urged the GOC to refuse to launch the offensive without air support, saying that the operation might fail. But the GOC Pakistan 18 Infantry Division replied that he would conduct the offensive anyway, because if he didn't, he would be labelled as 'a general who lost his nerve'.

The Pakistani Offensive Plan

In brief, the final plan for the offensive of 18 Pakistan Infantry Division was as under:

- The division to conduct an approach march of about 60 miles to the IB (International Border) on the night of 3 December.
- A further move of 40 miles from the IB to Ramgarh by 51 Pakistani Infantry with 22 Cav and 38 Baluch. After the capture of Ramgarh, the brigade to proceed to Jaisalmer to neutralize the airfield.
- 22 Cav to bypass Longewala and take up a position to counter any counteroffensive by 12 Indian Infantry Division.
- 206 Pakistan Brigade to leave one battalion for the defence of Rahimyar Khan and to secure Longewala as a Firm Base.
- 38 Cav less a squadron with 1 Punjab and a mortar battery to follow 51 Pakistan Brigade till the metal road to Jaisalmer is reached and then continue to Jaisalmer to carry out their task to neutralize the airfield.

Headquarters Southern Command (India)

Headquarters Southern Command, under Lieutenant General G.G. Bewoor, was responsible for the Sind–Rajasthan sector. He had two divisions under his command—11 and 12 Infantry Divisions. For ease of command and control, he had set up an Advance Headquarters at Jodhpur.

Southern Command had deployed one brigade each in the Barmer (11 Infantry Division) and Jaisalmer (12 Infantry Division) sectors to cover the move of the remainder of the divisions from their respective cantonments. Subsequently, both divisions were to launch offensive operations against Pakistan. Accordingly, one brigade was deployed in the Kishengarh–Tanot–Sadhewala area and another in the Munnabao–Gadra Road area. This was the first time that major operations were being conducted in desert terrain by Southern Command.

Commanded by Brigadier Ramadoss, 30 Indian Infantry Brigade was earmarked to lead the advance of the 12 Division offensive in the Thar sector and was located 2 km west of Sadhewala, where Brigadier Ramadoss had concentrated his three infantry battalions—17 Rajputana Rifles, 13 Kumaon and 6th Battalion of the 5th Gorkha Rifles. His task was to capture Rahimyar Khan and was to move at first light on 5 December. The Brigade had twenty Lancers (AMX tanks) and 6 Independent Armoured Squadron (T-55 tanks) as its armour complement, located at Kishengarh, 80 km to the north-east. It also had four tanks of the Replacement Tank Troop, located at Sadhewala for use in an emergency on orders of the GOC. Air cover for the division was being provided by six Hunters from the Armament Training Wing, Jamnagar, on detachment at Jaisalmer. The IAF Station at Jaisalmer was commanded by Wing Commander M.S. Bawa. Southern Command also had 10 and 220 Squadrons, with HF-24s at Uttarlai and Jodhpur for close air support. It could also call for support of Canberras located at Pune.

It appeared that both India and Pakistani forces in this area were launching offensive operations against each other, and neither knew about the other's offensives on axes that were parallel to each other but separated by vast desert terrain.

Sequence of Events

4 December 1971

On the night of 4 December, the Pakistani offensive force approached the Indian Border Post No. 635, at around 2330 hours.

On the night of 4–5 December, at around 2400 hours, the Indian Screen position ahead of Longewala reported the sound of enemy armour to his Company Commander, Major Chandpuri.

Major Chandpuri reported developments to his battalion and brigade.

5 December 1971

At 0030 hours, Pakistani artillery opened up on the post at Longewala in support of advancing Pakistani armour. Chandpuri's troops engaged Pakistan armour and infantry with their anti-tank and small-arms weapons.

The Indian force at Longewala was just one infantry company of less than 100 soldiers, with one jeep-mounted RCL gun, and MMGs and mortars.*

The Pakistani force consisted of 51 Infantry Brigade Group consisting of 22 Cavalry with T-59 Patton tanks and elements of 28 Recce and Support Battalion, 10 Punjab and 38 Baluch and were poised north of Longewala. Pakistani 206 Infantry Brigade with 38 Cavalry (Sherman tanks) were in depth. Their task was to secure Longewala after Pakistani 51 Infantry Brigade moved off for the capture of Ramgarh.

The aim of the force was to move ahead for the capture of Ramgarh and Jaisalmer after Longewala was captured.

The advance elements of Pakistan's 51 Infantry Brigade, probing for an expected minefield, came across the single strand of barbed wire. They mistook the barbed wire surrounding

---

* An area support weapon, often referred to as the Battalion Commander's artillery.

Kuldip Chandpuri's company to be a minefield marker and lost valuable time trying to breach a minefield that didn't exist.

At 0230 hours, messages of what was going on were relayed to HQ 12 Infantry Division. Major General R.F. Khambatta contacted Wing Commander M.S. Bawa at Jaisalmer for close air support to the company at Longewala, but Wing Commander Bawa said that the aircraft at his base did not have night-flying capability and that he could give support only at first light. The aircraft at the Jaisalmer airfield were Hawker Hunters.

This limitation meant that from 0230 hours on 5 December, to first light, Major Chandpuri's 'A' Company was on its own. While the forward Infantry elements of the Pakistan Brigade were busy trying to probe the depth and extent of the minefield, Pakistani artillery and tanks brought down heavy fire on the company holding Longewala.

Almost every defence structure of the company locality was blown to bits. The mandir, which is part of the Longewala locality, was the only structure that was left standing. The fodder for the camels caught fire, and by the light of its burning, the Pakistani artillery and tank fire became more accurate. However, it also lit up the Pakistani forces. Major Chandpuri's company was able to knock out one Pakistani tank while their medium machine gun and small-arms fire managed to keep the Pakistani force at bay.

For some reason, which came to be known much later through an interview of the Commanding Officer of 38 Cavalry, the Pakistan Infantry Brigade failed to press home their attack.

At 0700 hours, a squadron of armour and two companies launched an attack on the Longewala position. They were engaged by the Indians from Longewala with anti-tank guns, medium machine guns and small-arms fire.

'At this stage, enemy aircraft appeared on the scene. The tanks were out in the open without anti-aircraft protection and without any hope of friendly air cover. The Indian aircraft had a free run. 22 Cavalry lost eighteen tanks and several other vehicles. Frantic requests were made for friendly air cover. But there was no response.'*

Squadron Leader D.K. Das of the IAF spotted tanks ahead of the Longewala post. Initially, the IAF pilots did not fire at the Pakistani tanks, stating that they could not distinguish between Indian and Pakistani tanks. Lieutenant Colonel Atma Singh of the Air OP had to go up into the air and communicate with the IAF pilots and clarify that there were no Indian tanks in the area. Thereafter, the IAF had a clear run and began to take on the Pakistani offensive force north of Longewala.

By noon, IAF aircraft had decimated the attacking Pak force. Over 100 vehicles, including twenty-two tanks, were destroyed by the IAF.

Extracts from *Air Battle of Longewala*, an account by the Base Commander of the IAF Station Jaisalmer, Air Commodore M.S. Bawa:

> At about 0715 hours (7.15 a.m.), when the post at Longewala was about to be overrun, the first Hunter mission arrived on the scene scanning the road from Ramgarh to Longewala. The mission immediately reported the presence of T-59 tanks, confirmed also by the Air OP. The mission lost no time in engaging the tanks advancing towards Longewala post . . . Missions were launched one behind the other in

* Major General Shaukat Riza, *The Pakistan Army 1966–71* (Services Book Club, 1990). p. 208.

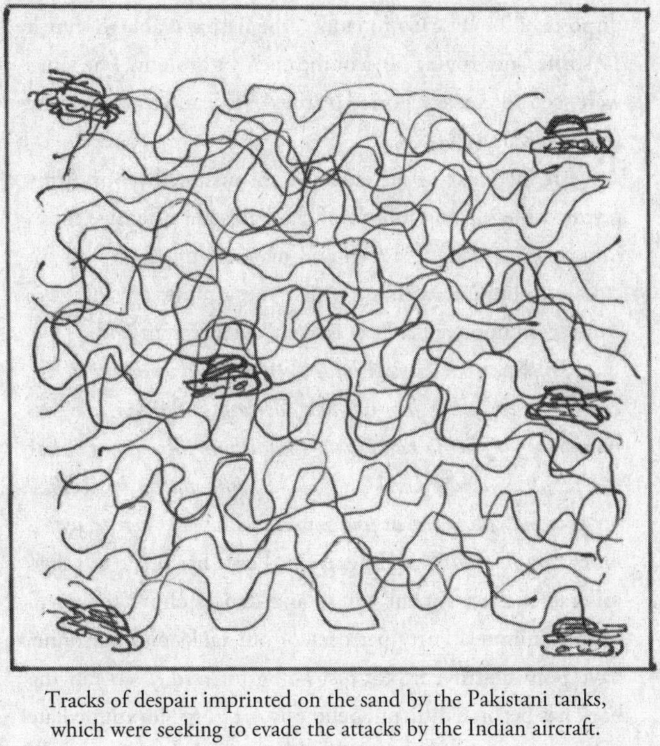

Tracks of despair imprinted on the sand by the Pakistani tanks, which were seeking to evade the attacks by the Indian aircraft.

quick succession to beat and destroy the enemy's armoured thrust. This turned out to be a clean battle, one of its kind, between Pakistan armour and the Indian Air Force. Never before in history was a more decisive battle fought of aircraft versus armour as was done at Longewala.

With a total of four Hunter aircraft available at the disposal of the Base Commander, the Base was able to launch 17 sorties, destroying 50% of the enemy's armour. The tanks were seen ablaze, as reported by the Air OP and the Company at Longewala.

An intercept of an enemy transmission by our Army revealed the sagging morale of the Pakistani offensive force, indicating casualties in men and material and SOS calls for close air support, without which the armour advance was considered impossible. This is what the intercept said:

'*Dushman ka Hawai Fauj ne nak me dam kardiya hai. Har ek hawai jahaz jata hai aur doosra atta hai aur bees bees minute oopar nachta hai. Chalis Fisadi Fauj aur saman hallak aur tabah ho chuka hai. Age jana ya peche murna be mushkil ho gaya hai. Jaldi hawai fauj madad ke lie bejo warna wapas murna na mumkin hai* (Enemy Air Force has made our lives miserable. Each aircraft comes and dances above for up to twenty minutes. Forty per cent of our tanks and personnel have been destroyed. Not just going forward, even moving back has become difficult. Send our Air Force for immediate help or else turning back will not be possible.'

6 December 1971

The Air Base once again mounted pressure at Longewala. The tanks were picked off one by one and were hit repeatedly till they began to burn. By the evening of 6 December, nearly thirty-seven tanks lay burning/damaged in this belt of the Thar Desert. The battle of Longewala was, in fact, over. Longewala, in the district of Jaisalmer in Rajasthan, became the biggest graveyard of Pakistani armour.

7–9 December 1971

During daytime on 7 December, the Air Base launched twenty sorties, pounding the area between Longewala, BP 638 and Ghabbar, depriving the enemy of its much-needed vehicles and guns, which lay burning. During the first mission of the day and his very first mission, Wing Commander Donald Melvyn Conquest, Officer Commanding 122 Squadron from Jaisalmer, sustained bullet injuries (from small-arms fire by the enemy) while engaging an enemy tank. But he brought the aircraft safely to the base. On 8 December, the Air Base launched a total of fourteen sorties in pursuit of its aim to destroy the enemy. It claimed the destruction of one tank and sixteen vehicles. On this day, the force was supplemented with additional aircraft from Jamnagar, raising the total force to fourteen Hunter aircraft, and the Base Commander flashed a message to state that the force was not being utilized fully, requesting better utilization. On 9 December, a total of twenty-two Hunter sorties were launched, and the Squadron claimed the destruction of nine tanks, three artillery guns, thirty-two vehicles and one armored personnel carrier, as well as damage to three tanks and six vehicles.*

---

* Air Marshal M.S. Bawa, PVSM, AVSM, VM, *Air Battle of Longewala*, Occasional Paper No. IV, Centre for Armed Forces Historical Research, United Service Institution, New Delhi, 2016.

By this time, close air support was needed for the offensives by 12 Infantry Division and 11 Infantry Division, in the areas of Rahimyar Khan and Nayachor–Gadra City, respectively, and the air effort was directed to these areas. Then, on the last day of the war, 17 December, the base at Jaisalmer launched fourteen Hunter sorties, including in the Longewala area, destroying fourteen artillery guns and other miscellaneous targets.

According to 122 Squadron, seventy-eight enemy tanks were destroyed/damaged, and two armoured regiments of the Pakistan Army were rendered inoperative. The enemy had entered the Longewala battleground with two armoured regiments, consisting of ninety tanks, and by the end of the battle of Longewala, less than a squadron of enemy armour was left intact. A large number of enemy artillery guns and innumerable vehicles were also claimed as destroyed.

Carl von Clausewitz, the nineteenth-century Prussian General and eminent military strategist, in his book *On War* repeatedly says that the aim of war should be the destruction of the enemy's war machine and his will to fight. With regard to the first, the Indian Air Force succeeded admirably in decimating two Pakistani armoured regiments. The desert sands around Longewala became their burial ground. Besides the tanks, artillery guns and over a hundred vehicles were also destroyed.

With regard to the destruction of the will to fight, it appeared that the Pakistan Army was itself responsible for its irresolute leadership. One often wondered why a huge force, of two Pakistan infantry brigades supported by two armoured regiments and the whole divisional artillery, was unable to destroy an isolated infantry company of less than a hundred men much before the Indian Air Force arrived on the scene.

Brigadier Z.A. Khan gives us a clue as to what actually happened in the context of Pakistan's wavering leadership that led to the debacle at Longewala. He was at that time the Commanding Officer of 38 Cavalry:*

> On the evening of 2 December 1971, I went to Headquarter 51 Infantry Brigade. Lieutenant Colonel Akram Syed, Commanding Officer 22 Cavalry, was already there. He told me that the Brigade Commander, Brigadier Tariq Mir was shaken and had lost his nerve (after hearing that air support would not be available). A little later the Brigade Commander came to the tent where the 'O' Group had assembled. He appeared shaken.
>
> The GSO3 (Junior Staff Officer) laid out the maps of the area of operations. The Indian territory was blank squares on the map. The Brigade had not collected the latest maps from the Division Headquarter. I placed my maps instead on the table which showed both sides of the terrain. The deployment of the Indians was not known and even the number of the Indian Division opposite us was wrongly given as 11 Infantry Division, instead of 12 Infantry Division.
>
> From the discussion that followed, it appeared that the mind of the Brigade Commander 51 Brigade had stopped functioning. I explained the divisional plan to the Brigade Commander. The Commander 51 Brigade accepted the plan.
>
> When the 'O' Group dispersed, the Commander of the Artillery Regiment in support, asked for the maps of 38 Cavalry, as his maps of the Indian terrain were also blank.

---

* https://www.strategicfront.org/forums/threads/battle-of-longewala-dec-1971-pakistani-perspective-brigadier-za-khan-pakistan-army-then-commanding-officer-38-cavalry.2495/

It appears that even before the offensive was to start, the Brigade Commander who was to lead the offensive had got demoralized on being informed that air support would not be available. Also, the preparations for the offensive appeared to be shoddy and many loose ends had not been tied.

Brigadier Khan continues:

On 4 December, at 0400 hours, when the Brigade had reached close to Longewala, I learned that the lorries carrying POL (petrol, oil and lubricants) were stuck in the sand near Darki.

During the day of 4 December, on advice of the Brigade Commanders the attack on Jaisalmer airfield was abandoned.

At about 0730 hours, explosions were heard in the direction of Longewala and columns of smoke were rising. I along with my adjutant drove towards the smoke and from a sand ridge overlooking Longewala I saw five tanks of 22 Cavalry burning. Four Hawker Hunters of the IAF were circling and after expending their rockets they went away.

This was the start of a series of continuous sorties that caused much damage to Pakistani armour, artillery guns and miscellaneous vehicles that has already been described.

At 2100 hours, Lieutenant Colonel Syed, Commanding Officer 22 Cavalry told me that Brigadier Tariq Mir was behaving very badly and that he had no intention of going beyond Longewala.

Next morning while we were still at Headquarter 51 Brigade, a helicopter landed with orders from the GOC ordering 51 Brigade to capture Longewala and Ghotaru, a place ten miles on the road to Jaisalmer.

> On receiving these orders, Brigadier Tariq Mir, Commander 51 Pakistan Infantry Brigade, announced that he would not comply with these orders as the Indians were too strong for a brigade attack. He later stated that two Indian armoured regiments were turning his flanks in order to cut him off! (Imaginary fears of the Brigade Commander.) While we were witnessing the Brigade Commander's refusal to obey the Divisional Commander's orders, Indian aircraft again attacked and we all took cover.

The description of the above is just to show the state of confusion in the preparation and conduct of the Pakistani offensive. Lack of air support for the offensive was not the only cause of their failure. It appears that there were major leadership and administrative failures that caused the operation to fail.

In all of this, we see the shining example of an Indian Army Infantry Company Commander holding his ground in the face of an attacking force nearly a division-strong. His bold courage, resilience and commitment to the call of duty is an example for every citizen to do what is right irrespective of the consequences. He was awarded the Mahavir Chakra for his qualities of leadership and courage that went beyond the call of duty.

The Indian Air Force proved beyond doubt the importance of air power and the need for close cooperation between the services. Among other awards, seven Vir Chakras were awarded to IAF pilots and two to Army Air OP pilots.

The Battle of Longewala exemplified the never-say-die spirit of the Indian Army, which turned the prospect of defeat into a decisive victory.

It was a long shot at Longewala, but it worked!

Postscript

1. This account of the battle of Longewala has been put together from, in addition to written narratives, accounts of Indian as well as Pakistani participants.
2. The offensives by 11 and 12 Indian Infantry Divisions were largely successful, and many hundreds of square kilometres were captured by them. Those are separate stories by themselves and are not discussed here. However, this battle demonstrates that it is more important to destroy an enemy than capture ground across the international border, which in any case we have to return after a ceasefire.
3. A single strand of barbed wire and the indomitable spirit of an Indian infantry company, led by a brave, determined officer, was all that it took to stop a huge Pakistani force of infantry and armour in its tracks.
4. The Indian Air Force played a prominent and critical part in the total destruction of the enemy force. Lack of air support to the Pakistani offensive contributed to the destruction of the Pakistani offensive and the demoralization of its Commanders. This effectively highlights the importance of air power.
5. Incidentally, 22 Cavalry was the armoured regiment that was once commanded by General Zia-ul-Haq.
6. General Mustafa was removed from command. The new GOC, Major General Abdul Hameed Khan, took command and ordered 18 Pakistan Infantry Division to withdraw to its original position.
7. Lieutenant General Eric Vaz, the iconic Commandant of the Indian Army's College of Combat, used to start his lecture on the Indo–Pak war of 1971 with these words: 'Two factors favoured our actions during this war: God and good luck! We had plenty of both at Longewala!'

Good Is Better Than Best

'An army of sheep led by a lion will prove to be far better than an army of lions led by a sheep.'

—Anonymous

It was the first week of October 1971, and Shimla looked resplendent in the glory of its last days of autumn. Trees had just begun to shed their leaves of gold and ochre, and in the upper reaches of the Shimla hills, bare branches pointed towards the sky in anticipation of a cold winter. Lieutenant General K.P. Candeth, GOC-in-C Western Command, however, had no inclination to take notice of nature's beauty at its best. He was instead in the Ops Room* of Headquarters Western Command, looking at the map that gave the dispositions of his formations that stretched from the deserts of Rajasthan through the plains of Punjab, the hills of Jammu and Kashmir up to the icy wastes of Ladakh. It was a long, extended border, and he had had great

* Ops Room: A high security room with sliding boards on which are pinned maps that cover the operation plans for each sector of a formation. Only those concerned with these operations have access to this room. In Army HQ, the Military Operations Directorate is known as the 'Cage'.

plans which he felt would deliver decisive outcomes. But now, that was not going to happen.

BSF posts which had to be recaptured by 6 Garhwal.

Some of his formations had been taken away from him by Sam Manekshaw, the Army Chief, for operations on the border of East Pakistan. This put him in a pensive mood, because it effectively cut down the offensive plans that he and his staff had worked out in anticipation of a war with Pakistan. He knew that as an Army Commander he needed to have sound plans and sufficient reserves. With the reserves taken away from him, he would not be able to implement his plans.

What was left, brought him to near parity with Pakistani formations on the Western Front. In fact, Pakistan was now stronger in armour and artillery. For offensive operations, he still had a Strike Corps* and two independent armoured brigades, but that was not enough to execute the plans he had in mind to teach Pakistan a lesson they needed to learn.

The overall strategy of the Indian Army was 'offence in the east and offensive defence† on the Western‡ and Northern§ fronts'. In compliance with this strategy and his reduced reserves,

* Strike Corps: a corps tasked to conduct offensive operations.

† Offensive defence: a defensive plan that includes limited offensive operations.

‡ Western Front: the plains of Punjab.

§ Northern Front: the plains and hill sector of J&K and the area of Ladakh.

he had directed the divisions that remained with him to work out their plans for offensives from within their own resources, in order to improve the overall posture of Western Command.

Somewhere along this long border, in the RS Pura sector of Jammu and Kashmir, was the 6th Battalion of the Garhwal Rifles. Its Commanding Officer, Lieutenant Colonel Ahobala Krishnamoorthy, was surveying the ground in front of him. The fields where wheat had recently been sown were just turning green. Beyond these fields were the enemy positions, and he could see what they were doing through his binoculars. Moorthy had worked out in his mind the various contingencies that could occur once the war started. He had discussed and rehearsed these with his companies and platoons, but he also told their commanders to be prepared for the unexpected. He did not realize at that time, that the unexpected was exactly what was going to happen.

Ever since he had assumed command of 6 Garhwal, Lieutenant Colonel Moorthy's only passion was to train every soldier of his battalion to be part of an efficient fighting machine, and he could just not wait to test his battalion in actual war.

As a Major, Moorthy had fought the Indo–Pak war of 1965 with the 1st Garhwal Rifles in the deserts of Rajasthan. In that war, 1st Garhwal, led by Lieutenant Colonel P.K. Lahiri, distinguished itself in operations to take Gadra City, putting up a fine display of infantry tactics in desert terrain without artillery support.

As the war continued, Moorthy was one day moving in his jeep when he was attacked by a Pak Sabre jet. Seeing a lone Indian Army jeep moving slowly along the sand dunes territory, the Sabre pilot made a low pass over Moorthy's jeep and let loose a sighter burst* from his guns. Moorthy and his driver,

* Sighter burst: a check by a fighter pilot to see whether his guns are properly aligned.

Naik Prem Singh, jumped out of the jeep and rolled into the sand dunes, with rocket and canon fire trying to seek them out. The Sabre made another pass, but the pilot, seeing the jeep at rest and the occupants on the sand, presumed that he had destroyed his target. Miraculously, neither Moorthy nor Prem Singh was hurt, nor was the jeep damaged. They got up, dusted themselves and continued on their journey. The Indian soldier believes in God and the efficacy of prayer. There is a saying: 'An army wife was praying for the safety of her husband, and somewhere, far away, a bullet missed its target.'

In that war, which continued from September to November, 1st Garhwal went on to capture Jesse Ke Par, Nawa Tala and Miajlar. The battalion was awarded the Battle Honour of Gadra City and the Theatre Honour 'Rajasthan'. In this operation, seven valiant soldiers were killed, and two officers and thirty-eight brave Bulas* were wounded. The Commanding Officer and Lieutenant Jasbir Singh were awarded Vir Chakras. Moorthy and Naik Prem Singh were lucky to get away alive, and word went around the langar† that, '*Moorthy Sa'ab ke saath jaoge toh bomb bhi nahin marega* (if you go with Moorthy Sir, even bombs won't kill you).'

It was now the end of November, and there were many indicators that war was in the offing. Moorthy believed that offence was the best form of defence, and that in addition to dominating 'no man's land',‡ an aggressive posture was necessary, which meant some sort of offensive action to intimidate the enemy.

---

* Bula: Regimental term for a Garhwali soldier. In the same way as a Gorkha soldier is called a 'Johnny'.

† Langar: cookhouse. 'Langar gupp' means barrack-room stories.

‡ No man's land: the ground between own forces and the enemy.

His problem, however, was similar to General Candeth's, although many levels lower in scale. Whereas the Army Commander was upset at some of his formations being moved away from him, Moorthy's issue was that personnel that had been taken away from him on attachment to various formation headquarters had not yet returned, although orders had been passed by Army Headquarters that they be reverted to their units immediately, due to the possibility of war.

Candeth, the Army Commander, was trying to create reserves from within his command for offensive tasks. Moorthy, the Battalion Commander of 6 Garhwal, was similarly engaged in trying to find some way in which he could scrape together at least a couple of platoons to aggressively dominate the enemy in front of him. Both these Commanders, at the level of army and battalion, were busy working out how best they could defeat the enemy and give him a bloody nose, despite the fact that their strength had unfortunately been drastically reduced.

Towards the south of 6 Garhwal, the Strike Corps of Western Command had got into its battle positions to carry out its tasks in the area of Basantar. To the north, the division of which 6 Garhwal was a part was rehearsing its plans for its own offensive operation, which came to be known as the 'Chicken's Neck' operation.

Moorthy was aware of these operations, but his focus was the defence of the area entrusted to his charge, and he went all out to ensure that not an inch of ground would be taken by the enemy. That, he felt, was not difficult but still not challenging enough. What he wanted was to get to grips with the enemy, to defeat him in his own area, across the border.

On 3 December 1971, Pakistan attacked Indian airfields in Rajasthan, Punjab and Jammu and Kashmir. Yahya Khan felt that he could replicate the success of a similar operation carried out by the Pakistan Air Force in 1965, but he failed this time because the Indian Air Force had protected its aircraft and launched counter air operations almost immediately. The PAF, however, continued to attack the Jammu airfield during the course of the war.

At their home in Miran Sahib, Moorthy's wife, Sharada, and their young daughter, Meghna, were for the first time experiencing the effects of war. They saw and heard with awe and some amount of fear the night sky lit up with the tracers of the air defence guns as they fired at the attacking PAF aircraft. As the walls of their home shook and the windowpanes shattered due to the bombs that fell, they followed the laid-down drill of moving to the bunker in their garden, where they spent cold and sleepless nights, listening to the news about the war on all fronts on their transistor radio. On the morning after the first air attack, the battalion Panditji came in full uniform and told Mrs Moorthy to pack a few clothes and move to a safer location. Many families had moved to their hometowns prior to the war, but Mrs Moorthy had decided to stay. Now, she quickly packed a few clothes, essentials and a picture of Goddess Durga, and moved with Meghna to the family quarters. On the way, they were witness to a sea of humanity on the move. The roads were packed with people carrying whatever they could on carts, cycles and on their heads. Rural folk from the villages, who had been displaced because of the war, were heading away from the scene of conflict. Able-bodied men and women were carrying frail elderly parents, little children, even lambs on their shoulders, while cattle and dogs accompanied their families on foot across the bridge over the Tawi River.

The newly built family quarters were located close to the Jammu airfield. Sharada Moorthy realized too late that they had moved literally 'from the frying pan into the fire' because now they were closer to the airfield, which was the constant target of the PAF bombing raids. Anyway, she was now together with the officers' and men's families from the brigade, and as the only Commanding Officer's wife, she took charge of the situation, raising their morale and organizing prayer services to Goddess Durga and also to Pir Baba, a revered Muslim saint, for the safety of the soldiers on the front and of Mother India.

The rooms were barely furnished with just a few cots and a couple of chairs. The windows had been covered with black paper, and there were only candles for light at night. From 4 December to the end of the war, the Jammu airfield continued to be subjected to air raids by Pakistani aircraft, but the children lost their sense of fear and rushed out of their homes as soon as the 'All Clear' was sounded, to search for shrapnel and bomb splinters. On one occasion, during the day, they were excited to see a dog fight in the sky between our own and enemy aircraft.

Ahead of 6 Garhwal, the Border Security Force (BSF) was holding two positions close to the border. In peacetime, the BSF is required to hold positions along the Indo–Pak border, to prevent cross-border infiltration and smuggling. These posts are taken over by the Army on the outbreak of war, and the BSF moves to alternative tasks in the hinterland. Two such posts were held by the BSF at Nawapind and Jogne Chak to the right and left of the 6th Garhwal defences. Unbeknown to Lieutenant Colonel Moorthy, on the night of 4 December the BSF had vacated their positions and moved out without being relieved. That same night, the Pakistanis, who were keeping a close watch on these locations, had quickly occupied the vacated positions that were gifted to them without firing a shot. The intrusion and occupation of Nawapind and Jogne Chak positions were detected at first light on the morning of 5 December by the battalion screen* position.

Early on the morning of 5 December, Second Lieutenant G.S. Rathore, who was manning the Screen position ahead of the defences of 6 Garhwal, reported that Pakistani troops had moved in and occupied the BSF localities, and that the BSF were nowhere to be seen. Lieutenant Colonel Moorthy moved immediately to the Screen position. Looking through his binoculars he could clearly see the Pakistani troops in their khaki uniforms busy improving their defences.

Intensely irritated by the behaviour of the BSF and his formation headquarters for allowing such a thing to happen, Moorthy immediately ordered his mortars and medium machine guns to engage these positions. A situation report was sent to the Brigade with a copy to the division, informing all concerned of what had happened and his proposed action to evict the Pakistanis from these two locations. Having done this, he moved back to his headquarters. Soon after he reached his headquarters, at about 0700 hours, Moorthy set into motion his plans to evict the Pakistanis.

At around 0900 hours, just as he was about to give his orders for the assault on these posts, the Brigade Commander arrived at Moorthy's headquarters. He appeared disturbed

---

* Screen: a small body of troops, normally a section, placed ahead of the forward companies to report on enemy activities. In the event of an enemy offensive, they report the strength and direction of the enemy attack.

about what had happened and apprehensive of Lieutenant Colonel Moorthy's plans to evict the Pakistanis. The Brigade Commander said that he would need to get permission from the General Officer Commanding the Division (GOC) to permit the Garhwalis to launch an offensive to recapture the BSF positions.

Moorthy was beginning to find the attitude of the Brigade Commander annoying. He said: 'Sir, I have copied my sitrep to the division as to what has happened, so they are aware of my plans. I can't wait for permission of the division to launch operations within our own area to recover positions that have been lost due to the BSF vacating their posts. If we wait for the division to analyse the situation and then decide on what action is to be taken, the enemy would reinforce its position with infantry and armour, and that would require a brigade attack organized and conducted by the Brigade. I am preventing that from happening, and you should be happy that I am saving you the trouble of having to plan and conduct such an attack.'

The Brigade Commander knew that Moorthy was right but was still apprehensive of the ability of the Garhwalis to evict the Pakistanis without proper support. He said: 'Are you aware that the division is launching an offensive tonight in the area of Chicken's Neck, and you will therefore not get the support of the divisional artillery. What shall I tell the GOC about your stubbornness?

'No, sir. You have not so far informed me about what the division is up to. I have committed support from the artillery in support of my battalion. That is for the Brigade to ensure. And even if that is not available, I will still go in with the support of my mortars, medium machine guns and RCLs.'

The Battalion 'O' Group* had meanwhile assembled at the viewpoint, ready to take orders, and the Battalion 'R' Group† had formed up some distance away, waiting to move forward.

At that moment, the Brigade Commander was called to the telephone and was told that the GOC had sent a message to him telling him to advise Lieutenant Colonel Moorthy to go in for a night attack rather than a day attack, as the former would reduce casualties. The Brigade Commander passed on the message to Moorthy.

Lieutenant Colonel Moorthy listened politely to the Brigade Commander and said: 'Sir, you can thank the GOC for his advice to launch my attacks at night to avoid casualties. I am aware that the cover of darkness helps in reducing casualties. However, by that time, the Pakistanis, who are already digging themselves in, would have reinforced these positions, and we would need many more men to do the same job. My battalion is responsible for defending other positions along the border, and I will not want to pull out my boys later on and risk an enemy attack elsewhere. I know what I am doing. My success depends entirely on attacking immediately, before they have time to settle down and be reinforced. The GOC would also know that counterattacks are successful only when they are launched immediately. We have already lost time, and I am not prepared to lose any more time.'

The Brigade Commander, who saw that Lieutenant Colonel Moorthy was adamant and not prepared to take no for an answer, said: 'All right. I will try to get our armoured squadron to shoot you on to your objectives.' With that, the Brigade Commander

---

* 'O' Group, or the Order Group, consists of commanders who take orders for the contemplated action.

† 'R' Group, or the Fighting Group, executes the action on the ground.

left for his headquarters, and Moorthy gave out his orders for the assault on Jogne Chak and Nawapind.

Naib Subedar Gopal Dutt Joshi was given the task of capturing Jogne Chak with his platoon. Jogne Chak was attacked at 1000 hours, and the platoon went in with their war cry of '*Bolo Badri Vishal Lal ki jai*', with the battalion mortars and medium machine guns in support. The platoon was well trained, and within half an hour the position was captured. The enemy just ran away as soon as the attack was mounted. Two enemy soldiers were killed and a few weapons captured.

The attack at Nawapind had to be staggered because the battalion mortars, medium machine guns and RCL guns could not support both attacks at the same time. For the attack on Nawapind, Lieutenant Colonel Moorthy had lifted a platoon from the Screen position commanded by Second Lieutenant G.S. Rathore and the Commando Platoon was under Captain P.K. Sinha. Both these officers were very junior but keen and spirited.

The platoons were quickly moved to their FUPs* behind the Screen Position to the north-west of the battalion defences and facing Nawapind.

The attack on Nawapind was to go in at 1100 hours, but the Brigade Commander asked for the postponement of the attack, as the troop of tanks he had asked for had not fetched up to support the attack. The time for the attack had to be changed to 1415 hrs.

The Mortar Platoon gave the platoons covering fire, and the battalion's RCL guns engaged the enemy MMG detachment,

* Forming-up place, where the assaulting troops collect to capture an objective. This place is normally square to the objective.

which was firing at the assaulting troops. The RCL guns accurately engaged the MMG bunker, which was destroyed and three enemy soldiers manning the MMG were killed. Second Lieutenant G.S. Rathore assaulted the enemy from the west and overran the eastern portion of the post. The enemy retreated to the western edge of the locality and occupied the trenches in that area. Second Lieutenant Rathore used one of his LMGs to block the enemy's route of withdrawal and closed in on the enemy, who continued to fire at him. At that moment, radio contact with Rathore was lost.

Lieutenant Colonel Moorthy quickly dispatched a wireless set with Second Lieutenant R.K. Tandon to re-establish contact with Rathore's platoon. When Tandon reported that he could not move forward because the enemy fire was too strong, the CO ordered Captain Sinha's platoon to attack from the north-east. The enemy was now encircled from the west and north-east, and Nawapind fell to the Garhwalis at 1500 hours after some hand-to-hand fighting on the objective.

Since there was no time to brief the tank commanders in detail, Major Tejinder Singh, a Company Commander, was sent to guide the armour. The tanks found it difficult to support the assault, and so they were used to engage the enemy, who was trying to retreat to the rear.

Three JCOs and fifteen enemy soldiers were taken prisoner. They belonged to Pakistan's 37 Frontier Force Rifles and 7 Engineer Regiment. They were moved to the Screen position, and then sent to the rear and handed over to the military police for dispatch to the prisoner of war camp. During the mopping-up of the post, dead bodies of one JCO, three NCOs and twelve enemy soldiers were found. The haul of sixty-five weapons included four LMGs, one MMG, one rocket launcher, three

Sten guns, thirty automatic rifles, seventeen rifles, and lots of hand grenades and ammunition.

The battalion lost two brave men during this battle.

As Lieutenant General K.P. Candeth states in his book *The Western Front: The Indo–Pakistan War 1971*, except for the Chicken's Neck operation, there was little or no activity in the 26 Infantry Division Sector. The only operation was the recapture on 5 December of the Nawa Pind post, which had been vacated earlier by the BSF, and some raids on various enemy posts.

Looking at the haul of sixty-five weapons, it was obvious that the Nawapind post was held by an enemy force of a Rifle Company, as the strength of a company in war is about that much. At the very least, it must have been held by two platoons in full strength. And so, an enemy position consisting of two platoons was destroyed by a force of equal strength, whereas the teaching is that in attack, the attacking force has to be in a ratio of 3:1. Therefore, it was only the boldness of the Commanding Officer and the fighting spirit of the battalion that won the day.

Also, it must be remembered that in this battle, the Commanding Officer resisted the temptation of using his Company Commanders (Majors) for this critical operation. He had full faith in his junior-most leaders, and he let them exercise their command in battle. After all, even though they were junior in rank, they were keen to lead their men in battle, and they were the commanders who had trained them. It was only right, therefore, that they lead them into battle. This experience would stand them in good stead in a future war.

Most important, the Commanding Officer knew that immediate action was of primary importance. He believed in his men, had trained them well and was confident that his plan to seize the moment with courage would yield the desired outcome, rather than delaying the attack and allowing the enemy to build up his strength. His success far exceeded the expectations of his Formation Commanders.

Far away from 6 Garhwal, General K.P. Candeth had to be content that the armoured brigades of his Strike Corps had destroyed the bulk of Pakistani armour that had been deployed against him. Lieutenant Colonel Ahobala Krishnamoorthy by his bold and timely action, had validated six of the ten principles of war. These were: selection and maintenance of aim; offensive action; surprise; concentration of force; economy of effort; and maintenance of momentum. His faith in his troops, belief in himself and conviction that what he was doing was right resulted in a victory far in excess of the meagre resources that were available to him. The recapture of the two posts vacated by the BSF, the capture of three JCOs and fifteen Pakistani soldiers, and the killing of one JCO, three NCOs and twelve enemy soldiers, as well as a huge haul of weapons—all of it goes to show what a Battalion Commander can do with minimum resources. After retaking Nawapind, the battalion carried the defensive battle into enemy territory, mounting three strong raids on enemy posts opposite its area. Gallantry awards received by the battalion were just one Vir Chakra and two Mentioned-in-Dispatches.

This story has a simple message—that a good plan, executed in time with courage and energy, is far better than a perfect plan carried out too late.

Postscript

1. Among the captured Pakistani JCOs was the famous Abdul Khaliq, an ace sprinter who had represented Pakistan at the

Olympic Games in Melbourne and Rome. He had won gold medals in the 100- and 200-metre races in the 1954 Asian Games and in the 100 metres in the 1958 Asian Games, but lost out to Milkha Singh in the 200 metres in the 1958 Asian Games. Both were Subedars in their respective armies. After being taken prisoner, Abdul Khaliq asked if he could meet Milkha Singh, India's 'Flying Sikh'. Milkha met him at the POW camp; though they met with the joy of fellow athletes, the circumstances this time were different.*

2. In a lighter vein, Moorthy's daughter had asked: 'But, Daddy, how did you catch him if he could run so fast?'†
3. The officers and men of 6 Garhwal knew that they had done a good job, and as is natural with soldiers, they hoped that the battalion would get its fair share of gallantry awards. Although the battalion received one VrC and two Mentioned-in-Dispatches, it felt it deserved better. Was it because the Formation Commanders felt that the Commanding Officer was too independent and insensitive to their advice? Nobody could answer this question, but the men were disappointed. They had fought well, and yet it appeared that the higher command did not recognize their acts of courage. The Commanding Officer, however, reminded them, 'It is better to deserve awards and not get them, rather than have awards you do not deserve.'

* Sagat Shaunik (ed), *Untold Battlefield Tales* (Navi Mumbai: Fauji Foundation, 2019), p. 80.

† Ibid.

A Touch of Luck

'In war, in addition to good generalship, great strategy, sound tactics and excellent leadership, sometimes luck plays its own part in deciding the fortunes of war. Before appointing senior generals to critically key appointments, Napoleon used to ask, "Is he lucky?"'

—Anonymous

Ever since Partition, Pakistan had been oscillating between military rule and civilian governments. However, as far as the Pakistani armed forces were concerned, irrespective of the form of government, it was the army that had arrogated to itself the role of decision-maker.

The Pakistan Navy decided that they needed to do something to make their presence felt and came to the conclusion that supremacy under the waves in the war at sea would be the best answer. From the early 1960s, they had decided to concentrate on building their underwater capability.* In 1964, the Pakistan

* Vice Admiral G. Hiranandani, *Transition to Triumph*, p. 108.

INS *Katchal*, an Indian naval ship, being targeted by a Pakistani midget submarine.

Navy acquired USS *Diablo*,* an ocean-going submarine, on lease and renamed it PNS *Ghazi*.

Their next move, acquisition of three Daphne-class submarines, was a masterstroke. The submarines were commissioned into the Pakistan Navy between 1 December 1969 and 5 August 1970. Named after species of three deadly sharks in Pakistani waters—the *Hangor*, the *Sushuk* and the *Mangro*—these French submarines were the best world-class submarines of that era. But not content with having established the Pakistan Navy in an already superior position in underwater warfare, the Pakistani Naval Chief went in for the purchase of midget-class† submarines and chariots‡ from Italy to consolidate and enhance that predominance.

---

* 'Diablo' is Spanish for 'the devil'.

† Midget submarines are small underwater craft built to carry frogmen into harbours where larger submarines cannot penetrate or to launch small torpedoes at enemy ships.

‡ A chariot is an underwater craft smaller than a midget submarine, with one or two men riding 'horseback' on it. These could be used as an underwater approach to an enemy ship, to attach a limpet mine and to move away before it blew up at a time set on its mechanism.

The Indian Navy was intrigued and wondered how the Pakistan Navy would use their midget submarines. These could not navigate the open seas on their own and would therefore have to be towed to the area of operations. This made it difficult to use them in offensive operations. Thus, the Indian Navy concluded that the midget submarines and the Chariots would be kept in reserve, and used for the defence of harbours or when suitable opportunities presented themselves.

Towards the middle of 1971 it was clear to the armed forces of Pakistan that there was every likelihood of their country going to war with India. So the Pakistan Navy began to finalize its operational plans. The focus of their strategy was to strike the first blow as soon as 'the balloon went up'.* With this, the Pakistani Naval Chief hoped to give the Pakistan Navy its rightful place in the eyes of his countrymen.

By the end of November 1971, it was clear that General Yahya Khan would attack very soon, but the date and time of the attack was not known. In anticipation of the signal to commence hostilities, the Pakistan Navy set her plans in motion. On 14 November 1971, PNS *Ghazi* left Karachi harbour in her quest to destroy the *Vikrant*, which was somewhere in the Bay of Bengal. The *Mangro*, too, left for Bombay around 14 November, and the *Hangor* left Karachi on 23 November for a patrol off the Kathiawar coast. The *Hangor* and *Mangro* were to take turns outside Mumbai harbour, so that they could destroy INS *Mysore* and the ships of India's Western Fleet once war was declared. But unbeknown to the Pakistani Naval Chief, Indian intelligence had got wind of the plans of the Pakistan Navy.

---

* The phrase 'balloon goes up' indicates that something is going to start. In this case, an indication that the war was about to commence.

Being aware of Pakistan's intentions, the Indian Naval Chief, Admiral S.M. Nanda, ordered the Western Fleet out of Bombay harbour a day before Pakistan launched its attack on India. While the previous stories in this book—'The Hunt for the *Vikrant*' and 'Mission Karachi'—serve as a background to this one, the focus here is on one of the midget submarines of the Pakistan Navy.

The midget submarines were small 62-tonne underwater craft, which could not carry a torpedo. This inability to carry a torpedo limited their role to transporting frogmen* to enemy harbours, into depths where larger submarines could not penetrate. The naval element of the Pakistani Special Service Group manning the midget submarines were an elite, rigorously trained force. Midget crews were trained to be towed underwater by larger submarines. For sorties longer than three days, the relief crew took over on passage, and the attack crew took over just before being detached to attack.

In order to enhance the capability of these midget submarines, the Pakistan Navy improvised a system by which the midgets could launch torpedoes at enemy ships. Trials were carried out, and the system worked admirably. The torpedoes were of French origin and were fixed externally to the Italian-designed midget submarines by means of locally made torpedo cages. The torpedoes could be launched by air-operated pistons that were actuated from within the submarine.

The procedure for firing these torpedoes was very basic. They had to just point the midget submarine at an enemy warship and shoot, allowing for the speed of the enemy warship

* Frogman: a swimmer, normally from the navy, equipped with breathing apparatus and other equipment, such as a rubber suit and flippers, to execute underwater operations.

and the direction in which it was travelling. The torpedo's homing head would do the rest.

During the 1971 war, on 6 December, one of these midget submarines was on a patrol off the coast of Kathiawar, on the lookout for a suitable target to confirm its ability to destroy an enemy naval craft.

Meanwhile, after the Indian Navy's successful attack on Karachi on 4 and 5 December 1971, Lieutenant Commander Kailash Nath Zadu, Captain of the Indian Navy's INS *Katchal*, was tasked to sweep down the coast of Kathiawar along with the missile boats *Nirghat* and *Nashak,* on the off chance that there could be some enemy activity in those regions.

After forty-eight hours of intensive patrolling, Lieutenant Commander Zadu, who had been given overall command of the *Katchal, Nirghat* and *Nashak*, came to the conclusion that there was no possibility of enemy submarines operating off the Kathiawar coast, so far from their base at Karachi. After the first attack on Karachi on 4 December, the Pakistan Navy had bolted into Karachi harbour and had refused to fight.

But Commanders of the Petya and the missile boats did not realize how wrong they were!

After the first attack on Karachi, the *Katchal*'s engine was heating up, and Zadu decided to task his crew with the servicing of the engine, which had been used extensively on the mission to Karachi. After the engine had been serviced, the three ships were cruising at a comfortable speed towards their rendezvous off Porbandar, in preparation for the next attack on Karachi, scheduled for 8 December.

The sea was calm and the day was sunny, with clear blue skies. Zadu decided that he now had the time to look at the letters delivered to him by the Fleet Mail Office, just before the Western Fleet had taken off for the attack on Karachi.

At that moment, he did not have the faintest idea that his ship, the *Katchal*, was being watched through the periscope of a Pakistani midget submarine, which was following the *Katchal* at a safe distance.

Zadu closed his eyes, sat back and decided to take a break.

Meanwhile, the Pakistani midget submarine was getting into position to destroy the *Katchal*. The ship was right in the middle of the cross hairs of the submarine's aiming device. The *Katchal* was sailing along at a comfortable speed, its crew oblivious that the ship was being stalked by a Pakistani submarine.

It is best that we now let Pakistan's Vice Admiral S.T.H. Naqvi, the Captain of this midget submarine at that time, tell the rest of the story:*

> We had been on patrol for some days; now it was 6 December and we were off Veraval on the Kathiawar coast. A short while ago, at the start of the first dog-watch,† we'd been operating at a deep depth when our very basic type of sonar picked up some propeller noises seaward‡ of us. My crew of five was alert and ready as I pointed the midget towards the noise and groped our way to periscope depth. As my periscope broke surface, there was the ship filling my entire periscope view,

* The Pakistani account of this story is from a Pakistani naval book titled *Bubbles of Water* (Islamabad: PN Book Club, NES Directorate, NHQ, 2001).

† Dog-watch: a period of time aboard a ship when only a part of the crew is assigned to duty.

‡ Seaward: moving or lying in the direction of the sea.

> right ahead of me. I recognized her as a *Petya*, a Russian-built, anti-submarine frigate of the Indian Navy. She was at a distance of 1200 yards only. I had been waiting for such a ship to show up, and now one had tumbled into my lap.
>
> The Captain of the *Petya* was very relaxed as he sat on the bridge* of his ship. It was a pleasant and sunny day in winter and the sea was calm. The signalman came and stood beside him with the signal log† and the Captain flipped through those pages as Captains do all over the world. There was peace and tranquility on the upper decks, a couple of sailors were smoking and shooting the breeze amid ship‡ near the funnel area, as sailors are wont to do. One of them was wearing a blue boiler suit.§ It was a picture-postcard scene of a ship sailing towards the sunset.

When one looks at an enemy target through a periscope, time is at a premium, because the head of the periscope is above the water and if discovered, the roles would be reversed and the submarine would become the 'hunted' instead of being the 'hunter'. Having observed the scene for a few seconds, the midget submarine's crew commenced action drills for destruction of the *Katchal*:

> Excited, I ordered a quick alteration of course to starboard for the aim off and as we turned, I took in the details of

---

* Bridge: a crossways platform or area above the main deck of a ship, from which the ship is controlled.

† Signal log: a book in which a record of a ship's speed, progress, radio transmissions and events of navigational importance is kept.

‡ Amid ship: middle of a ship.

§ Boiler suit: a worker's suit combining shirt and overalls in one piece.

the *Petya*. I could see the whole length of her starboard side and her bow wave indicated that she was doing moderate, economical speed. The ship's hull number had been obliterated, which is normal practice in wartime. She was proceeding with normal, cruising watch-keepers closed up; the guns were not manned, and we could hear no sonar transmissions emanating from her.

The *Petya* simply had no idea that I was around. The moment we arrived at the correct heading, I ordered, 'Shoot', and the crew went through their carefully drilled movements. I held my breath and waited for the moment of truth.

'Shoot! Damn it!' I yelled, tearing my eyes from the telescope.

'Use more air pressure.'

There was a flurry of further activity; somebody swore loudly, but still—nothing!

The crew tried everything—and I exhausted my favourite collection of profanities reserved for such occasions—but there was no making that fish* swim out of its cage. It had become an obstinate mule that no amount of flogging could budge.

The Captain of the midget submarine once again looked at the *Petya* through his periscope and was surprised to now see a pair of OSA missile boats that were escorting the *Petya* and were moving on either side of her. One of them suddenly changed course and started heading for the midget submarine at full speed. The submarine Captain realized that he had been probably discovered and quickly ordered the submarine to dive

* Fish: naval slang for torpedo.

fast and deep to avoid being run over by the OSA missile boat. By the time the midget submarine was able to come back to periscope depth, the *Petya* had moved away, and as far as the submarine was concerned, the chance of a lifetime had passed. The Captain of the midget submarine went on to say:

> Later, there were the inevitable recriminations all round. Some blamed the torpedo. Others said that it was the up-angle of the midget at that precise moment that had prevented the torpedo from swimming out. There were many conjectures and theories. But when all was said and done, I couldn't but marvel at the luck of the Indian Captain I had watched through the periscope that day.

The Captain of the Petya was a lucky man indeed. He did not even know what a close shave he he'd had.

However, Vice Admiral Hiranandani of the Indian Navy says in his book *Transition to Triumph*: 'There were also reports that the Pakistan Navy, on their own, fitted two midgets with external torpedo tubes for firing MK-44 torpedoes. During the war these midgets were deployed 30 miles from Karachi. When one of them tried to fire against an Indian ship, the fire-control system did not work.'

After the second successful attack on Karachi, the Western Fleet returned to Bombay. On conclusion of the war, Admiral Gorshkov, who had come to Bombay with part of the Russian fleet, asked to meet the commanders of the *Petya* and the missile boats. He wanted to congratulate them on the innovative use of the Russian naval craft. Among them was Zadu, who was awarded the Vir Chakra for his courage and tenacity during the attack on Karachi. He was lucky to be alive to receive his award.

Maybe someone's prayers had saved him on that fateful day when a torpedo aimed to destroy him failed to get ignited.

Postscript

1. When asked about this incident, Vice Admiral Hiranandani, author of *Transition to Triumph*, stated, 'A torpedo fired by a midget, close to Karachi, failed to swim away. I feel that the author of the story [Vice Admiral S.T.H. Naqvi of the Pakistan Navy] may have got the dates wrong when he says the incident took place on 6 December 1971.'
2. Zadu was promoted to Captain's rank and continued to serve the Indian Navy with distinction, and it was expected that he would reach higher ranks. It was at this time, that the Ministry of Defence passed an order that no person from the armed forces could marry a foreign national. If the marriage had to take place, then the lady would have to adopt Indian nationality, or the officer had to resign. Faced with this situation, many officers were forced to resign, and the Indian Navy lost some excellent officers. Some of them were potential Naval Chiefs—Zadu was one of them.

Vazir

'There are many things that are beyond our understanding.'

—Ian Cardozo

The Pakistan Air Force's F-86 Sabre jets circled for a second time before going in for the kill. They were a pair. They always came in pairs.

Earlier that morning, when a patrol from the 4th Battalion of the 5th Gorkha Rifles (FF) had left the battalion firm base, they had seen a pair of fighter jets roaming the skies, unchallenged. Like quicksilver, they glinted in the sun, streaking in and out of scattered cumulous clouds, and then climbed high till they became small silver specks in the canopy of the blue sky. *Are these fighters ours or those of the enemy?* the patrol leader wondered.

The patrol was operating in the mountains of Jammu and Kashmir. They had been tasked to locate and destroy caches of arms and ammunition hidden by the infiltrators in the area of Pir Kalewa.* The infiltrators had crossed over into J&K from

* Pir Kalewa: A high mountain peak which is part of a range south of Rajauri. A battle was fought here during the Indo–Pak war of 1947.

The attack by Pak Sabre jets.

Pakistan-occupied Kashmir (PoK) a few days earlier. Later in the day, when the patrol was returning after carrying out its mission, they saw two Pakistani Sabre jets attacking targets far away. The patrol leader wondered whether they were the same ones they had seen earlier that morning. Several pine-covered ridges separated the patrol from the attacking Sabre jets. They could, however, even at this distance, see the flash of their blazing cannons and hear the thunder of their jet engines. But the intervening ridges prevented the patrol from seeing the targets that were being engaged.

Five days had passed since Pakistan had launched Operation Gibraltar, on 5 August 1965. A Pakistani force of 30,000 guerrillas, under the overall command and control of Major General Akhtar Hussain Malik, General Officer Commanding of Pakistan's 12 Infantry Division, had crossed the ceasefire line (CFL) in a second attempt by Pakistan to take J&K by force.

Field Marshal Ayub Khan, President of Pakistan, had himself addressed this force at Murree in the second week of July 1965, before it crossed the CFL. Ayub had decided that the best way to consolidate his power in Pakistan was to capture J&K. He reckoned that India had yet to recover from the reverse suffered during the Sino–Indian War of 1962. Jawaharlal Nehru had passed away, and the diminutive Lal Bahadur Shastri did not fill Ayub with a sense of awe. Pakistan, on the other hand, had been in receipt of massive economic and military aid from the United States of America, and Ayub felt that the situation could never be better and that this was just the right moment to strike. Part of the military arms and equipment received by Pakistan were four squadrons of F-86 Sabre jets. It was two of these aircrafts that the Indian Army patrol saw that morning. India had raised objections to the

USA's transfer of these aircrafts and gift of a huge amount of military hardware to Pakistan. In response, General Dwight Eisenhower, President of the United States, sent a message to Pandit Nehru, dated 24 February 1954, which said:

> . . . and I am confirming publicly that if our aid to any country, including Pakistan, is misused and is directed at another in aggression, I will undertake immediately, in accordance with my constitutional authority, appropriate action both within and without the United Nations to thwart such aggression.*

Needless to say, no action was taken by the US at this flagrant violation of its agreement with Pakistan and the world that these arms and equipment would not be used against any country, which in this case was specifically India.

So much for the duplicity of Pakistan and the credibility of a President of the United States of America!

The capture of Pakistani Junior Commissioned Officers (JCOs) and Non-Commissioned Officers (NCOs) of Pakistan's Gibraltar Force by the Gorkhas during subsequent days of these operations rebutted the Pakistani claim that this was purely an uprising of the people of J&K. These captured personnel of the Pakistani armed forces revealed to the Gorkhas that the aim of Operation Gibraltar was to create a law-and-order situation behind the front line and to call it a civil uprising.

Once this happened, Pakistan would initiate a strong military offensive (Operation Grand Slam), with regular Pakistani troops to capture Akhnur, which was part of the district of Jammu.

---

* General K.V. Krishna Rao, PVSM, *Prepare or Perish* (New Delhi: Lancer Publishers, 1991), p. 119.

Akhnur was strategically important because of its proximity to Jammu and because its capture would sever the Indian line of communication between Pathankot and Poonch. They hoped that the Indian Army would be sandwiched by the Pakistan Army from the front and by the infiltrators from the rear.

On the morning of this incident, the patrol leader from the 4th Battalion of the 5th Gorkha Rifles (FF) was oblivious of Pakistan's grand strategy. War, in fact, had not even been declared, and here was Pakistan attacking them on the ground and from the air. *Were the mandarins in Delhi aware of what was happening in J&K?* he wondered.

It was only when the patrol leader reached their base that he learnt that the Pakistani Sabre jets that they were watching from afar had, in fact, been attacking his own Battalion Headquarters! An Army Supply Corps (ASC) vehicle column had parked their vehicles 'line ahead' on the road running alongside their battalion. It was this collection of vehicles that had attracted the attention of the Pakistani Sabre jets. The target was no doubt attractive. Damage inflicted was considerable, but what was unacceptable and a blot on the conduct of the Pakistan Air Force was that they had used napalm bombs to destroy their targets. Napalm bombs create great walls of fire which move with the momentum and force of their delivery, burning anything and everything in their path to cinders. Use of napalm was banned by the Geneva Conventions, to which India and Pakistan were both signatories.

Pakistan, however, has never cared for conventions and agreements. After agreeing to abide by them, its leaders would disregard them and go into denial mode if questioned; and if caught in a lie, they were thick-skinned enough to refuse to admit their misdemeanours. A few months earlier, Pakistan had launched Operation Desert Hawk in the area of Kutch. India protested at the use of force. Harold Wilson, Prime Minister of Great Britain, brokered a ceasefire in April 1965 between the two countries, and Pakistan had endorsed the idea that force should not be used to resolve territorial disputes. In fact, while the ink of their signature on the Kutch Agreement had yet to dry, she was preparing her second invasion of J&K, which was launched a few months later, in August of the same year. It was this invasion that the Indian Army was now facing.

Survivors recounting this action stated that the Sabre jets had initially used their cannons and rockets, causing considerable damage. Not satisfied, they came around once more and used napalm bombs with deadly effect. Great clouds of orange fire and black smoke engulfed the targets on the ground. In addition to the vehicles, they burned to death the Second-in-Command of the Gorkhas, who was trying to organize the protection of his Battalion Headquarters. Nothing much was left of him.

This was the first Second-in-Command of the 4th Battalion of the Fifth Gorkha Rifles to die since the battalion was re-raised in January 1963. The battalion was now without a Second-in-Command.*

A replacement for the Second-in-Command was difficult to find due to the expansion of the Indian Army after the 1962 Sino–Indian war. The 4th Battalion, in fact, was raised as part of this expansion, and the other battalions of the regiment had already been milked to find the necessary officers to man them.

* A Second-in-Command (2IC) is the right-hand man of the Commanding Officer, and takes over command as and when the Commanding Officer is absent or when he becomes a casualty. He is therefore an important part of a battalion team.

Eventually a major posted at Khadki, a cantonment of Pune, was posted in as Second-in-Command. The battalion, by this time, was holding a string of picquets on the CFL after the Indo–Pak war of 1965, including a high-hill feature called Bir Badeshar on which was located an ancient temple and a pir's grave. The Commanding Officer's Tactical Headquarters was located on a lower ridge, and the newly posted Second-in-Command was asked to report here.

It was known to the battalion that this officer was on the verge of retirement, but nobody from the battalion knew that the major was very unwell. Despite his failing health, the officer, knowing that the battalion was involved in a conflict with Pakistan in Jammu and Kashmir, did not want to make his ill-health an excuse to not join the battalion. He made the effort to climb to the Headquarters, which involved a steep climb of nearly 2000 feet. The effort was too much for an officer who was ailing, had been away from active duty for a long time and was soon to retire. Just short of the Tactical Headquarters, the major fell down, never to rise again.

Two Seconds-in-Command had died within a space of two months.

Army Headquarters once again began searching for a replacement. This time, they found a regimental officer who was located at a Station Headquarters in Lucknow. The Commanding Officer made it a point to meet him down below at the base. He initiated him in the role and tasks of the battalion. The new Second-in-Command was taken to all the picquets and given adequate time to get accustomed to the hilly terrain and develop an understanding of the battalion's counterinsurgency plans. After three months, the officer was fully acquainted with all that he needed to know. The year, however, was coming to an end, and the officer asked for a few days' leave to spend Christmas with his family.

His leave was sanctioned, but he never came back. He was run over by a bus in Lucknow. The battalion had now lost three Seconds-in-Command in a matter of six months!

Military Secretary's Branch (MS Branch), which is responsible for the career planning of officers and the staffing of units and formations, now began to get concerned. Word had got around that the appointment of the Second-in-Command of the unit was jinxed. The battalion, however, needed a Second-in-Command urgently. The situation on the border was once again getting tense. There were reports of infiltration attempts in the border areas of Poonch and in the area where the battalion was located. MS Branch once again began their search for an officer not already posted to a battalion on active duty or to a sensitive post. This time, they were able to find a considerably young officer. The officer was on his way back to India from the UK, where he had been posted as India's Assistant Military Adviser.

By this time, the Subedar Major and Junior Commissioned Officers of the unit were also getting perturbed at the rapid rate of attrition when it came to the Seconds-in-Command of the unit. The Subedar Major is the senior-most JCO of the unit. This rank is the highest that a soldier can aspire to, other than getting a commission as an officer. The Subedar Major is usually a JCO with a lot of service, loads of experience, and he advises the Commanding Officer on matters concerning the morale and welfare of the men and their families. He is therefore a JCO who is respected and whose advice on such matters carries a lot of weight.

The Subedar Major decided that he needed to speak to the Commanding Officer on the matter concerning the

Seconds-in-Command of the battalion. It was strictly not his area of responsibility, because it was a matter that concerned officers. But it affected the morale of the unit, so he decided to voice his concern.

Soon after the new Second-in-Command arrived from the UK, the Subedar Major reported to the Commanding Officer and said that the high casualty rate of Seconds-in-Command of the battalion was beginning to get disturbing. He suggested to the Commanding Officer that the newly arrived officer be sent to the ancient temple at Bir Badeshar to pay his respects to the deity, which had been installed there more than a thousand years ago, and also to the pir who was buried close to the temple. The pir was reputed to grant favours to those who visited his grave, and people came from distant villages to seek his blessings. The temple at Bir Badeshar was within the battalion-defended area and so was the pir's grave. The CO spoke to the newly arrived Second-in-Command and told him what the Subedar Major had said. The newly arrived officer acted on the advice of the Subedar Major, and all went well. The officer not only survived but, after a year, was promoted in command of another battalion of the regiment.

On the departure of this officer, another officer had to be found and posted as the Second-in-Command of the battalion. This time, as soon as he arrived, the officer was dispatched to the temple at Bir Badeshar and to the pir's grave. He, too, survived and in later years rose to the rank of Lieutenant General. All now seemed well as far as the appointment of Seconds-in-Command of the unit was concerned. The jinx appeared to have been put to rest.

Sometime later, the battalion had to move away from Bir Badeshar, towards the border with East Pakistan, in the third quarter of 1971. This was the period just prior to the 1971 war.

In December 1970, Sheikh Mujibur Rehman had won a landslide victory in the elections in East Pakistan. Based on this election, major positions in the Pakistani government would be held by Bengali Muslims. But Zulfikar Ali Bhutto and President General Yahya Khan were not prepared to accept this. They initiated Operation Torchlight, leading to the extermination over a million East Pakistanis, and followed up with the persecution of the Bengali personnel of the Pakistan Army. This led to the formation of an East Pakistan government in exile and the formation of the Mukti Bahini, or Freedom Fighters, who were determined to free their country from the stranglehold of West Pakistan. Mukti Bahini personnel commenced guerrilla warfare against Pakistan, and these clashes sometimes spilled over across the border into Indian territory.

When these skirmishes resulted in casualties to Indian Army personnel, the 4th Battalion of the 5th Gorkha Regiment, which had moved to this part of the border with East Pakistan, also got involved in confrontations with the Pakistan Army. The Second-in-Command, who at this time was the sixth Second-in-Command of the battalion, took part and led counterattacks against the Pakistanis, who had encroached into Indian territory. There was, however, no temple or pir's grave in the battle zone where this Second-in-Command could offer prayers, as had been the case with the two Seconds-in-Command at the previous location.

The sixth Second-in-Command got killed when leading an attack. He received a bullet in his head and died on the spot. It appeared that the Second-in-Command jinx had returned to haunt the battalion once again!

MS2, the section of Military Secretary's branch that dealt with infantry officers, once again had to resume its search for a

Second-in-Command for the unit. By now, the jinx had become well known. Between 10 August 1965 and 10 December 1971, the battalion had a turnover of six Seconds-in-Command in six years. Four of them had succumbed to fate and circumstance, and only two had survived, possibly because they had the opportunity to pray at a temple and a pir's grave.

The officer in charge of infantry postings at Military Secretary's Branch, Army Headquarters (AMS2) called for the panel of officers of the regiment. He had to pull out someone from somewhere to be posted as Second-in-Command of this battalion. However, all the battalions of the regiment were committed to battle either in the Western or the Eastern sectors. The officer to be selected had also to have the required level of seniority and experience to take over as Commanding Officer, if required. An in-depth search indicated that one such officer was available. He was doing the staff course at the Defence Services Staff College at Wellington, in the Nilgiri Hills in Tamil Nadu.

In the meanwhile, orders had been issued by Army Headquarters for the termination of all courses in anticipation of a war that seemed imminent. This officer's posting on staff had already been issued to a formation in the Eastern Sector. The need of the battalion, however, was greater, and necessity demanded his return to the unit. If posted, he would be the seventh Second-in-Command at the battalion in six years.

Lieutenant Colonel Madhok, the officer in charge of the career planning of infantry officers, could not help wondering whether these unfortunate events were a matter of pure coincidence or there was really a jinx at work. He decided to check with Military Operations (MO Directorate) as to what was happening on the ground. MO Directorate was the department that monitored all military operations—they knew exactly what was happening on both fronts. They would also know the situation in the battalion, as to where they were, what they were doing and what operations had been planned for them.

He rang up Lieutenant Colonel Rai Singh, who headed the Section that dealt with the north-east and East Pakistan.

Lieutenant Colonel Rai Singh, after checking, stated that the battalion was doing extremely well but in the process had taken a lot of casualties. It had eighteen officers at the start of the war, and in less than a week, three of its officers had been killed and four officers wounded. Among those killed was the Second-in-Command. Lieutenant Rai Singh also stated that it would be necessary to post a Second-in-Command immediately and also some more officers, because the Corps Commander had detailed this battalion for another important task. He also stated that he would be forwarding to MS Branch signals from the Corps Headquarters and Eastern Command, requesting that the officer situation in this battalion be addressed on an 'Op Immediate' basis.

Lieutenant Colonel Madhok thanked Rai Singh for the information. He wondered as to what important task could be given to a unit that had already suffered such heavy losses. He wondered also about the officer who had now to be posted as the Second-in-Command to this unit. What would be his fate? Would he meet the same end as his predecessors? However, Lieutenant Colonel Madhok needed the approval of Deputy Military Secretary (A) to cancel the earlier posting on staff and issue a new order posting the new Second-in-Command to his battalion.

The Brigadier was busy. He was looking at the officer situation of an army at war. Messages were pouring in about officer casualties on the Eastern and Western fronts, and formations were clamouring for replacements. The telephones on his table were all ringing simultaneously, demanding immediate attention. Officers of the Indian Army led from the front, and so officer casualties were bound to be heavy.

The Brigadier looked up and said, 'Yes, Madhok. What is it?' The Brigadier, like many other officers, had been in office the whole of the previous night. He had gone home only for a shave and to change his uniform, and was back at his desk early that morning.

Lieutenant Colonel Madhok explained the situation. The Brigadier took no time to decide. He said, 'Post the officer from Staff College as Second-in-Command immediately. Also look at the panels of other battalions of this regiment and see who else can be posted to this battalion as it has already suffered heavy officer casualties. This battalion has been tasked to conduct the army's first heliborne operation. They are bound to take more casualties. I've been receiving urgent messages from Corps and Command.'

The Brigadier waved him off and turned to the bunch of telephones that were all ringing together.

Lieutenant Colonel Madhok went back to his office. He now knew the important task given to this battalion! The war in the east was moving fast—too fast. He issued the order posting the officer as Second-in-Command to the unit and also rang up the Defence Services Staff College with instructions to convey the message personally to the officer before he moved. He once again wondered what the fate of this officer would be.

On the ground, far away in the Eastern Sector, the Commanding Officer of the Gorkha Battalion was wrestling with the problems connected with the heliborne operation for the capture of an airfield, a bridge and the junction of two roads at a place called Sylhet. Only a limited number of helicopters were available for the heli-lift. It was a daunting task that his battalion had been given. Considering the spread and size of the targets, the Commanding Officer would have to divide his force, and the necessity of a Second-in-Command became all the more important. The operation was a hazardous one. The CO's battalion was to be inducted nearly a hundred kilometres into the heart of the enemy defences. He recalled the Chindit operations of World War II on the Burma front, where a division-sized force was flown in gliders deep behind Japanese lines. They did a great job, but there were very few survivors! Also, what would happen if he himself became a casualty? Command and control were crucial in an operation like this. Where, he wondered, was the Second-in-Command that had been promised to him? This was the army's first heliborne operation and success was vital.

But unbeknown to the CO, the officer from the Staff College was already on the move to join the battalion.

The battalion, meanwhile, was gearing up for the heliborne offensive. Since only eight MI-4 helicopters were available for the heli-lift, only a limited number of troops could be heli-lifted for the operation. The area was a frenzy of activity. Load tables were being made; arms, ammunition, rations and equipment were being weighed because the helicopters could take only a limited load, and every additional load, however small, mattered. The tactical plan was being worked out and battle drills rehearsed. The officers and men were excited at their battalion being chosen for the first heliborne operation of the Indian Army, and the section and platoon commanders were busy briefing their commands on their tasks.

The CO, however, was alone with his thoughts. Once again, he wondered whether he would get the Second-in-Command he had asked for, and whether he would arrive on time for the operation. There was much to discuss and innumerable contingencies to be worked out.

The battalion was to be landed deep inside enemy territory, but there was a commitment from the corps that they would be linked up within forty-eight hours. What would happen if the link-up did not happen as promised? If they were on their own, what would be more important—ammunition, or food and water? How would casualties be evacuated? What about the dead? There were bound to be heavy casualties.

These and a number of other concerns ran through his mind, and there was no one senior enough to consult and discuss this with. He finally decided that the men would carry as much ammunition as possible, and that food and clothing would take a lower priority. After all, military teaching and practice accepted that a heliborne or para-dropped force had to be linked up within forty-eight hours, failing which that unit would be considered as having been destroyed. He had been assured that the battalion would definitely be linked within forty-eight hours, so he felt that ammunition was more important than food and clothing.

In the meanwhile, the officer from Staff College was doing his best to reach the battalion as early as possible. He arrived at Kalaura, the launch pad for the heliborne operation, early on the morning after the launch of some of the Rifle Companies and the Battalion Headquarters and he was able to catch the last wave of helicopters to battleground Sylhet.

The helicopters landed amid heavy fire from enemy artillery, mortars and medium machine guns. Some of the Gorkhas, who were on duty to protect the helipad, seemed to be aware that the Major was on board one of the choppers and came searching for him. This officer had led his company in a number of actions in the 1965 Indo–Pak war, and his men were glad to have him back. The Gorkhas are fearless and also fun-loving. Oblivious of the bullets and shrapnel flying around, they hoisted the Major on their shoulders and started dancing to celebrate his arrival.

The Major was as glad as his soldiers to be back with them once again, but they were in the middle of a battle and he had a job to do. He asked them to put him down so that he could go and meet the Commanding Officer, but it took some amount of persuasion before they finally put him down. The Major went in search of the CO and found him in a clearing, speaking on the wireless set and directing the battle. The CO was communicating with his rifle companies in Gorkhali so that the Pakistanis, trying to intercept his messages, would not be able to understand what he was saying.

The choppers took off and the small-arms fire was once again directed at them. Luckily, they managed to get away safely.

The CO was glad that his Second-in-Command had finally arrived, and that the dead and wounded had been evacuated in the returning choppers. Soon, silver streaks of dawn lit up the horizon and birds began to chirp. The CO wondered whether the birds knew that there was a war on. Were they heard only when the firing stopped and silent when the battle raged?

The Major, who belonged to the battalion, was meeting the CO for the first time, as the latter had come from another battalion of the regiment. The CO welcomed his Second-in-Command and started briefing him on the battle situation so that he was 'in the picture'. Soon after he finished, the CO's runner reported that the senior Subedar had come up to speak to the CO.

The JCO appeared, saluted and, speaking in Gorkhali, said, 'We are happy, sahib, that Major Sahib has returned to the battalion, but we don't want anything to happen to him. The JCOs who had served with the battalion during World War II in Burma told us that during that war, two Seconds-in-Command of the battalion were killed one after the other, and two other Seconds-in-Command, who went on to become Commanding Officers during that war, also died in battle. Recently, we have lost four out of six Seconds-in-Command. I have been talking to our JCOs, and it is our suggestion that since there is no mandir out here for Major Sahib to do puja, we should not call him 2IC or Second-in-Command.'

'So, what should we call him?' asked the CO.

'Sahib,' said the JCO, 'we can call him by any other name. The Pakistanis call their officers by code names like Bada Imam, Chota Imam, Kazi and Vazir. We should call him by some such name.'

'Tell me then,' said the CO. 'What do you suggest?'

'Vazir, sahib. It is the suggestion of the JCOs that we call him Vazir, because this word is closest to the role of a Second-in-Command.'

The CO looked at the Major and asked him if it was all right to call him Vazir?

'Yes, sir,' said the Second-in-Command, 'it's not an issue. You can call me whatever you like.'

So, word was passed to the companies that the term 'Second-in-Command' would not be used, and that henceforth the term for Second-in-Command would be Vazir.

But the CO, unfortunately, would often forget the word 'Vazir' and would call for 'Kazi' instead, and the troops would get confused. In one such incident, the battalion missed ambushing an enemy convoy, and the CO spoke to the Major and said: 'Looks like I have a mental block on the word "Vazir". I keep saying "Kazi" instead of "Vazir". It has been happening too often. Is it all right if we call you Kazi instead of Vazir?'

The Second-in-Command said that it was all right to call him by any name that he wished.

So, orders were passed accordingly, and the CO began using the word 'Kazi' instead of 'Vazir'. This, however, caused more confusion because the troops had earlier been told that 'Vazir' was the word to be used for Second-in-Command. The companies were widely separated, and patrols and ambush parties were moving in and out, so it was difficult to get the change of the codename across. In exasperation, the CO spoke to the Second-in-Command once again and asked him whether he believed that bad luck was associated with the term 'Second-in-Command' and if it was okay to revert to the official nomenclature of 'Second-in-Command'. The Major said that it was okay to call him anything that the CO felt was appropriate.

And so, the battalion reverted to calling the Major 'Second-in-Command', in keeping with official terminology.

A few days later, the seventh Second-in-Command was blown up in an enemy minefield. He was lucky to be alive but was badly wounded, and his left leg had to be amputated.

The battalion was upset but there was nothing they could do about it, except to revert to the term 'Vazir' instead of Second-in-Command. And so, it was decided from that day, amid the din and dust of the battle of Sylhet, that the Second-in-Command of 4/5 Gorkha Rifles would be called Vazir on a permanent basis.

The war terminated on 16 December 1971, and the unit, like all other units of the Indian Army, kept moving to other stations. For a while, all went well. As long as 'Vazir' was the term used to refer to him, the Second-in-Command of the unit continued to be safe.

Some years later, around 1978, during the course of a unit inspection, the Formation Commander, a Brigadier, who was the inspecting officer, noticed the name board saying 'Vazir' outside the Second-in-Command's office.

'What's that?' he asked, pointing to the name board.

The Brigadier was given the background. He wasn't happy, as he did not like the sound of the word 'Vazir', but he let it pass. In his inspection report, he wrote:

> The Battalion has performed very well during the period of this report. During the last one year, this unit has won almost all professional and sports competitions in the Brigade and Division. Its morale is high, and it executes all tasks very efficiently. There is, however, a strange legacy in this unit, where the Second-in-Command is called 'Vazir' due to a series of unfortunate incidents resulting in the death/disability of a series of previous Seconds-in-Command. Although this is a departure from accepted nomenclature, I have let it remain, giving due regard to the sensitivities of a fine, highly efficient and motivated unit.

Some more years passed. Successive Vazirs survived and went on to other postings and promotions. In 1985, however, during a unit inspection, a month prior to its move to Sri Lanka, the Formation Commander, once again a Brigadier, objected to the term 'Vazir' in place of the official terminology of 'Second-in-Command'. He, too, was given the background of the story, but he refused to accept the battalion's point of view. He ordered the unit, in writing, to remove all traces of 'Vazir' from its name boards, stationery, bills, receipts, etc., and to revert to the term Second-in-Command. The battalion's sensitivity on this issue was ignored.

Immediately after this inspection, the battalion was moved to Sri Lanka for Operation Pawan and hit the ground running. Immediately on landing, it was tasked with the rescue of another unit that was trapped in a major ambush. In the fierce fighting that followed with the Tamil Tigers, the Commanding Officer and a senior Company Commander were both killed. The deaths occurred less than a month after the battalion had been ordered to change the nomenclature from 'Vazir' to 'Second-in-Command'.

The battalion felt angry, but there was nothing they could do. With regard to the future, they decided that they could not let this state of affairs continue. It was all very well for others to say that all this was a matter of coincidence, but as far as the battalion was concerned, obedience had its limits, and enough was enough. Losing five Seconds-in-Command one after the other was no joke. It decided to inform the Brigade that they were reverting to 'Vazir' instead of 'Second-in-Command', and that if anyone had any questions, they should contact the Colonel of the regiment at Army Headquarters.

Army Headquarters now had to find replacements for both the Commanding Officer as well as the Second-in-Command. The battalion was in an operational area in Sri Lanka, and it was imperative that a Commanding Officer be posted without delay. All available Colonels, however, were already commanding units or had finished command. It was finally decided by Army Headquarter to post a Lieutenant Colonel as Second-in-Command to the unit as Officiating Commanding Officer, till a Colonel could be pulled out from somewhere to command the battalion.

After an in-depth search, there was only one Lieutenant Colonel available who could fit the bill. He was posted as Second-in-Command as well as Officiating CO.

By a strange coincidence, the seventh Second-in-Command, who had been wounded and had lost a leg at Sylhet, was posted at this time as Deputy Military Secretary (A), i.e., the Brigadier in charge of postings at MS Branch, Army Headquarters. He knew only too well the story of the Seconds-in-Command of the battalion, and the portent of using the term 'Second-in-Command'. So, he drafted the signal himself and made it 'Op Immediate'. This is what he wrote:

> Lt Col Ravinder Singh posted as 'Vazir' 4/5GR (FF). Offr to assume appt of Officiating CO till further orders. Offr to move immediately without relief. Confirm. All ack.*

The Brigadier signed the posting order himself and sent it down to the section dealing with infantry postings which was located in the basement of South Block, for immediate dispatch. The Colonel in charge of MS2, however, came rushing up from the basement to meet the Brigadier and said: 'Sir, what is this word "Vazir" that you have included in the signal. Is it a typographical error or does it mean something?'

The Brigadier and the Colonel were both due to go to Air Headquarters for a meeting. The Brigadier said, 'Just send the signal off quickly and come back soon or we will be late for the meeting. I will brief you in the car.'

---

* 'Ack' means acknowledge.

The Colonel sent the signal off to the Army Headquarters Signal Centre for dispatch to all concerned, and, with the Brigadier, proceeded to Air Headquarters for the meeting. En route to the meeting, the Brigadier told the Colonel the story of the Seconds-in-Command of 4/5GR (FF), and the significance of the word 'Vazir'.

In the meanwhile, personnel at the Army Headquarters Signal Centre were puzzling over the word 'Vazir' in the signal they had just received. They consulted their book of code names but could not locate the word 'Vazir' anywhere. They next looked at their list of nicknames but failed to find the word. They consulted their officer in charge of the Signal Centre, who in turn consulted the Duty Signal Officer, who said, 'Send it back to the originator for clarification.' And so the signal came back to MS Branch.

Other than the Brigadier and the Colonel dealing with infantry postings, no one knew the meaning or significance of the word 'Vazir'. The signal had been signed by the Brigadier himself, which was unusual, and he had marked it as 'Op Immediate'. This meant that the signal had to be sent off at once. The officer who had to now act on the signal had some idea from the text of the message that 'Vazir' probably meant Second-in-Command. However, he did not want to change the text of the signal because the Brigadier and Colonel had both cleared the signal and therefore knew what they were doing. So, he decided to take the signal to the Major General, who was the overall in-charge of postings. The Major General asked the officer what he thought 'Vazir' meant. The officer said that he thought it meant Second-in-Command. The General scratched out the word 'Vazir' and replaced it with 'Second-in-Command', and told the officer to send the signal off as this was an urgent matter.

As directed by Army Headquarters, Lieutenant Colonel Ravinder Singh reported to the battalion in Sri Lanka as Second-in-Command, Officiating CO. Within a week, he became a casualty and had to be evacuated. It was only emergency medical intervention that saved him.

The Brigade Headquarters, the Divisional Headquarters, Army Headquarters and all those who had to deal with the battalion now began to realize that possibly there was some meaning and merit in the request, the need, of the unit to use the term 'Vazir' for the battalion's Second-in-Command.

Thereafter, Army Headquarters posted a Colonel who had already finished command of another unit and had volunteered to take command of the battalion in its hour of need. The battalion did extremely well under the new Commanding Officer, and the senior-most Company Commander took on the appointment of Vazir.

Since then, the battalion has had only a 'Vazir' and not a 'Second-in-Command', and it has never had to look back.

If you ever happen to visit the 4th Battalion of the 5th Gorkha Rifles (FF), and if you look for the Second-in-Command, you won't find him. You will only find a Vazir.

Postscript

Those who hear the story for the first time often ask, 'Is there really a jinx on the Seconds-in-Command of this battalion?' No one really knows. But the battalion does not want any more proof and to take any more chances. They say, 'Just leave it as it is. We have had enough!'

A Bullet for Breakfast

'*Often the test of courage is not to die, but to live.*'

—Conte Vittorio Alfieri (1749–1803)

Lieutenant Colonel 'Bulbul' Brar* looked at Jamalpur through his binoculars. It stood there far away, shimmering on the horizon, seemingly suspended in mid-air in the early morning mist. Its early capture was important. The war needed to be wrapped up quickly, before outside help could arrive, and this was one of the obstacles that needed to be removed to speed up the advance of 95 Indian Infantry Brigade.

Intelligence reports indicated that Jamalpur was strongly held by 31 Baluch, along with a battery of 120 mm mortars, a detachment of six-pounder anti-tank guns and a large number of medium machine guns. The Commanding Officer, Colonel Sultan Ahmad, had built his battalion-defended locality on

* Nobody knows why he was given this name. But then, why was General Francis Dias called 'Dick' Dias, or General Christopher Baretto called 'Bobby' Baretto? It appears that the armed forces find it amusing to add a rhyming name—an alliteration—to certain names that lend themselves to such imaginative wordplay.

the north bank of a river that covered the approaches from the north. A railway embankment covered the southern approach. Maximum use had been made of built-up areas. The weapons were sited in strong concrete bunkers, with enough ammunition to last him weeks. The garrison had a strong defence potential that would make it difficult to capture.*

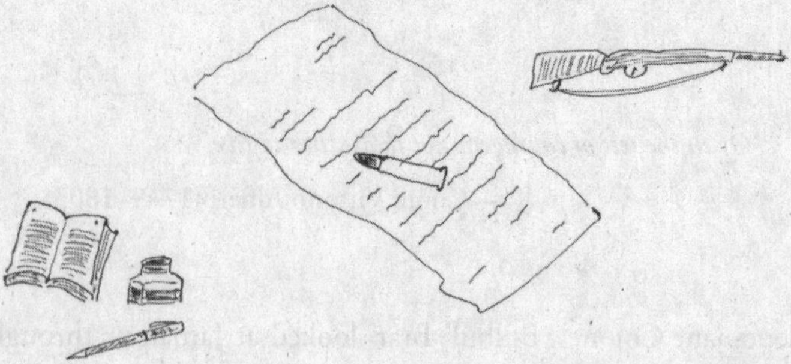

Sketch of the letter and the bullet sent by the Pakistani Garrison Commander.

Lieutenant Colonel K.S. ('Bulbul') Brar, the Commanding Officer of the 1st Battalion, the Maratha Light Infantry, was tasked with the capture of Jamalpur. His battalion had an enviable reputation of war-fighting. It was known as 'Jangi Paltan', which indicated that it was a battalion that always did well in war.

Brigadier H.S. Kler, Commander, 95 Indian Infantry Brigade, was the Brigade Commander. He had sited his Tactical Headquarters alongside the Battalion Headquarters of the Marathas. He was from the Corps of Signals.

Kler was under pressure to capture Jamalpur at the earliest. To accomplish this task, the battalions of his Brigade had

* Major General Sukhwant Singh, *The Liberation of Bangladesh* (New Delhi: Vikas Publishing House Pvt. Ltd., 1981), pp. 195–96.

laid roadblocks on the approaches and exits to the Jamalpur Garrison. But after doing that, he had no reserves to assault it. The only option was to lay siege to the garrison. However, that would be a time-consuming process, and time was at a premium. The 101 Communication Zone Commander wanted Kler to get on with the capture of Jamalpur and then move on towards other objectives that blocked the way to Dhaka.

In preparation for the attack, patrols sent out by the Marathas on 8–9 December, to find out details of the enemy defences, clashed with Pakistani soldiers from the Jamalpur Garrison. Lieutenant Colonel Sultan Ahmad learnt of the roadblocks behind and in front of him only when a vehicle carrying Captain Jamsher Ahmad, a Para Commando officer, was ambushed by the Marathas. The vehicle was captured, but the officer managed to escape to tell Lieutenant Colonel Ahmad that his garrison had been encircled by the Marathas and a battalion of the Guards.

Aware of the strength of the Jamalpur defences, and the time and effort that would be required to capture this strong fortress-like structure, Brigadier Kler decided it would be better to use a bit of psychological warfare and push the Commander of the Jamalpur Garrison to surrender, rather than to spend a lot of time and effort in assaulting a very strong defensive position. He and Lieutenant Colonel Brar sat down and dictated a note, which they sent to Lieutenant Colonel Sultan Ahmad, informing him that his battalion had been surrounded and it would be better if he surrendered, as many lives would be saved. This is what the note said:

9 Dec 1971
To,
The Commander
Jamalpur Garrison

1. I am directed to inform you that your garrison has been cut off from all sides and you have no escape routes available to you. One brigade with its complement of artillery has already been built up and another will be striking by the morning. In addition, you have been given a foretaste of a small element of our Air Force, with a lot more to come. The situation as far as you are concerned is hopeless. Your higher commanders have already ditched you.
2. As a soldier to soldier, I give you an assurance of safety and honourable treatment when you surrender—since that is the only course left to you. I am sure you will not be foolhardy in risking the lives of the men under your command for your personal ego. You may have heard of the appeal of our Army Chief and I once again reiterate, if you wish to be re-united with your families—the only course open to you is to surrender. We will arrive at formalities as soon as I get your reply. It may be pertinent to point out that if you fall in the hands of the Mukti Fauj or their sympathizers, they are unlikely to spare your lives. Your colleague, Captain Ashan Malik, wisely surrendered to me at Kamalpur on 4 December. He and his men have been well looked after as per the Geneva Conventions. I expect your reply by 6.30 p.m. today, failing which I shall be constrained to deliver the final blow, for which forty sorties of MiGs have been allotted to me. In this morning's action, the prisoners captured by us have given us your strength and dispositions and are in a position to let you down. They are being well looked after. The treatment I expect to be given to this civil messenger shall be according to a gentlemanly

code of honour and no harm should come to him. An immediate reply is solicited.

Sd/Brig. H.S. Kler*

This note was given to a Mukti Bahini volunteer. He was sent to the Jamalpur Garrison on a cycle with a white flag. The Marathas were on the Jamalpur–Tangail road and the distance to the Jamalpur Garrison was about four kilometres. The messenger was stopped and taken to the Garrison Commander. Lieutenant Colonel Ahmad read the note and sent a note back in reply. This is what he said:

Jamalpur
Dec 091735
Dear Brig,

1. Hope this finds you in high spirits. Thanks for the letter. We here in Jamalpur are waiting for the fight to commence. It has not started yet. So, let's not talk and start it.
2. Forty sorties, I may point out are highly inadequate. Please ask your Government for many more.
3. Your remark about your messenger being given proper treatment was superfluous. Shows how you underestimate the hospitality of Pakistan troops. I hope he liked his cup of tea. Give my love to the Mukties. Hoping to find you with a sten gun in your hand next

* 'Reminiscences of Three Wars', an article dated 27 July 2016, written by Lieutenant Colonel K.S. Puntambekar, 1st Battalion, the Maratha Light Infantry. pp. 30–1.

time instead of the pen—as you seem to have so much mastery over.

I am your most
Sincerely,
Lt Col Sultan Ahmad
Jamalpur Forces*

The note came wrapped around a bullet, possibly to signify the need for combat on ground rather than the combat of words. The Marathas, as would anyone else in uniform, were impressed by the spirited reply of the Commander of the Jamalpur Garrison. It was what any good military commander would have said.

Brigadier Kler realized that he was being sandwiched between his higher formation commanders, who wanted him to get on with the quick capture of Jamalpur, and the Jamalpur Garrison Commander, who was enticing him to attack him. An interesting situation was developing, and the officers of Jangi Paltan wondered what would happen next.

Colonel Sultan Ahmad had given a good account of himself earlier at the battle of Bakshiganj. He had withdrawn from that position only after he had caused considerable delay. His aim was to fight the main defensive battle at Jamalpur. Although Bakshiganj was captured in the early hours of 5 December, Kler was not able to follow up fast enough, allowing the Pakistani defenders to withdraw unhindered to their main defensive position at Jamalpur.

The decision to attack or not to attack Jamalpur, however, was taken out of the hands of the main protagonists in this

* Ibid., p. 31.

stand-off between Brigadier Kler and Lieutenant Colonel Sultan Ahmad. General A.A.K. Niazi, General Officer Commanding-in-Chief of all forces in East Pakistan, realized that the promised intervention by the Americans and the Chinese might not happen, and that he needed to do something for the defence of Dhaka. He had not earmarked troops for its defence, confident that Pakistan's allies would come to his rescue. However, that had not happened. He therefore asked Brigadier Qadir, Commander, Pakistan 93 Ad Hoc Brigade, whether he could send some troops for the defence of Dhaka. Brigadier Qadir passed on the request to Lieutenant Colonel Ahmad, and asked him whether he could break through the siege and reach Dhaka. Lieutenant Colonel Ahmad stated that it would be better for the Indians to break their heads against his strong defensive position at Jamalpur, which he had prepared with such diligence. However, when he was explained the problem of the highest Pakistani Commander in the field, Lieutenant Colonel Ahmad stated confidently that he saw no problem of breaking out of the cordon established by the Indians. However, he made the mistake of trying to soften up the likely roadblock locations with artillery fire. This gave away his intention that he would attempt to break out that night. The 1st Marathas and 13 Guards, one of the other battalions of the Brigade, made their plans to ambush* any enemy troops trying to exit the Jamalpur Garrison.

At about 2350 hours on 10 December, some movement was heard along the Tangail road approaching the forward-company-defended localities. The Marathas held their fire till the Pakistani troops came well within range and then opened

---

* Major General Sukhwant Singh, *The Liberation of Bangladesh* (New Delhi: Vikas Publishing House Pvt. Ltd., 1981), p. 197.

fire, mowing down all those who were in the vicinity of the ambush site. The Pakistanis came in, wave after wave, shouting their war cries of 'Allah-hu-Akbar, Pakistan Paindabad'. The Commanding Officer and the officers, JCOs and NCOs of the Marathas, however, displayed leadership skill of a high order in a classic, cleverly laid and well-executed ambush. The battle at the ambush site ended only at dawn of 11 December. With sunrise, the fog lifted from the ambush site. The area was littered with bodies of the soldiers of the Jamalpur Garrison. Three hundred thirty enemy soldiers were killed, twenty-three wounded and sixty-one Pakistani soldiers were captured as prisoners. Lieutenant Colonel Sultan Ahmad, however, seemed to have a charmed life. He had managed to escape along with 200 of his men.*

Later that morning, a wireless intercept picked up an appeal from a Pakistani officer. It was the Second-in-Command of the Jamalpur Garrison and of 31 Baluch, asking for acceptance of surrender.

Lieutenant Colonel K.S. Brar directed Major Satish Nambiar, Company Commander, 'Y' Company,† to go and accept the surrender. The Commanding Officer's party followed closely along with Captain H.K. Malhotra, the Regimental Medical Officer, who commenced giving first aid to his own troops as well as to that of the opponents.

Three hundred seventy-six all ranks of the Pakistani Army surrendered, of which two officers, nine JCOs, 209 other ranks

---

* Lieutenant Colonel K.S. Puntambekar, *Reminiscences of Three Wars*, p. 37.

† 1 Maratha is the only unit in the Indian Army that has a 'Y' Company, so named when 'B' Company continued to consistently receive heavy casualties during World War II in Italy, so much so that it changed its name to 'Y' Company.

and a doctor belonged to 31 Baluch. Nine others belonged to the artillery and paramilitary forces. A large number of small arms, three 120 mm mortars, one 106 mm and three 57 mm recoilless guns, as well as a huge amount of ammunition and rations also fell into Indian hands.*

Interrogation of prisoners later revealed that Ahmad's Brigade Commander, Brigadier Qadir, had ordered Ahmad to pull out on the night of 10–11 December. Although Ahmad was reluctant to leave his well-prepared defences, he was obliged to obey this order. He personally led the breakout the same night and managed to get away with about 200 of his soldiers. Although the Pakistani soldiers tried to provoke the Marathas to make them fire and reveal their positions, the Maratha fire discipline was good. They held their fire, and the Pakistanis thought that the Marathas had vacated their positions. The withdrawing Pakistani soldiers were allowed to enter deep into the killing zone before the orders to open fire were given.

Brigadier Qadir's decision to make Ahmad withdraw from the Jamalpur defences was fortunate for Kler, as it removed the need to assault this very strong position, and this probably saved many lives. As it is, ten soldiers of the Marathas were killed and eight were wounded; the Guards lost one JCO, who was killed during the conduct of the ambush.†

The Marathas had moved on man-pack basis‡ and had to be replenished. But when they resumed their advance on 12 December, Lieutenant Colonel Sultan Ahmad and his

---

* Maj. Gen. Sukhwant Singh, *The Liberation of Bangladesh*, p. 198.

† Ibid., p. 198.

‡ Man-pack basis: a unit sometimes moves for short-duration operations on a self-contained basis, where each soldier carries the wherewithal for the operation, which includes weapons, ammunition, food and clothing.

approximately two companies of 31 Baluch had disappeared from the scene and had moved for the defence of Dhaka.

Kler's 95 Infantry Brigade continued to advance towards Dhaka. By the night of 15–16 December, Kler's brigade came across strong opposition holding up their advance. It was none other than Lieutenant Colonel Sultan Ahmad of 31 Baluch. He, together with 400–500 men and three tanks, was holding a crossroads against the Indian troops advancing towards Dhaka.

About midday of 16 December, while preparations were being made for Niazi's formal surrender of all Pakistani forces in East Pakistan, Lieutenant Colonel Ahmad attempted to break through the Indian forces and join the defences at Tungi. This bid failed, with heavy casualties on both sides. Apparently, Lieutenant Colonel Ahmad had not been told to halt hostilities. Fighting continued till late in the afternoon, when emissaries with white flags communicated that a ceasefire was in effect and that the war was over. This officer, who had earlier desired a showdown at Jamalpur but was ordered to leave for the defence of Dhaka, now refused to surrender and decided to break through with men from his own battalion and some others. With this last encounter, hostilities came to an end in East Pakistan.

Brigadier Kler, a paratrooper himself, linked up with Lieutenant Colonel Pannu, Commanding Officer of the 2nd Para Battalion, who had the previous day been paradropped at Tangail. Brigadier Sant Singh, who was leading with the Mukti Bahini, also joined them. All three met at the Mirpur Bridge. By this time, 2 Corps, 33 Corps and 4 Corps had already reached the outskirts of Dhaka.

Sometime later in the day, Kler reached Niazi's headquarters, along with Major General Nagra, GOC, 101 Communication Zone. Noticing that Kler was wearing a purple turban and para wings, Niazi asked him whether he was commanding the Para Brigade that had been dropped at Tangail. Kler replied that only one para battalion had been dropped and not the brigade. But Niazi found this difficult to believe. He then asked Kler to name his regiment. Kler replied that he was from the Corps of Signals. Niazi stated that in the Pakistan Army they did not give brigades to Signal officers. Kler retorted: 'No wonder you lost the war.'*

After the surrender, Brigadier Kler went looking for Lieutenant Colonel Sultan Ahmad, who was his opponent initially at Jamalpur and subsequently on the outskirts of Dhaka. They finally met in a makeshift prisoner-of-war camp and faced each other for the first time. From a scenario of a combat of shadows, they finally met in the flesh. Lieutenant Colonel Ahmad saluted Brigadier Kler, who returned the salute and shook his hand. Kler regarded Ahmad as a worthy opponent on the battlefield.

They sat down and discussed the action at Jamalpur. During the discussion, Lieutenant Colonel Ahmad said that being a staff college graduate, he could not comprehend how the Indians could put across the river in front of the Jamalpur position anything more than a weak battalion, with no bridging or rafting equipment. Brigadier Kler, ever ready with a reply, said with a smile: 'The only snag in your thinking, Ahmad, is that you were only a student at Staff College, whereas I had been there as an instructor! Your second mistake was to use artillery fire on the night you attempted to break out, because that gave your intention away.'

The 1st Marathas once again did well. For this war, among other awards, the Commanding Officer Lieutenant Colonel

* Ibid., p. 214.

K.S. Brar, Major Satish Nambiar, Major R.S.V. Dafle, Havildar Laxman Rane and Havildar Krishna Gaurav were awarded Vir Chakras for conspicuous courage and leadership in battle. Brigadier Kler was awarded the Mahavir Chakra.

It was admitted that Lieutenant Colonel Sultan Ahmad was a good officer. The problem was that he was on the losing side!

Thus, ended a duel that commenced with an exchange of written notes. The note from Lieutenant Colonel Sultan Ahmad was wrapped around a bullet. A bullet for breakfast!

Postscript

The duel of words in the exchange of notes between Brigadier Kler and Lieutenant Colonel Sultan Ahmad ought to have been followed up with combat on the ground. However, the three battles that ought to have followed sequentially, at Jamalpur, Mymensingh and Dhaka, never took place. Jamalpur capitulated, the battle for Mymensingh evaporated and the battle for Dhaka fell through with the surrender of all Pakistani forces in East Pakistan. The rest is history.

And Then There Was One

'Destiny—is it a matter of choice or a matter of chance?'

—Ian Cardozo

8 January 1972

There were four of us in the beginning. Actually, it was the beginning of the end! But we did not know it—not at that time!

We arrived at the Artificial Limb Centre on the same day, 8 January 1972. We had lost our limbs on various battlefields across the war zone of the 1971 war—in East Pakistan, the Punjab, the Rajasthan desert and Jammu and Kashmir, and had converged from diverse military hospitals across the subcontinent to Poona, because that was where the Artificial Limb Centre was located.

That morning, the four of us in wheelchairs reported at the Reception Centre of the Command Military Hospital, Southern Command, Pune. Although the Limb Centre would give us our artificial legs, it did not have beds for patients, and so we had to be admitted to the Command Hospital. That is where we stayed from the time the corrective surgery was done, our wounds healed, measurements for our artificial legs taken and we were given our wooden* legs to walk out of hospital and face life anew.

Artificial Limb Centre, Pune.

The 1971 war for the liberation of East Pakistan was fought with a sense of urgency, as there was a need to wrap up the war quickly, before other countries could arrive to assist Pakistan. But the price we paid was heavy. Three thousand eight hundred forty-three Indian armed forces personnel were killed and 9851 were wounded. The four of us belonged to the latter category.

The four of us were: Major Abu Taher of the Baluch Regiment of the Pakistan Army and, later on, part of the Mukti

* At that time, an artificial leg consisted of a plastic socket into which the stump was inserted. The socket was attached to a piece of wood and to this, a rubber foot was attached by means of a metal bolt. The wooden leg was shaped to look like a leg and attached to the thigh with a leather strap.

Bahini of Bangladesh; Major S. Kipgen, SM, of the 2nd Battalion of the Assam Regiment; Major J.V. Raju of the artillery; and me.

Being senior majors, the four of us were quartered in the new wing of the hospital, built after the Sino–Indian war of 1962. Each of us had an individual room to ourselves, with an attached bathroom, which was a luxury not given to us in any other hospital we had been to before this.

After reaching Pune, Kipgen, Raju, I and some others had to undergo another amputation for various reasons—either the stump was not shaped properly by the amputations carried out on the battlefield, or the length of the stump needed modification, or, as in my case, infection had set in due to lack of medication during the chain of evacuation. So, the first few months were spent by all of us in the hospital, till the limb healed and the stump was in a fit state to be measured for the artificial limb. During this period, we had to live by the hospital rules and routines, which were quite strict. The officer battle casualties were mostly young and, notwithstanding the loss of limb, bursting with energy. We wanted to break out of the strict discipline of the hospital regime which we were being subjected to. The hospital authorities, however, understood our predicament and closed their eyes to the many small infringements of laid down rules and procedures.

It is to their credit that they still managed to maintain discipline and to our credit that we did not cross the Lakshman Rekha.*

For the first month, we were restricted to our beds. Time passed slowly, and the hours were whiled away playing scrabble, reading books brought to us by the Red Cross sister, or just

* Lakshman Rekha: a line that one should not cross. Part of the story of the Ramayana where Sita was told not to cross a particular boundary has now become a phrase reminding us to remain within limits.

talking to each other about what the future held for us. After a while, however, we were seen all over Poona with our bandaged stumps and on crutches—we were at the Poona Race Course, betting on horses as though our lives depended on it; watching the Asian Lawn Tennis, which that year was held in Poona; at cinemas; at the Southern Command Officers' Mess bar; and at the restaurants on Main Street.* We were everywhere, and the citizens of Poona not only got used to us but also accepted us as their own. We lived beyond our means by borrowing money from a moneylender off Main Street at exorbitant rates of interest. Looking back, we lived like this perhaps because we were told that the army might not keep us, and this was something we did not want to face. So, we lived as if there was no tomorrow, because what was left of the future seemed so bleak.

The world over, hospital routine must be the same. We were not allowed to loll around in our beds. We were woken up at 6 a.m. with a cup of tea. We had to complete our ablutions by 7 a.m., finish breakfast by 8 a.m. and, once our wounds had healed, be ready to move to the ALC at 8.30 a.m. Thereafter, our measurements were taken and the sockets for our stumps were made. A piece of willow wood† was attached to the socket and a rubberized foot was attached to the piece of wood with a metal bolt, and we had to walk, walk and walk, all the while being closely scrutinized by a battery of limb fitters and technicians who made adjustments to our artificial legs till our gait was just right. Once this was done, a duplicate limb was made, because we needed a reserve leg in case anything untoward happened to

* Main Street has now been renamed as Mahatma Gandhi Road or MG Road.

† Willow wood: wood from the willow tree out of which cricket bats and hockey sticks are made.

the first one. At around 12.30 p.m., an ambulance would come and take us to our wards for lunch and rest, and then back to the ALC for more trials till 4.30 p.m., after which we were generally free. Leaving the hospital premises required an 'out' pass, but we had to be back latest by 9 p.m. and in bed by 10.

Abu Taher was in a hurry to get back to his country. He was the only one among us who was not in need of corrective surgery. He asked that the making of his limb be prioritized. This was sanctioned, and he moved ahead of us in the programme of limb-making. Although all four of us were Majors at the time we were admitted to hospital, Abu Taher was promoted to Lieutenant Colonel and once again to Colonel's rank while we were still waiting for our limbs, and so he became as senior in rank as the Commandant of the Hospital and the Commandant of the Artificial Limb Centre.

A few days after he was promoted, Abu Taher left for his country—Bangladesh. The three of us saw him off at the Poona airport. As he was leaving, he turned around and said: 'So, when are you guys coming to Dhaka? What you have done for my country needs to be reciprocated. Do come with your families. I would, on behalf of my country, like to host you.' The three of us looked at each other, undecided. I answered for myself and said, 'Yes, Abu, I would love to come. However, things need to settle down a bit. If I am still in the army, it will be difficult.' Raju said that he was thinking of leaving the army and would need to settle down in his job on Civvy Street and that would take time. Kippy said that instead, he would like all of us to come to Manipur. I kept my thoughts to myself. During the war I did not need a passport to go to East Pakistan, but I knew that if I was still in the army, going to a foreign country in peacetime would be a big hassle. Finally, the three of us decided that we would go to Dhaka after a period of ten years, and the date was fixed for 16 December 1982. Abu, Kippy, Raju and I placed our right hands one on top of the other and sealed our decision. With that, Abu walked away. He did not look back even once. He walked out of our sight and out of our lives! We did not realize that we would never see him again. We came to know about his adventures only four years later, when his story appeared in newspapers worldwide.

In the meanwhile, Kippy,* Raju and I spent our remaining days at the hospital, trying to figure out what we should do with our lives. Our percentage of disability, which was calculated according to international standards, was the same. It depended on the length and health of the stump. This worked out to 60 per cent for all three of us.

Grateful governments—central and state—were offering generous concessions in return for the sacrifices that the armed forces had made during the war, but to access most of these concessions, we had to be invalided out of the army. That, I was not prepared to accept. The army was the only life I knew, and I had no desire to leave a life that I had grown to love. My battalion and my regiment meant the world to me, and I could not imagine living any other sort of life. Kippy held a similar view, but Raju said he had had enough. His state was offering him land and many other concessions. Raju had earned a degree before joining the army and was academically bright. He felt confident that he would do well in civilian life and agreed to be invalided out. Kippy and I were products of the National Defence Academy and unlike cadets of today, we had no degrees.

During our stay in hospital, the Red Cross sister, who visited us once a week, gave me a book to read: *Reach for the Sky* by

* Kippy: short for Kipgen.

Paul Brickhill. It was an inspiring story about Squadron Leader Douglas Bader, DFO, DFC, a British Royal Air Force fighter pilot who had lost both legs in an accident but continued to fly Spitfires during World War II and became an 'air ace' by shooting down twenty-one German planes. I said to myself that if he could do this after losing both his legs, what was there to prevent me from fulfilling my role as an infantry officer? However, I did not know at that time how I would make this happen.

All four of us had earlier agreed that none of us wanted to spend the rest of our lives as 'babus' in uniform, but each of us was ordained to find different solutions to this issue. Abu Taher had not only been accepted as a valuable asset to his army but had already been promoted twice while he was still in hospital! As soon as he reported to his Army Headquarters at Dhaka, he was appointed as Adjutant General of the Army of Bangladesh. Raju felt that although the Indian Army had gone through World Wars I and II, the wars of 1947–48, 1962 and 1965, it had not allowed a single battle casualty who had lost a limb to command troops. So, how and why would the system change now?

By the first week of September, all three of us were discharged from the Limb Centre. Raju was invalided out of the army and had already been offered a job in a corporate house in Hyderabad. He was happy to leave. Kippy was posted to his Regimental Centre at Shillong. And I was posted to Army Headquarters, Delhi.

By the time we joined our new postings, Abu Taher was well on his way in his attempt to reorganize his army and shape the future of his country.

During our time together in hospital, Abu never once gave us an insight into his thoughts and philosophy; we came to know later that they were, in fact, quite radical and revolutionary. Strangely, while we were in hospital, none of us ever discussed the stories of our battle experiences of the war. Probably, we had had enough of the war and did not want to regurgitate what happened during those thirteen fateful days. I learnt about the stories of Abu Taher, Kippy and Raju from other sources. These are our stories.

Our Stories Before We Met

Abu Taher

Abu Taher was commissioned into the Baluch Regiment of the Pakistan Army.* Bengali officers from East Pakistan were normally recruited into the East Bengal Regiment and the East Bengal Rifles, but Abu was specially selected for an elite regiment of the Pakistan Army, which indicates that he was, from the very beginning, someone who was considered to be special. As part of the Baluch Regiment, he once again proved his worth by being selected for the Special Services Group and as the only Bengali officer of that time to be sent to the USA to do two courses at the Ranger Training Command at Fort Benning, Georgia and the Special Forces Training Institute, Fort Bragg, North Carolina. While he was with the Special Services Group, he had done 135 static-line jumps and was awarded the Purple Para badge in recognition for the number of jumps to his credit.

On termination of these courses, Abu returned to Pakistan from the USA in December 1970, to hear that the Awami League in East Pakistan had won the general election with an overwhelming majority. Two months after the election result, he sensed that there was going to be trouble, so he sent his wife to his hometown in Mymensingh, in early February 1971.

---

* All information on Abu Taher has been gleaned from *Taher's Last Testament: Bangladesh: The Unfinished Revolution* by Lawrence Lifschultz.

On 25 March 1971, he was attending a course at the School of Infantry and Tactics in Quetta when he learnt of the crackdown by the Pakistan Army on the citizens of East Pakistan. He was very disturbed and spent the whole night walking on the deserted streets of Quetta, unable to sleep.

On 28 March, the course was called off and the officers told to join their units. As he was preparing to leave, Abu was detained and charges were brought against him, because he had expressed his displeasure at the atrocities being committed against his people in East Pakistan.

At that time, there were over a thousand Bengali officers in West Pakistan. Many junior officers came to him for advice as to what they should do. He told them quite categorically that they should escape from West Pakistan and join the War of Liberation. He himself and a few others had decided to do so. After two failed attempts, Abu Taher bought a second-hand car and with two others, drove to the Sialkot cantonment, crossed the border on foot to India and then made their way to East Pakistan. On reaching East Pakistan, he was put in charge of 11 Sector, consisting of the districts of Tangail and Mymensingh.

While we were together in hospital in Poona, we did not know that Abu Taher was an expert in guerrilla warfare and a firm believer in Marxist philosophy. He had concluded that as far as the Mukti Bahini was concerned, the only way they could win against a vastly superior Pakistan Army, was through guerrilla warfare. His views ran against the thinking of the military hierarchy heading the government of Bangladesh in exile. He pointed out to his superiors the weaknesses of the prevailing concepts of the military hierarchy in the conduct of operations by the Mukti Bahini. He stated firstly that political leadership was essential in guerrilla warfare and that the Awami

League had failed to provide that leadership. Secondly, the current military leadership in the Mukti Bahini had no concept of guerrilla warfare. Thirdly, in a liberation war, the focus had to be on guerrilla warfare and to turn to conventional warfare only when the war had achieved sufficient success. Fourthly, the Provisional Government of Bangladesh and the Sector Headquarters needed to move into East Pakistan rather than remaining on Indian soil. His views, understandably, provoked a lot of antagonism among the hierarchy of the Mukti Bahini and did not endear him to them.

Abu Taher was prepared to align himself with anyone who understood the advantages of guerrilla warfare. One of them was Subedar Aftab, who was handling a sub-sector under Taher. Together, they planned a raid against a Pakistani unit lodged on a river island. They lured this force into a killing ground and destroyed them when they fell into their trap. The rest fled. Encouraged by the success of this guerrilla attack, Abu planned a raid in mid-September on a strong defensive Pakistani unit at Chilmari held by two Pakistani Infantry Companies. A force led by Abu Taher raided the Chilmari position and came back after a successful operation with a huge haul of arms, ammunition and prisoners. On 13 November, Abu Taher ordered a full-scale attack on Kamalpur and led the assault himself. Kamalpur was captured, but, in the process, he was grievously wounded and lost a leg.

Abu Taher was deeply disappointed at being wounded, primarily because he felt that now he would not be able to realize his dream to lead his beloved country to freedom.

He was evacuated through a chain of medical units and his main amputation was done at Guwahati Military Hospital. Finally, he landed up at the Artificial Limb Centre and Command Military Hospital in Poona, at around the same time as the three of us.

All of Abu Taher's six brothers and two sisters fought in the War of Liberation. Due to the involvement of his family in the struggle for freedom, their village was ransacked and their parents put in prison.

Kipgen

After the four of us met for the first time at the Reception Centre at the Command Military Hospital, we met again an hour later, in the corridor of the New Wing of the Upper Officers' Ward. We were waiting for our rooms to be prepared. We rolled our wheelchairs towards each other and began talking. Kipgen came across as very open and friendly. He had a round face, with twinkling eyes and an infectious smile. He was bald but the lack of hair only emphasized his cherubic countenance and his friendly disposition. Kipgen was his surname. His first name was Shehkogin, and his nickname, in his village, was Pagin. But we found it more convenient to call him Kippy. He was born in June 1942 in Manipur, at the height of World War II, when the Japanese had invaded Burma and were on their way to take Imphal, the capital of Manipur, by force. Kippy's family braced themselves for the expected war, but the battles fought in Imphal were in areas fortunately away from his village.

Kippy joined the NDA in January 1960 and proved to be an excellent sportsman. He was awarded a football 'Blue' at the NDA and captained the NDA football team.

He was commissioned into the 2nd Battalion, the Assam Regiment, from the Indian Military Academy in June 1963. In January 1967, he successfully captured a group of army deserters, for which he was awarded the Sena Medal for gallantry. His first posting outside his battalion was as a Divisional Officer at the National Defence Academy, Khadakvasla—an excellent posting for a young officer. Kippy enjoyed shaping the orientation and character of the cadets under his charge. By the end of his tenure, there were indications that a war was brewing, and he moved to his battalion.

On arrival in the battalion, he was promoted to the rank of Major and given command of a Rifle Company. The battalion was in Jammu and Kashmir, holding pickets on the Line of Control near Baramulla. Soon after the '71 war started, Kippy was tasked to take a strong patrol to raid an enemy post and to bring back information about the strength of the enemy and their firepower. The enemy, however, detected their presence and brought down heavy fire on the patrol. One of his soldiers got blown up on a mine. Kippy went to his rescue and got blown up on a mine himself. He managed to crawl to safety, but his leg was in a bad way. By this time, the enemy picket brought down heavy fire on the patrol. It appeared that the patrol had been caught in the killing zone of the enemy. Kippy realized that the patrol needed to move out of the area as quickly as possible, and ordered the patrol to leave him and move to safety. His men, however, refused to leave him and carried him and the other injured soldier to safety. The battalion stretcher-bearers came and took him to the Regimental Aid Post. From there, he was evacuated to Army Hospital in Srinagar, where his leg was amputated, and from there to Delhi. From Delhi, he was once again moved to Poona. Corrective surgery was done—yet another amputation—at Command Hospital, Poona, where we all met.

Raju

Major J.V. Raju was commissioned soon after the Sino–Indian war of 1962. He already had a degree in commerce before he was commissioned. During the 1971 war, he was the FOO (Forward Observation Officer) accompanying an infantry battalion in an attack on an enemy objective somewhere in the Western Sector. His job was to bring artillery fire on to the enemy position. While assaulting the enemy position, he stepped on an anti-personnel mine and his leg blew up. The attack had gone in at night, and the fighting on the objective took till morning, when the enemy position was finally captured. All that while, he remained where he fell, and it was only in the morning that a mine-clearing party, followed by the unit's stretcher-bearers, was able to retrieve him and some others from the enemy minefield. By this time, he had lost a lot of blood. He described those moments waiting for help as the worst moments of his life. He thought that he would not survive.

Ian Cardozo

My story has been scripted in two preceding stories in this book—'The Beeb's Best Broadcast' and 'Vazir'. However, in order to bring some form of completeness to this story, I will very briefly recapitulate.

I reached the battalion on the night of 7–8 December, just in time to catch the last wave of helicopters that was inducting the battalion into Sylhet in what was to be the Indian Army's first heliborne operation.

The battalion had been wrongly informed that the Pakistani Brigade that was holding Sylhet had moved for the defence of Dhaka and that there were just a few razakars (irregular soldiers) holding Sylhet. Not only was 202 Pakistan Infantry Brigade still holding Sylhet, but 313 Pakistan Infantry Brigade too had landed up to reinforce Sylhet, and there was also the Sylhet

Garrison in location. So, when we landed, we were facing a force approximating three enemy brigades. Fortunately, we did not know this. All we knew was that we were facing a strong enemy force. The strength of our battalion, when we landed, was just 384 all ranks, due to the heavy casualties suffered in two earlier battles and also because our leave parties had not yet fetched up from Nepal.

We were assured, however, that we would be linked up within forty-eight hours. Despite the best of intentions of all involved, the link-up never took place till after the surrender. We fought an enemy who were overwhelmingly superior to us for nine days and nights. During that time, a BBC war correspondent mistakenly made a broadcast that a 'brigade' of Gorkhas had landed at Sylhet. Using this bit of misinformation to our advantage, we deployed our limited force to project that we were a brigade.

After fierce fighting for nine days, on 15 December, the Pakistani force decided to surrender. They were astonished to learn that we were an understrength battalion and not a brigade, and we were equally astonished when three Brigadiers, two Colonels, 173 officers, 290 JCOs and approximately 8000 troops surrendered to us. By this time, our strength had reduced to 352 all ranks. We had suffered severe casualties. By the end of the war, we had lost thirty killed (including four officers and three JCOs) and 123 wounded (including seven officers and three JCOs). I was among the wounded, having lost a leg on a Pakistani minefield.

During the battle, our Regimental Aid Post (battalion-level medical facility) was destroyed by Pakistani artillery, and when I got wounded, there were no instruments to amputate my leg. So, I cut it off with my khukri. A proper amputation was done later in the day, by a Pakistani doctor, as by that time all Pakistani forces in Sylhet had surrendered to my battalion. Subsequently, I moved through a series of medical facilities, at Kalashehr, Dharmanagar, Silchar, Guwahati and finally Poona, where Abu Taher, Kippy, Raju and I met for the first time.

The Challenges We Faced after Hospitalization

Abu Taher

Colonel Abu Taher had returned to his country more than five months after he got wounded. During that time, the situation in Bangladesh had undergone a drastic and dramatic change. It appeared that the officers of the Mukti Bahini heading the different sectors of East Pakistan felt that those who had not fought the war did not deserve to be holding the most important posts in the country. They had a similar opinion about those senior officers who headed the Bangladesh government in exile. This was an unhealthy and dangerous trend, as it meant not only that they were ignoring the part played by these persons in the struggle for freedom, but also that some officers in the military were aspiring for political power.*

On returning to East Pakistan from the Limb Centre in April 1972, Abu Taher was appointed as the Adjutant General of the Bangladesh Army. Part of his charter of duties was the morale and discipline of the army. Abu put into practice his values and beliefs. In this, he antagonized not only the top hierarchy of the Mukti Bahini, but many others who had used their authority to illegally grab property belonging to the Pakistanis who had returned to West Pakistan. He took up cases

* Lawrence Lifschultz, *Taher's Last Testament: Bangladesh.*

not only against the senior hierarchy but also against anyone who had taken equipment which was not theirs. Anything that had been acquired illegally had to be returned.*

Sometime later, Abu Taher took over 44 Brigade, and his friend Ziauddin, with whom he had crossed over from Pakistan to India, took over the Dhaka Brigade. In the execution of their duties, both Taher and Ziauddin propounded their beliefs that Bangladesh needed to be self-reliant, and they worked towards this aim within their brigades.

By this time, foreign powers were attempting to enter the political arena to control Bangladesh. In the two and a half years since independence, Bangladesh received more financial aid than it had received in the previous twenty-three years. Corruption was making itself felt in the life of the country. Dependence on outside aid and lack of self-reliance resulted in a man-made famine in Bangladesh, where thousands of people perished. This did not sit well with many in the army; Abu Tahir was one of them.

In 1975, Bangladesh entered a new phase of disastrous political upheavals. Three coups and countercoups took place in quick succession on 15 August, 3 November and 7 November 1975.

The coup of 15 August 1975 was led by six army Majors, during which Sheikh Mujibur Rahman and many of his family members were assassinated. This putsch did not have the support of the people. Taking advantage of the situation, Brigadier Khaled Musharraf staged a countercoup on 3 November 1975, and Brigadier Ziaur Rahman was arrested.

Khaled Musharraf did not have the support of the rank and file of the army, who were fed up with their senior officers

* Ibid.

looking at personal benefit rather than the good of the country. Immediately after the coup by Khaled Musharraf, the rank and file of the army converged on Narayanganj and came to Abu Taher, asking for a countercoup. Most of them belonged to the Revolutionary Soldiers' Organisation. Rather than allowing a rebellion by a mass upsurge of soldiers, Abu Taher took charge, and the first thing he did was to rescue Brigadier Zia, who had been held by the insurrectionists.

Together, Zia and Taher were able to restore some semblance of law and order, but subsequent developments proved that Abu Taher was considered a threat due to his radical views by senior army officers.

On 15 November, Zia ignored all that Taher had done and had him arrested on grounds of treason. Zia had betrayed the very person who had put him in power. Perhaps he feared the magnetic hold Taher had over the officers and men of the army, and he wanted him removed.

On 7 November, Zia had backed Taher. Within two weeks, he had him arrested. Locked away in a Dhaka jail, Taher was placed in solitary confinement, tried by a Special Military Tribunal, charged with mutiny and high treason, and a news blackout was imposed on the conduct of the court martial under tight security.

At first, Taher refused to attend the tribunal, calling it an instrument of the government to commit crimes in the name of justice. Taher's lawyers, however, persuaded him to participate. This was a mistake. Taher's sentence was decided even before the trial commenced.

Abu Taher's problem was that he was too clean, too patriotic and too honest. But he was also too radical. If he was allowed to survive, he would have become a cult figure. He was, in fact, already on the way to becoming one when the others decided to lock him up in jail, bring a case of treason against him and have him executed.

On 17 July, at three o'clock in the afternoon, the verdict was delivered—a death sentence for Taher . . . People all over the country were shocked, because the government could not prove anything. Taher told the barristers: 'This government, which I have brought to power—you are not to ask anything from them.'

At the same time, hearing them declare the sentence, he broke into laughter. He told everybody: 'If lives are not sacrificed this way, how will the common people be liberated? Don't bow your heads. I do not fear death. If you can feel proud—that is enough.'

On 18 July 1976, Abu Taher wrote his last letter to his father, mother, his wife, Lutfa, and his brothers and sisters, and his children, Nitu, Jishu and Mishu. Three days later, on 21 July 1976, he was hanged.

Extracts from his letter are given below:*

> Respected Father, Mother, my dearest Lutfa, my brothers and sisters,
>
> Yesterday afternoon the tribunal announced its verdict against us. I have been sentenced to death . . .
>
> . . . I made it clear to them that no appeal will be issued. We had installed this president and I would not petition my life from these traitors.
>
> . . . I was taken to Cell No. 8. It is the cell assigned to prisoners who are to be hanged. In the cells next to mine

* Lawrence Lifschultz, *Taher's Last Testament*, pp. 2–4.

there are three other victims for the gallows. It is a small cell. Quite clean. It is all right.

. . . When standing face to face with death, I turn to look back at my life and find nothing to be ashamed of. Instead, I see many events that unite me irrevocably with my people. Can I have a greater joy or happiness than this?

Nitu, Jishu, Mishu . . . everyone comes crowding into my memory. I have not left any wealth or property for my children, but this entire nation is there for their future. We have seen thousands of naked children deprived of love and affection. We wanted a home for them. Is this dawn too distant for the Bengali people? No, it is not too far off. The sun is about to rise.

I have given my blood for the creation of this country. And now, I shall give my life. Let this illuminate and infuse new strength in the souls of our people. What greater reward can there be for me?

No one can kill me. I live in the midst of the masses. My pulse beats in their pulse. If I am to be killed, the entire people must also be killed. What force can do that? None . . .

This morning's papers have just come in. They have published the news of my death sentence and the sentences of the rest on the front page. The description of the proceedings that have been published are entirely false. It has been alleged during the trial and on evidence of State witnesses that the Sepoy Revolution of the 7th November occurred during my leadership. This I do not deny.

It is my ardent hope that our lawyers, Ataur Rahman, Zulmat Ali and all others who were present will expose the secret behind this trial and protest this false propaganda. I do not fear death. Zia is a traitor and a conspirator and has taken refuge in lies to discredit me in front of the people. Tell Ataur Rahman and others that it is their moral responsibility to expose the truth – and if they fail in this duty, history will not forgive them.

My greatest respect, my love and my everlasting affection be with you all.

Taher

The day after the verdict, banner headlines screamed 'Taher to Die'.

In London, Amnesty International issued an appeal to the President of Bangladesh to grant Taher clemency. It said: 'A martial law trial held in camera inside jail falls short of internationally accepted standards as laid down in the United Nations Declaration of Human Rights. Before criminal courts, the case against the accused can be established according to the normal process of law and with all legal safeguards, including right of appeal to the highest judicial authorities.'

Amnesty called for a complete retrial for Taher and other Jatyo Samajtantrik Dal (JSD) leaders. Its appeal to the Bangladesh President went out on 20 July.

The next morning, at 4 a.m., Taher was hanged in Dhaka Central Jail.

On the evening of 20 July, Taher had been informed that on 21 July, early in the morning at four o'clock, the death sentence would be carried out. He accepted the news and thanked those who had delivered the message. After that, he took his dinner completely normally. Later, the maulvi was brought to seek absolution for Taher's sins. Taher said: 'I am not touched by the evils of your society nor have I ever been. I am pure. You go now. I wish to sleep.' He went to sleep quietly. At three o'clock, he was woken up. He asked how much time was left. After knowing the time, he cleaned his teeth, shaved and bathed. Some came forward to help him. He forbade them to do so, saying: 'I don't want you to touch me. My body which is pure.'

After his bath, he told the others to prepare tea and to cut the mangoes his friends had sent. He put on his artificial limb, his trousers, his best shirt, his wristwatch and smoked cigarettes with all those present. Looking at his courage, some burst into tears. He consoled everyone, saying: 'Come on, laugh. Why are you so gloomy? Death cannot defeat me.'

He was asked for his last wish.

He said: 'In exchange for my death—peace for the common man.'

After that, Taher said: 'Is there any time left?'

They answered, 'A little bit.'

He said: 'In that case, I shall recite a poem to you.'

He read out a poem about duty and his feelings. And then he said: 'All right. I am ready. Go ahead. Do your duty.' He walked towards the gallows and put the noose around his neck with his own hands.

He said: 'Goodbye, my countrymen. Long live Bangladesh! Long live revolution.'

He then told them to press the button, but nobody came forward.

He said: 'Why don't you have courage?'

Then someone did it. It was all over.

That day, not a single prisoner among the 7500 there took their meal. Taher's body was given to the relations at 2.50 p.m. in the midst of the tightest security.

A car was taken into the jail, and his body was put into it. Five trucks and buses filled with heavy security guards escorted the car to the helipad, and he was lifted into the helicopter. At around 7.50 p.m., he was buried in the family graveyard.

A special camp was set up near the gravesite, and the grave was guarded for twenty-one days. The government of that time feared him even in death. He has left the people of Bangladesh but has left behind a rich legacy of courage, honour and truth.

Kippy

Kippy, Raju and I reviewed the news of Abu Taher's death with disquiet, little knowing that there was to be more in store for us.

Kippy accepted with equanimity his appointment as a staff officer at the 101 Communication Zone Headquarters in Shillong. He picked up golf once again and being the excellent sportsman that he was, he soon achieved a single-figure handicap of 4, which was quite remarkable. He was so good that he represented Eastern Command at the Army Golf Championships in Delhi in 1973 and 1974.

There were, however, two aspects in his life where something was missing. He missed serving with his troops, and he missed a partner in his personal life. There had been a girl who was close to him, but she moved away after he lost his leg. He was anxious to prove that he was as good as the next man but did not want any sympathy.

His Regimental Centre was also in Shillong. He would go there quite often to be with his men. No party or barakhana was complete without him, and he was the life of every party. He wanted to serve with his troops but felt that he could not give them his best.

Though he felt that he was no less than anyone else, he did not relish the thought of serving at desk appointments for the rest of his life. He continued to feel he was a 'passenger' unable to contribute fully, and so, against the advice of his friends and colleagues, he left the army and Shillong in 1975. He was invalided out of the army on 7 May 1975, as a battle casualty of the Indo–Pak war of 1971. Later on, he learnt that command appointments opened up for battle casualties and some achieved high rank, but he never regretted his decision. He had made up his mind to work for the simple village folk of Manipur and returned to civilian life.

The first few months of retirement were a nightmare for Kippy. Having become used to the discipline and rigours of life in the army, he was lost in the easy-going pace of rural Manipur. However, he decided to work to improve the grassroots-level economy of Manipur's villages—especially of his own village, Haipi.

The first thing he did after being invalided out of the army was to get academically qualified. He appeared for the BA examination at Guwahati University as a private candidate and got qualified on 30 August 1976.

He decided to invest his hard-earned pension money in the printing of Christian hymnbooks for a Baptist association in Manipur with a firm conviction that not only would he be doing something for the community, but that he would also get a return on his investment. In fact, he did not even get back his capital.

Refusing to get discouraged, Kippy threw himself wholeheartedly into welfare schemes. He assisted the Ministry of Social Welfare of the Government of India in setting up 'Disability Cells' to help the disabled people of Manipur. He established contact with the All India Institute of Medical Sciences, New Delhi, the Artificial Limb Centre, Poona, and many other institutions caring for persons with disabilities.

He also set up economic development schemes with the aid of Canadian and German international aid agencies to help villagers in the isolated hills of Manipur. These practical schemes gained much popularity in the villages of Manipur, putting many households on firm economic foundation. The people of Haipi started selling their produce in local markets. He instituted schemes for running water in the villages, as well as for bathrooms and indoor latrines.

Through his voluntary organizations, twenty-four villages, with a total of 7000 people, were covered. Kippy motivated the villagers to take up cultivation of cash crops on a commercial scale. He initiated the introduction of winter crops and social forestry, set up public health camps and helped the needy to get bank loans for self-employment schemes. Through his army connections, he got a football ground made for his village, which was an instant success with the youngsters. He also facilitated the building of a new village church, which was something the villagers had wanted for a long time. Kippy's popularity grew not only in his own community but all over Manipur and beyond.

Although Kippy was doing well in his work, he was lonely, and his family perceived the need of a companion. Kippy was perhaps reluctant at first because of his earlier experience, but to his family's great joy he met a beautiful young lady from a neighbouring village. Her name was Maman, and they were married at the Centre Church in Imphal on 10 September 1983. Subsequently, they had three children—the eldest, a son, was born in 1984, followed by a daughter in 1986 and another son in 1988.

Meanwhile, people who saw the tremendous good that he was doing with his community work and welfare schemes felt that he could do much more if he belonged to a political party.

Politics was abhorrent to him, but he was persuaded by the thought that he could do better work for the people of Manipur in general, and for the rural folk in particular, if he had political power. With this in view, he joined the Manipur People's Party (MPP) and later became the president of Ex-Servicemen's Congress in the Manipur Pradesh Congress (I). He did an excellent job in handling the general election in 1984, and his role was highly appreciated by the party high command. He contested for a Lok Sabha seat as a party candidate of the MPP in 1980 but was placed second, and as a Congress (S) candidate in 1992 but lost once again. He also contested for the state assembly seat from the Kangpoki constituency, which he lost by a narrow margin of nine votes.*

By this time, the political situation worsened, with several underground movements springing up all over the state. The state government could no longer contain the situation. Kippy was in no way involved in these political movements. He was therefore amazed when he received a threatening letter from the National Socialist Council of Nagaland demanding that he disassociate himself from the Kuki National Front (KNF). He did not take the warning seriously, because he had never been involved with the KNF in any way.

In April 1993, he attended a conference of Action for Food Production in New Delhi. After the conference, he stayed back in Delhi for a few days, with his eldest brother at Pandara Road, to make arrangements for the schooling of his eldest son, Jem. While he was there, he was asked to lead the family prayers. He spoke well and chose verses from the Bible which later

* *A Life in Service*, biography of Major S. Kipgen, SM, p. 44. Published by family members of the late Major Kipgen in 1998.

assumed some significance. The verses were from Chapter 3 of Ecclesiastes.

The verses began like this:

For everything its season, and for every activity under heaven its time:
A time to be born and a time to die;
A time to plant and a time to uproot . . .

No one realized the significance of these words. However, Maman, Kippy's wife, sensing a premonition of disaster asked him to stay on in New Delhi, but Kippy had too much work in Manipur. He returned to Manipur to find that the law-and-order situation had worsened, with curfews in force and life brought almost to a standstill. Frustrated by the enforced inactivity, Kippy decided to visit a sick friend who lived just a few houses away.

It was early on a Sunday evening, 9 May 1993, that Kippy, his wife, Maman, and their little girl took the short fateful journey to his friend's house. They were followed by three Naga militants who had been lying in wait for him, and when the family returned sometime later, they shot Kippy at point-blank range, pumping a total of twenty-seven bullets into him, right in front of his wife and daughter. He was rushed to hospital, but he had lost too much blood and died within half an hour, at 7.45 p.m. '*Henno, annai* (Mother, it is painful)' were his last words.

The brutal assassination by Naga hostiles, for no reason whatsoever, was so unexpected that it shook the people of Manipur, and there was a sudden emptiness all around. The family, community and locals were shattered.

Kippy's mortal remains were laid to rest in the cemetery at Haipi, the village for which he had sacrificed so much of his time and effort. The funeral took place on Tuesday, 11 May 1993, at 4 p.m. Hundreds of mourners attended the funeral—people from all walks of life, from all communities, irrespective of caste, creed or background, came from across Manipur to pay their last tribute to their leader, benefactor and friend. Mourning continued for weeks as streams of visitors came from various parts of India to pay their last respects to a man they loved and acknowledged as a friend, a man who had worked selflessly for his people.

In many ways, it was an irreparable loss. The grief-stricken family lost a beloved husband, father and brother. Haipi villagers lost a distinguished member of their chief's family. His clan lost a kinsman who had devoted himself to the cause of their economic and social well-being. The social welfare organizations lost an effective spokesman for their cause. And the disabled lost a mentor who was kind, compassionate and caring. Kippy will be missed for his qualities of constructive leadership, straightforwardness, integrity, clarity of thought, understanding, vision and direction. Manipur and indeed India lost a distinguished son. Following his demise, there was a deathly hush at home, in the village and indeed in the land.

Sometime before this happened, Priscilla, my wife, was to spend the Dussehra holidays with me at Tezpur, where I was the Chief of Staff of 4 Corps. I was waiting for her at the Guwahati airport when the airplane overflew Guwahati and went on to Imphal, as there was some sort of strike at the Guwahati airport. She had to spend the night in Imphal. While there, she contacted Kippy, who drove over and took her to his home for dinner. There she met Maman and their children, and spent a pleasant evening with them, talking about old times and about our days spent together at the Artificial Limb Centre and Poona MH.

It took a week for the report of Kippy's death to percolate down to us. Maman was in touch with Priscilla, and it was she who told us about what had happened. I retired from the army on 31 August 1993, a few months after Kippy had been assassinated.

J.V. Raju

Raju continued to prosper in his post-retirement life. He belonged to the state of Andhra Pradesh, and his hometown was Hyderabad. The company he worked for, which was in the business of making fruit juices, jams and similar products, was also located in Hyderabad. His competence, hard work, integrity and commitment impressed his employers to no end, and he rose rapidly from the position of production supervisor to production manager to general manager and CEO. The company thrived and grew exponentially under his care. So much so that the owner offered him a partnership in the firm. This, along with the concessions from the central and state governments, put him in a very comfortable position.

Raju would often come to Delhi on business and would drop by at home whenever he learnt that I was in town. The deaths of Abu Taher and Kippy, and the manner of their dying had upset him considerably. He would recall our days spent together at Poona MH. Priscilla had spent a month in Poona while I was in hospital, so she knew most of the battle casualties. The hospital was short-staffed for nurses, and Priscilla used to help out. So there were lots of shared experiences to talk about.

However, it appeared to Priscilla and me that for Raju, work had become an obsession.

We also noted a radical change in Raju's behaviour. He could now never sit still and had become a chain-smoker. When talking to us at home, he would be pacing up and down puffing away at a cigarette. He would come to our house by taxi and keep the taxi waiting, and after a couple of drinks he would take us to his hotel for a meal. The hotels he used to stay at were always five-star. Raju was doing well, but we could see that the stress of business was taking a toll on his physical and mental health and well-being.

We tried to tell him to slow down, that he had done enough in his life and had nothing more to prove—but it was of no use. A couple of years later, Raju passed away of a massive heart attack.

Raju was also sentimental. He was deeply affected by the violent deaths of Abu Taher and Kippy, and felt that the world had gone mad to have allowed the lives of such wonderful persons to end so violently. During our conversations, he used to say that only two of us were now left of our 'gang of four' and that I'd better look after myself. I now wonder if he was also thinking about himself and whether he had some premonition of his own death.

Ian Cardozo

And now there is only one left of the four of us who started life together as amputee patients at the Artificial Limb Centre on that faraway day of 8 January 1971. Each of us has had a checkered life, vastly different but dramatic all the same, shaped by our individual destinies but controlled by the collective destiny of war. I often think about war and the effects of war on those who are left behind. So many have died for a cause and for their country. But has the sacrifice made the world a better place for our children? Why do wars take place? Why can't countries be happy and content with what they have? And if the world cannot learn the lessons of history, then why can't leaders understand that the best way to prevent war is to be prepared for it?

After the war, the fates of the four of us, as well as of the other war-disabled at military hospitals all over India, were uncertain. At that time, Army Headquarters came to the conclusion that the war-disabled could not serve in command appointments. It took me seven years to prove to Army Headquarters that the war-disabled needed the opportunity to prove themselves and that some of us were as good as the non-disabled! Army Headquarters eventually changed its policy and permitted battle casualties to serve in command of troops. Three war-disabled officers went on to become Army Commanders, and one of them had lost both legs! The war-disabled now wait for the day when a war-disabled army officer will become the Army Chief.

Each of the four of us proved that destiny was a matter of choice, but fate or chance also intervened to play its part in what the future would hold for us. As far as our individual destinies are concerned, each of us—Abu Taher, Kipgen, Raju and me—was dealt with our own set of cards, and we played our hands to the best of our individual abilities. Chance, however, intervened in different ways and took us to our eventual destinations.

What is it that we can learn from this story? Maybe it is that each one of us should do whatever is right, irrespective of the consequences, and leave the rest to fate or destiny or whatever one may call it.

Que sera sera! Whatever will be, will be!

Postscript

The High Court of Bangladesh has declared the constitution of the military tribunal by General Ziaur Rahman as illegal, and dismissed the trial and execution of Colonel Abu Taher.*

* Syed Badrul Ahsan, 'The Strange Case of Colonel Taher', *Indian Express*, 22 Mar 2011, https://indianexpress.com/article/opinion/columns/the-strange-case-of-colonel-taher/

The Sinking of INS *Khukri*: A Captain's Dilemma

'The great battles for supremacy have been fought for centuries on the sea. For a period, they have been fought over the sea. Perhaps in future, they will be fought under the sea.'

—Anonymous

Colaba, Bombay, 7 August 1971

Dark clouds covered the sky and the colour grey dominated the seascape, making it difficult to separate sky from sea. The south-west monsoon had hit Bombay six weeks earlier, and the deluge had turned the Arabian Sea to a shade of gunmetal as it moved and heaved like a huge living being. A dense sheet of rain rapidly approached the Yacht Club which fronted the Apollo Bunder. The deluge beat a tattoo on the roof of the veranda, forcing torrents of water from its eaves to gurgle down its ancient drainpipes. A strong breeze that accompanied the rain invaded the wide veranda, spreading water on the floor and making it a very wet scene.

INS *Khukri*.

Seated at a table were two naval officers who seemed oblivious of the rain and the wetness all around. What they were discussing remains unknown, but it was known that the Flag Officer commanding the Western Fleet had had a conference that morning, and it is possible that their talk centred on future operations on the western seaboard. There were problems on the Indo–Pak border in the east, and Pakistan was openly making statements that there was every likelihood of its going to war with India.

So animated were their discussions that although the waiter attending to them kept refilling their mugs with beer, the officers did not seem to notice. Their names as signed in the register of the Yacht Club that morning were—Captain Mahendra Nath Mulla and Lieutenant Commander Manu Sharma.

A week earlier, the Naval Chief, Admiral S.M. Nanda, had directed the Flag Officer Commanding-in-Chief, Western Fleet (FOC-in-C West), Vice Admiral S.N. Kohli, to make his plans for an attack on Karachi, and Admiral Kohli did not think this to be a great idea. Karachi harbour had two air force bases at Drig Road and PAF Masrur, in close proximity. These, he felt, would be a major threat to the Indian warships attacking the Pakistan Navy in the vicinity of Karachi harbour. The large number of ships would make ideal targets for the Pakistan Air Force. INS *Vikrant* had developed a crack on one of her boilers, and it was doubtful whether she could give air cover to the Western Fleet.

Those who had been called for Admiral Kohli's conference that morning were the Captains and Executive Officers of the ships of the Western Fleet—mostly Commanders and Lieutenant Commanders of the Indian Navy. Most of them supported the concept of the Naval Chief's option to attack Karachi. A few, however, doubted the wisdom of going on an offensive from the sea without air cover. The comparative ability of Indian warships against Pakistani submarines was another issue. It is possible that the two naval officers were discussing these issues so animatedly.

Captain Mulla and Lieutenant Commander Manu Sharma were the Captain and Executive Officer, respectively, of INS *Khukri,* which was part of a three-ship squadron of frigates. INS *Kirpan* and INS *Kuthar* were the other two frigates. The squadron was part of the Western Fleet. These frigates were Blackwood anti-submarine frigates built in Britain in the 1950s and inducted into the Indian Navy towards the end of 1959. They would be nearly twenty years old and close to obsolescence by the time the war would take place.

According to Admiral Raja Menon, the Indian Navy was unhappy with the short-range sonars that were being given with the Blackwood-class anti-submarine frigates and had asked Britain for better medium-range sonars.* The reply given, according to the Admiral, was that the better range sonars were being given only to NATO countries. This was strange, considering India's contribution to both the World

* Sonar: an apparatus used in submarines that uses acoustic waves to detect submerged objects.

Wars, and the fact that India was part of the Commonwealth and that the sonar was not a lethal weapon. However, that was how it was.*

The three frigates were part of 14 FS Squadron, and Captain Mulla, being senior-most, was placed in command. Its role was the protection of the Western Fleet from enemy submarines.

New Delhi, 12 October 1971

Admiral Nanda, the Chief of the Indian Navy, believed that unless 'the selection and maintenance of aim'—the first principle of war—was clear, nothing of consequence would follow. He was also firm in his conviction that only 'offensive action' would obtain conclusive results. Keeping in mind these two principles of war, he felt that the best option to win the war on the Arabian Sea was to attack the Pakistan Navy in its own waters. He had got wind of the doubts expressed at the conference held by the FOC-in-C West. A number of meetings were held to resolve these differences, but he made it unambiguously clear that he would brook no half-hearted attempt to achieve his aim. Gradually, these differences got buried, and all those who had expressed their doubts about the offensive now fell in line. All agreed to follow the Naval Chief's plan to attack Karachi.†

In the conduct of anti-submarine warfare, two basic parameters are of paramount importance. Firstly, naval ships need to be able to move fast; and secondly, they need to have a sonar system that can detect enemy submarines at a reasonable

* Major General Ian Cardozo, *The Sinking of INS Khukri: Survivors' Stories* (New Delhi: Roli Books, 2016), pp. 69–70.

† Admiral S.M. Nanda, Padma Vibhushan, PVSM, AVSM, *The Man Who Bombed Karachi* (New Delhi: HarperCollins, 2004), pp. 212–213.

distance. The *Khukri*, *Kirpan* and *Kuthar*, when handed over to India by Britain, were designated as 'second-class anti-submarine frigates' and were deficient in both these important parameters. Built in the 1950s, these Blackwood-class frigates could work up a maximum speed of only 14 knots in ideal conditions, and their sonar capability was just 2500 metres.

Opposing them were the Pakistan Navy's French-made state-of-the-art Daphne-class submarines, which had a sonar detection capability of 25,000 metres—that is, ten times more than the Indian frigates. And Pakistan had three of them. They were so incredibly swift under the waves that they were named the *Hangor*, *Mangro* and *Sushuk*, after species of deadly sharks found in Pakistani waters. Considering the interoperating parameters between the two opposing weapon platforms, the submarines were to prove vicious and dangerous. They could sense the presence of the frigates when they were over twenty miles away.

Captain Mulla and Lieutenant Commander Manu Sharma supported the planned offensive against Karachi. What worried them, however, was the ability of their frigates to protect the Western Fleet from these particularly dangerous denizens of the deep.

Admiral Nanda's views on the war at sea were well known. His talks and discussions with his officers projected a strong conviction, bordering on obsession, to take the offensive should war come, to throw everything the navy had into battle and to destroy the Pakistan Navy in its own territorial waters.*

---

* Vice Admiral G. Hiranandani, *Transition to Triumph: History of the Indian Navy 1965–1975*, pp. 118–20.

The conference held on 7 August 1971 by Admiral Kohli was the first of a series that would culminate in the presentation of plans to the three Service Chiefs and the Defence Minister in Delhi on 23 November 1971.

Conscious of the limitations of the aging anti-submarine frigates of the 14 FS Squadron to protect the Western Fleet, Captain Mahendra Nath Mulla put forward his views frankly at these discussions but was told that the navy had to fight with what it had, and that this was all that was available.

Being aware of the limitations of the sonars of the anti-submarine frigates, Headquarters Western Naval Command had requested the assistance of the Bhabha Atomic Research Centre in Bombay (BARC), to find some way to increase the range of their sonars. The BARC had done some research and modification on the sonars held by the Indian Navy. Results looked promising, but further improvements were needed and live trials considered necessary. But the time to experiment was extremely limited as war was close at hand.

1 December 1971

A week after the Fleet Commanders had presented their operational plans to the Service Chiefs at the Combined Chiefs of Staff Committee on 23 November, intelligence intercepts indicated that Pakistan was close to waging war against India. These intercepts also revealed that the Daphne-class submarines—the *Hangor* and *Mangro*—had been tasked to take turns to destroy ships of the Western Fleet in Bombay harbour, once war was declared. The *Ghazi* had already moved out of Karachi on 14 November for its task to destroy the *Vikrant*, and the *Mangro* had moved towards Bombay around the same date to lie in wait outside the harbour. The *Hangor* sailed from Karachi on 23 November for a patrol off the Saurashtra coast and on 1 December was ordered to relieve *Mangro,* her sister ship, who had by this time finished her patrol outside Bombay harbour.

Aware of the need for urgent and immediate action, Admiral Nanda made a flying visit to Bombay on 1 December, to address the officers and sailors of the Western Fleet and to move the fleet out of harm's way into the open sea.

The Western Fleet moved out of Bombay harbour on the night of 2–3 December 1971. It consisted of the cruiser *Mysore*; the 15th Frigate Squadron *Trishul* and *Talwar*; the 14th Frigate Squadron *Khukri*, *Kirpan* and *Kuthar*; *Betwa* (an anti-aircraft frigate); *Kadmatt* (a Russian Petya); *Ranjit* (an old destroyer); *Deepak* (a tanker); *Sagardeep* (a requisitioned light-house tender); and two missile boats, *Vijeta* and *Vinash*.

In his assessment of the comparative strengths of the opposing navies, Admiral Kohli, FOC-in-C West, had accepted that the Pakistan Navy's Daphne-class submarines were far superior to our submarines and our surface ships. Accordingly, all naval ships coming to or leaving Bombay hugged the shallow waters of the coast, north and south of Bombay, and altered their routes landwards/seawards at random, so that enemy submarines could never predict where to wait for targets.

On the night of 2–3 December, the *Hangor* detected the Western Fleet approaching from Bombay harbour. She had the mortification of sensing the whole fleet above her but could not launch her torpedoes, as war had not yet been declared. It was learnt later that the Executive Officer of the *Hangor* tried to persuade Commander Tasnim Ahmed, the Captain of the *Hangor*, to launch her torpedoes at the ships as such an opportunity would never occur again, but Ahmed decided against it. Tasnim Ahmed was to learn that it was only around twelve hours later that Pakistan attacked Indian airfields, at 5.45 p.m. on 3 December; which in fact was a declaration of war.

The Western Fleet, in the meanwhile, was on its way towards Karachi when, on 4 December, the *Kuthar* suffered a boiler explosion and the Fleet Commander ordered the *Kirpan* to tow her back to Bombay, escorted by the *Khukri*. On 5 December, on the way back to Bombay, the *Khukri* detected the presence of an enemy submarine and carried out an attack. A hit was recorded, but the *Khukri* did not linger around in the area, as the three ships were in a vulnerable position and the squadron proceeded southwards to Bombay. The squadron arrived in Bombay on 6 December, and the *Kuthar* was taken in for repairs. Captain Mulla made a report of the encounter with an enemy submarine and stated that a hit was recorded, but he added that he could not wait to collect evidence, as the squadron was in a very vulnerable position.

Soon after, there were reports of submarine sightings off Diu Head and confirmed bearings of a submarine that had transmitted a wireless message to Karachi. It was decided by Western Naval Command to eliminate this threat. The *Khukri* and *Kirpan* was the only force available for this task, along with the Sea King helicopters. After considering the gravity of the situation and the decreased anti-submarine capability without the *Kuthar*, FOC-in-C West ordered the *Khukri* and the *Kirpan* to join the Navy's latest anti-submarine Sea King helicopters operating from Bombay, to eliminate the submarine threat off Diu. Orders were issued to Captain Mulla to sail on 8 December towards the last known position of the submarine, to hunt and destroy it. By the morning of 9 December, the

Khukri and *Kirpan* were approaching the reported location of the enemy submarine.

This submarine, in fact, was the *Hangor*.

With a sonar range capability ten times better than that of the *Khukri* and the *Kirpan*, the *Hangor* detected the presence of the frigates that were searching for her early on the morning of 9 December, when they were twenty miles away. The hunt had begun.

By the evening of 9 December, the *Hangor* was able to discern that the frigates were carrying out a rectangular pattern of search. Her sensors also warned her of the presence of the Sea King helicopters, which too were looking for her with their 'dunking sonars'.*

The *Hangor* was able to discern not only the search pattern being followed by the frigates but also that they were operating at a slow speed of 12 knots. The distance between the *Hangor* and the frigates began to close. The *Hangor* still kept a safe distance because of the Sea King helicopters. However, close to dusk, by 1830 hours, the Sea King helicopters left the scene. The *Hangor* saw the opportunity she was looking for. Forecasting the position of the frigates along the well-known rectangular pattern of search, she was able to position herself at around 1900 hours in a tactically advantageous position on the path of the approaching frigates. The crucial moment that the *Hangor* had waited for had arrived, and she was in a position to attack.

While the *Khukri* was in Bombay after escorting the *Kuthar* to safety, Admiral Kohli had ordered the experimental mechanism developed by the BARC to increase the range of the

---

* Dunking Sonars: sonars that are let down into the sea from the Sea King helicopter. *The Sinking of INS Khukri: Survivors' Stories*, p. 79.

sonar capability of the frigates, to be taken on board the *Khukri*. Lieutenant V.K. Jain, who was working on this project, boarded the *Khukri* on 6 December.*

On board the *Khukri*, Captain Mulla was having difficulty coping with the sonar, as this equipment, still in its experimental stage, required him to reduce his speed, whereas when conducting hunter-killer anti-submarine operations, speed was essential to outmanoeuvre and destroy a lurking enemy submarine. He was also aware that according to laid-down practice, he was required to zigzag—a procedure followed to frustrate enemy submarine commanders. This would, however, further slow the *Khukri* down. Captain Mulla was already irked at having to reduce his speed from a maximum speed of 14 knots to 12 knots because of the errant experimental sonar; zigzagging would reduce his speed further. Captain Mulla was therefore in a dilemma. He was faced with two contradictory requirements—zigzagging to evade the submarine or speed to destroy it.

Commander Manu Sharma, the Executive Officer, states that the *Khukri* was in fact zigzagging, and this, along with the needs of the sonar, had reduced its speed considerably. Captain Mulla expressed his exasperation to Lieutenant Jain, who decided to once again explain to Captain Mulla how the experimental sonar functioned. He moved off to get some red and blue pencils from the sonar room, to explain this on a chart.

The *Hangor*, meanwhile, waited for the *Khukri* and the *Kirpan* to come to the area she anticipated was the best to fire her torpedoes at. The first target, in fact, was not the *Khukri* but the *Kirpan*, the first to come within the designated target area. The *Hangor*'s torpedoes were meant to activate below the keel

---

* *The Sinking of INS Khukri*, p. 71.

of the target ship, so that it would break the keel. The torpedo homed in on the *Kirpan* but failed to explode, due probably to a faulty mechanism. With the firing of this torpedo, the presence and position of the *Hangor* was given away, and she had the option of slipping away or to fire another torpedo. Since both the frigates were still quite some distance away, the *Hangor* decided to fire another torpedo. But the *Kirpan*, now alerted, took evasive action.

The *Hangor* then turned her attention to the *Khukri*, which was moving towards her, and fired a torpedo, her third, at her. This time, the torpedo found its mark and exploded below the keel of the *Khukri* near the magazine, breaking it in two. The time was 2045 hours, 9 December 1971. The *Khukri* sank within minutes.

An Account of What Happened on the Night of 9 December, by Commander Manu Sharma

'After the Sea King helicopters left, Captain Mulla was apprehensive about the situation. Being on action stations continuously since 2 December was a great strain. Officers were required to be relieved for meals and sleep. The Operations Room had to be continuously manned, communications had to be constantly maintained, as also all the weapon platforms. Therefore, instead of a day of three shifts of four hours each, the crew was constantly at action stations, where duties became 50–50, i.e., four hours on and four hours off. Captain Mulla, however, was constantly on the bridge, as also the Officer of the Watch, the Navigation Direction Officer, the Midshipman on Training and the Quartermaster who was doing the steering just next to the bridge. At around 8.30 p.m., Captain Mulla went down for about ten minutes, and on his return he asked whether there was any news about the replacement of the Sea King helicopters. I confirmed that they had not returned, which in effect meant that their area of search was not being patrolled. He was also concerned about the speed of the ship and to what degree the sonar capability was affecting it. He wanted to know whether the speed could be increased without adversely affecting the functioning of the sonar. At that time the *Khukri* was doing 12 knots. The message was passed on to Lieutenant Jain, who felt that he could best explain with the help of coloured pencils and proceeded to the sonar room, which was close to the bridge. Soon after, the *Khukri* was struck by a torpedo.

'There were two massive explosions, one after the other, and the *Khukri* keeled over to one side by about fifteen degrees. Captain Mulla was thrown off his chair. He hit the bulkhead and cut his head quite badly. Immediate loss of power followed the second explosion. Captain Mulla ordered "Full Ahead"—for both engines—but there was no response. Due to loss of power, no communication was possible between the bridge and the engine room.

'The *Khukri* by now was down by the stern and flames were coming from the funnel. The ship started tilting to starboard, presumably because of intake of water caused by the hole made by the torpedo. I recommended to Captain Mulla that we should "abandon ship" as the *Khukri* was definitely sinking. There was, however, no means by which we could communicate these orders to the crew of the ship, as there was no power supply. So Kundan Mall and I started yelling these orders to abandon ship through the ship's blower and outside.

'Meanwhile, Captain Mulla and those of us who were on the bridge were trying to help the sailors coming up the only escape route, which was open from the decks below to the top. However, the sailors coming up through this narrow stairway choked the staircase. The situation was made worse by those who were wearing their life jackets, which were very bulky causing further delay when every moment was so precious.

'The ship by now was sinking fast and had tilted dangerously towards starboard. Water flooded the bridge and created a major hazard by sealing the only escape route. The escape route was limited to only one because during "action stations" all hatches and doors are closed, leaving just a few stairways open. In this case, the stairway near the stern was already underwater, and the only stairway that was open was choked by sailors trying to clamber to safety. Kundan Mall and I continued to pull out sailors from this hatch, and some of them started jumping into the sea.

'Once the level of the water had reached the bridge and the tilt of the bridge was nearly 90 degrees, Captain Mulla pushed Kundan Mall and me off the bridge. We tried to take him along with us, but he refused and ordered us to jump to safety. We both jumped into the sea from the starboard side. The sea was on fire, with all the fuel ablaze, so we had to dive under the fires in order to swim to safety. When I cleared the part of the sea which was on fire and came up the other side, I looked for Kundan Mall, who was a good swimmer, but I could not see him anywhere.

'I looked at the ship at this point of time and saw that its bow was pointing upwards at an angle of 80 degrees and sinking slowly. The light of the fires illuminated the ship. I got a glimpse of Captain Mulla. He was hanging on to a railing. I could also see a few sailors hanging on to the fo'c'sle (the forward part of the ship) of the *Khukri*, which was by now close to vertical.

They were clinging on to the guard rails desperately, trying to stay above the water. Most of them remained hanging and went down with Captain Mulla as the *Khukri*, with a great sigh, finally slid into the water. As the *Khukri* sank, there was a great suction effect, taking a lot of sailors and debris in the vicinity down with her. A number of sailors, who had tried to swim through the fires, were badly burnt, and many of them who had been thrown off the ship by the explosion had lost their limbs. There was much shouting for help, but after the *Khukri* went down there was an eerie silence for a moment, as all of us were awestruck by the sinking of our ship.

'As the ship went down, a number of fires were put out by the resultant suction. The cries for help now resumed. Those who were not injured tried to help their injured comrades to hang on to some of the debris floating in the vicinity. I, along with some uninjured sailors, tried to get as many as possible on to the safety of the rafts, but as the capacity of the rafts was limited, most of us opted to hold on to the edge of the rafts and put the injured on board. Two of the rafts remained close to each other, whereas the third raft had drifted quite far. This being December, the water was icy cold, and the sea was rough with waves five to six feet high.

'We were hoping that the *Kirpan*, our sister ship, would come to rescue us, but we saw her sailing away from the area. Knowing there were no other ships in the vicinity, we now realized that we would have to fend for ourselves. Some of us took turns to get on to the raft as the water was very cold and while on the raft, we had to keep a lookout for ships and aircraft which we hoped would come to look for us. We were also concerned about the enemy resurfacing and taking us as prisoners of war, so I got rid of my epaulets (badges of rank). At one stage, in the middle of the night, a maritime reconnaissance plane flew quite low over us. We fired a flare to attract its attention, but we remained undetected.

'The next morning, another aircraft flew over us and threw us some supplies, but we could not retrieve them because the sea was too rough. It was a great relief the next morning, around 1000 hours, when we saw a Petya closing in on us. This was INS *Katchal*, which took us on board. All the survivors were given blankets and hot beverages. Meanwhile, one of the sailors had died on the raft. We gave him a sea burial, conducted by Captain Zadu, the Captain of the ship. The body was wrapped in the national flag, and the ship's bell was rung as a mark of respect for the dead.

'In light of my qualification as a Communication Officer, I helped Captain Zadu in his search-and-rescue effort for other survivors. It was while I was doing this duty that I came to know that the hunt for the enemy submarine had commenced. I came to know later that this exercise was codenamed Operation Falcon. This operation continued till 16 December when the ceasefire took place.

'Sometime later, I was posted to the Cabinet Secretariat, and I had the opportunity to have an informal meeting with the Second-in-Command of PNS *Hangor*. He was an officer from East Pakistan and was placed under house arrest when the *Hangor* reached Karachi. He had escaped from there and was on his way to Bangladesh via Delhi. He made the following statements which are relevant to what had happened. He said:

> PNS *Hangor* had a mechanical problem on 5 and 6 December and had made a radio transmission for permission to return to Karachi. (This ties up with the report by Captain Mulla

that it had had an encounter with an enemy submarine and had recorded a hit and that this could have been the cause of *Hangor*'s problem which caused her to make a transmission to Karachi. It was this transmission, which was intercepted, that gave indication that an enemy submarine was in the vicinity of Diu Head.)

The crew of the *Hangor* was very apprehensive of taking action against the *Khukri* and the *Kirpan* because of the presence of the Sea King helicopters, and it was only when the Sea Kings did not reappear that she realized that she should take on the Indian frigates before the Sea Kings returned and then head for Karachi, for which permission had been received.

'Operation Falcon came very close to destroying the *Hangor*. Two depth charges had bracketed the *Hangor*, and they waited for the next depth charge that would have destroyed them, but that destructive blow never came.

'*Operation Falcon* pulled out all the stops to hunt and destroy the *Hangor*, but we failed to get her.

'The *Hangor* survived probably because it headed out to the open sea and did not return to Karachi by following a route close to the coast, for if she had, the Sea Kings would have detected and destroyed her.'

Excerpts from the Account of Sub-Lieutenant Anil Kakkar, Another Survivor Who Was on Board the *Khukri*

'I was given duties on the bridge as Officer of the Watch. Due to a bit of a science background, I was subsequently appointed to assist Lieutenant V.K. Jain.

'On the evening of 9 December 1971, the system produced an echo indicating the presence of what could be a submarine, and Captain Mulla decided to take evasive action. After taking evasive action, Captain Mulla altered course so as to prosecute the target; however, there was no further confirmation of the presence of a submarine. The *Khukri* and the *Kirpan* now decided to carry out an anti-submarine search operation, adopting the rectangular pattern for this purpose.

'Just before the torpedo struck the *Khukri*, Captain Mulla, Lieutenant Jain and I were on the bridge as the ship was at "action stations" for quite a while. In fact, Captain Mulla was mostly on the bridge—he very rarely, if ever, left it. When the torpedo hit the *Khukri*, the ship shuddered and the lights went out. The emergency lights came on, and I noticed that the ship's gyro-failure alarm started ringing. I lifted one of the ship's blinds that covered a porthole and looked out, and I was astonished to see that the after part of the ship was burning. I now heard a series of loud explosions that shook the ship violently. This must have been the anti-submarine ammunition which was stored just above the propellor exploding, or it could have been that the *Khukri* was struck by another torpedo. Soon after the second explosion, the ship started listing very rapidly towards starboard. By the time I had climbed ten steps of the companionway (ladder) that connected with the bridge, the *Khukri* had listed more than 30 degrees towards starboard. I now found it difficult to climb up the companionway, and I had to hold on to the railing with both hands. I realized that the ship was sinking rapidly and that the best escape route for me was via the bridge. The ship had by now listed to about 45 degrees. I remembered I had placed my life jacket below the radar, but now, when I searched, it was not there!

'I sensed that the port side would be the better side to get off the ship, and with great difficulty I managed to cross over to the bridge. At this moment, I saw Captain Mulla on the bridge. He was calm and collected, as if he had made up his mind to go down with his ship. The *Khukri* had listed to about 45 degrees, and Captain Mulla was holding on to the guard rail. The ship started sinking very rapidly. It was now totally dark, and the water was close to my head. I was trapped between the awning and the bulwark of the bridge, the gap between them being about one and a half feet. The ship now began to sink vertically, and I thought that this was the end. Then, all of a sudden, some air trapped in the ship tried to escape, and this escaping air with great force pushed me out from where I was trapped. While I was going down with the ship, I must have swallowed a lot of water and fuel. I came up coughing and spluttering, and my left eye was burning, due probably to the ship's fuel. In retrospect, I think I was very lucky not to have been able to locate my life jacket, which was made of some synthetic material with a thick canvas cover. If I had found and worn my life jacket, I would have remained stuck between the awning and the bulwark of the bridge, and the air escaping from below would not have been able to push me out.'

Excerpts from the Account of Sub-Lieutenant S.K. Basu

'On the morning of 9 December 1971, we got underwater submarine contacts. All these contacts were homed in on and attacked, when the contacts were within attacking range of the ship, with projectiles and depth charges. All these attacks, however, had no positive outcome.

'At 2000 hours, I handed over watch to Sub-Lieutenant Khanzode and went to the "cowshed" to catch up on some sleep as I was again on duty at midnight. The cowshed was a small compartment on the *Khukri* where junior officers used to stay.

'As I switched on the radio at around 8.45 p.m., I heard a tremendous explosion, and the entire ship shook. The gyro room was next to the cowshed, and the gyro alarm started ringing. I thought it was "action alarm" and rushed to my action station, which was the bridge. While I was on my way, there was another explosion, and the ship's propulsion and power generation systems failed. There was total darkness everywhere.

'When I reached the bridge, I heard Captain Mulla telling the Chief Yeoman to make a signal to FOC-in-C West that we had been hit. Chief Yeoman Prosperin was taking down the message when there was yet another explosion, and the ship started listing to starboard.

'Captain Mulla was telling others on the bridge to leave the ship. I saw Lieutenant Kundan Mall crossing the guard rail and jumping into the sea. Some others were also jumping into the sea. I collected my life jacket and prepared to follow suit.

'The bridge was on the fourth deck and approximately forty feet above the waterline. Captain Mulla looked at me and said, "*Bachcho, utro* (Son, go down)". I got into the choppy Arabian Sea, leaving the solid safety of the steel deck.

'The moment I got into the water, I started swimming away from the ship and from the fires in the water. The huge mast was leaning towards the starboard side as the ship had taken a starboard list. Once I got clear of the ship, I saw the forward part of the ship suddenly go straight up with a loud noise. Personnel were shouting for help, but nobody could see anybody in the darkness.

'In the background of all this noise and confusion, the *Khukri* started sinking with her stern down. In a matter of moments, it vanished from our sight forever. We had lost our battleship. It was a very sad moment for us. That night, eighteen officers and 176 sailors lost their lives.

'Among the survivors picked up by INS *Katchal* from the second life raft, one of the crew had died. His name was Thomas, and he was from Kerala. He was on duty near the projectile room, and he must have got injured when the torpedo hit the ship. He died that night on the life raft. A sea burial, with full military honours, was given to him, and the Christian burial ritual was followed.

'All the survivors remained on board the *Katchal* while it joined the search-and-destruction operation for the submarine that sank the *Khukri*. On 14 December, we set course for Bombay and disembarked on 15 December, at around 2030 hours, at Break Water Berth. We went thereafter to INS *Angre* for our accommodation. I had my medical done there.

'A court of inquiry was held. All the survivors were full of great praise for Captain Mahendra Nath Mulla. We were sent on special leave for a month. There were sixty-six survivors, which included six officers.'

Reminiscences of Her Father: Recollections of the War and Its Aftermath, by Dr Ameeta Mulla Wattal

This story would be incomplete without an understanding of the person and psyche of Captain Mahendra Nath Mulla. This is best told in the words of his elder daughter, Dr Ameeta Mulla

Wattal, the iconic principal of Springdales School, Pusa Road, Delhi. It is important for the reader to see what she says, because this is not only the story of a war and of a ship, but also of a man who lived and died by his strong values—very important in today's confusing times. It is also an account of the aftermath of war in the lives of those who lose their loved ones—something which the average citizen of India knows very little about.

'I have often wondered what made my father go down with his ship after it was torpedoed during the 1971 Indo–Pak war. Did he want his name to be enshrined in history books as a man of valour? Did he do it because of an old archaic naval tradition? Or did he accompany his ship to the womb of the sea, because he felt it was the right thing to do?

'My sister and I had come home from school for the winter holidays just before the war. Earlier, we children used to play war games with tin sailors and paper boats, which, if broken, could always be put together again. The anti-aircraft guns that opened up on the night of 5 December at Bombay were, for us, an enchanting display of bright fireworks, which we looked at with glee from our balconies of Navy Nagar. To us, war, destruction and death were just fast-moving images of World War II movies seen in the security of the United Services Club, from where one could easily escape by walking out of the darkened auditorium. It was this innocence which was torn apart on the night of 9 December 1971, for the torpedo that struck the *Khukri* was no toy and the ship, which was not made of paper, could never be put together again. Unlike the reel-life adventures shown at the club auditorium, this real-life battle had no exits.

'The news of the sinking of the *Khukri* was brought home to my mother along with weak assurances that the Captain of the ship had also been rescued. However, to this day, I recall that my mother felt a hopeless despair, because she knew that her husband was not the type of man who would put his own safety before the safety of his men.

'As the list of survivors started arriving, news was also received that the Captain was last seen helping men out of the sinking ship with silent and calm determination, which in turn transferred to his men. When the last life raft pulled away from the doomed ship that was rapidly sinking to its watery grave, they saw their Captain on the bridge—a sentinel to his battleship for eternity.

'Five decades have by now rolled by, and we have all been involved in the journey of growing up; our household was then all women—my mother, my younger sister and me.

'I remember my sister Anju's reaction to the news of the sinking of the *Khukri*. She was merely a child of eleven. She took the news with silent calm, her eyes not leaving my mother's face. Anju had the inner strength, which she has inherited from my father. She would get up every new day and lay out Papa's uniform and attach his medals and epaulettes with such intense care that I felt her faith alone would bring our father back. She would answer every doorbell and telephone call with the firm conviction that it would be our father at the door or at the other end of the line.

'Our house seemed to be a multitude of humanity, and the days rolled by and mingled into one another. My mother became deeply involved with the widows of the crew of the *Khukri*, seeing to their emotional and physical needs. She put away her own tragedy and worked with grim determination to bring solace and comfort to the families of those who had lost their men of the house. Their needs seemed to obsess her, for she felt she had taken the place of their Captain.

'When all the tumult and the crowds faded away, we were left, just the three of us—one brave woman and two scared children. I remember asking my mother as to what she would do and where we would go, and she replied, "The world is big and has room for everyone, and the three of us are strong enough to find our own place in the sun." That day I knew that there was nothing that the three of us couldn't do.

'How do I remember a parent who died fifty years ago but who continues to deeply influence my every living moment? I was six years old when I became conscious that the tall handsome man with light-brown eyes was my father.

'Father was a Kashmiri Pandit and belonged to one of the most illustrious families of the state of Uttar Pradesh. He could count among his kith and kin Chief Justices, poets, Constitution framers, criminal lawyers and even a dignified scoundrel or two, but they were all brilliant people, uniformly addicted to the romance of living. Veeru (as he was affectionately called) was a man of deep faith. He accepted religion as part of his being, but he never let it prejudice him. He believed that an understanding of different faiths was important because essentially all of them preached the innate goodness of mankind.

'I remember being once influenced by a pamphlet titled "Soldiers of God", in which there was a line that read, "make a sacrifice and save a sinner". I righteously went about putting this into practice. One day, my father noticed me refusing something he knew I was particularly fond of, with an expression of pained tragedy. He asked me why, and I replied, "Sacrificing." He smiled and said, "Never call your best action a sacrifice. If one fights for a cause, it is because one is prepared to live without certain things." I never understood him then, but I do now, that is, that the cause has to be such that one should not count the cost.

'Our father was a voracious reader and encouraged us to read as well. When he returned from a trip, I never expected a doll or a bauble. It always had to be a book.

'*The Rubaiyat of Omar Khayyam* was the first book that I received from him at the age of eight, inscribed with the words, "To my dear daughter. To thine own self be true and the rest follows as the night the day, then thou cans't be false to any man." Six months before his death, on my fourteenth birthday, he wrote to me at school, "These are the formative years of your life. Your sole aim should be to imbibe knowledge, let not your mind wander . . . The time for life, love and laughter will come later. For those who fritter away this precious time, the good things will never seem to arrive. Their future is blighted. This is the inexorable law of Karma." He also remarked that the business of war, if left to the unintelligent, could only result in disaster, and so it was with every profession. I wonder now whether he had a premonition of his end when he made those remarks to me.

'Papa was not always serious; he loved a good laugh. Mother used to say that you can always vouch for the sincerity of a man who laughs openly and without inhibition. However, with me his humour was always tempered with an injunction. Complaining about the severity of life at the Convent of Jesus and Mary, I wrote to him that the food was not even fit for worms. "My dear worm," he replied, "I am glad to learn that the food is fit for you. I am also happy to be informed that there are not frequent outings on the Mall, where misguided young ladies promenade in unbecoming apparel. I am delighted that you are kept 'far from the madding crowd's ignoble strife'. I think it is excellent training."

'Because of Papa, whenever I was home in Navy Nagar, I never saw boys. They were terrified of him and vanished when his silver-blue Renault appeared. I guess I could not have been very popular with the young crowd, but I did not mind. I wanted to spend every waking hour with my father, talking to him, going for long walks through the countryside or trying to beat him at Scrabble. Whenever I challenged him on a particular word, not only would he show it to me in the dictionary, but he would also give me its etymology. He once explained that the reason why English was a progressive and a living language was because it borrowed freely from all languages without fear of losing its own identity, a principle which could be sensibly applied to life as well.

'My father had a histrionic talent too, shared by many members of the family, but he delighted in playing the villain. At the Defence Services Staff College, he played the role of Henry Touchard in *We Are No Angels.* He apparently was very successful in his portrayal and he began to be recognized by the educated gentry of the Nilgiris. He said that to act well, it was more important to get into the character's mind rather than to be concerned about style and nuances of voice.

'Most children have a lifetime with their parents; I had only fourteen years. Yet Papa taught me all the games that I enjoy playing, all the songs I still love to sing and all the stories I relate to my son. I think he was born 200 years too late. His thoughts were medieval, and his compulsions dated to a period in Indian history where parents were the sole arbiters of a child's future. Though well-read, well-travelled and well-informed, he still fervently believed in the religious tenets of faith, duty and accountability, which have largely taken a back seat in the present-day world. He began treating me as an adult very early in life. When other children read comics and Enid Blyton, I was introduced to Chaucer and Wordsworth. He also made it a point never to neglect our religious upbringing. "Hinduism is a way of life," he used to say. "It has been a repository of the wisdom and culture of this subcontinent for thousands of years. Never forget this, and never belittle your priceless heritage." Today, when I witness crimes being committed all over the world in the name of religion, I realize that it is faith alone that preserves the dignity of mankind.

'Our move from the busy metropolis of Bombay to Shimla was not the longest we had taken in our lives, but it seemed an enormous distance in terms of moving from one life pattern to another, and the trauma stayed with us for a long time. In Shimla, the healing process started for bruised and battered spirits. I remember the minuscule two-room flat that my mother had rented and how she joked that we were lucky, for who had a parlour, a bedsitter and a kitchen all rolled into one? Thereafter, we grew up in that flat. It had in it all our dreams and illusions, and it now houses all the memories of our adolescence. It also had in it my father's books on religion, poetry and humour. I feel that P.G. Woodhouse—coupled with a song our father had taught us, '*We are going to sink the Bismarck and the world depends on us*'—ironically enough, helped see us through a lot of grey patches.

'I remember the winters in Shimla used to be terribly severe. Everyone would leave for the plains, and a blanket of snow would cover everything. Water was a problem as the pipes would freeze and burst. My sister or Mom would fill the aluminum *bukhari* with coal, and we would crack walnuts, drink innumerable cups of tea and generally lead a mole's existence. My sister, however, was one of those tireless workers who seemed to be always around, giving us emotional strength. My father's death had affected her deeply. I often felt that she realized our mother had become the "man" of the family, so she took on the mantle of a mother. It was ironic how her doll's house existence before the war took on a real-life dimension afterwards. In many ways, it was Anju who made our cold, rented house a home. Often at night, when it was still and we were wrapped up in our thoughts, she would silently come close to my mother and stroke her face to see if there were any tears, and then she would go back to bed. I wonder now whether Anju's eyes were ever moist when she went back to sleep.

'The Forest Hill Road was a five-kilometre winding road that linked our flat to the school and college. My mother, sister and I used to traverse that road twice a day. Those walks are etched in my mind. They were difficult days for my mother, for she was trying to come to terms with her existence, and I with mine, and often my intensities would catch fire and burn. That road and that house have been silent spectators to many a storm that passed over our lives.

'Nearly fifty years have passed. We have long since moved out of that flat on the hill and moved to broader horizons, newer lives with different people; towards being wives, mothers, teachers, executives, writers, but always striving to be women of strength. My entire life has been a testimony to a man who died for his country, and I believe that I have to live for it. The irony, however, is in never being able to come up to his expectations because of the exemplary way in which he lived and died.

'On 9 December when his ship was struck by a torpedo and started to sink, he spared no effort in getting as many sailors and officers to the safety of the life rafts and the sea. And when he had done his duty, he took the decision to go down with his ship. I suppose he saw himself as the master of a ship hundreds of years ago, nurtured by the traditions of the sea that required him to stay with his vessel. Not because it was the right thing to do, nor because it was expected of him, but because knowing him as I did, it was the only thing to do. He was the first Captain of independent India's navy to go down with his ship and hopefully the last. One such man is enough to bring honour to an entire nation for a lifetime.

'I imagine him now striding purposefully through the vast void of space and his words reach out to me, "Let not your dreams be transformed into nightmares—remember the honour of the Mullas."'

Vice Admiral Hiranandani, in his book *Transition to Triumph: History of the Indian Navy 1965–1975*,* states that after the war, there was considerable debate on:

- Whether two ships were a viable enough force to send on an anti-Daphne Hunter Killer mission without anti-submarine air effort in direct support.
- Whether the *Khukri*'s doing so slow a speed was related to the experimental Sonar 170 modification.
- Whether the Sea Kings could have been used more offensively.
- Whether the *Kirpan* was justified in withdrawing from the scene after the *Khukri*'s sinking, instead of immediately going to rescue the *Khukri*'s survivors.
- Why Operation Falcon was unable to locate the Pakistani submarine.
- Since the Daphne-class submarine's anti-ship capability was known to be, and accepted to be, superior to our anti-submarine capability, should the anti-submarine operation have been launched at all?

* *Transition to Triumph*, pp. 210–11.

- Were the two frigates and Sea Kings deployed on 8 December adequate to cope with a Daphne-class submarine?

The answers to some of the questions were as follows:

- The consensus was that in war, it is unacceptable to let an enemy submarine threaten you on your doorstep—it has to be hunted.
- The Sea King helicopters, which were the navy's latest and best anti-submarine system, could have been better utilized operating from Diu (instead of from Bombay), although they were considered defenceless if attacked by Pakistani aircraft. However, Super Connie maritime recce aircraft and Alize anti-submarine aircraft should have been utilized in support of the operation from the moment it started on 8 December.
- It is of utmost importance that any new sensors which have a direct bearing on the safety of the ship should not be experimented with during war, when the ships are engaged in active operations, especially so, if this experimentation would place restrictions on the speed and movement of the ship.

The questions that were asked and only some of which have been answered, indicate the following:

- That Captain Mahendra Nath Mulla was aware of the issues mentioned above but had to do whatever was within his power to do his duty to hunt and destroy the Pakistani submarine.
- That Captain Mulla had to do whatever he could to increase the range of the experimental sonar that was

ordered on board by Western Naval Headquarters, despite the disadvantages inherent to the experiment.

- That Captain Mulla was in a dilemma as to whether he should focus on speed to avoid destruction by enemy submarines or to increase the range of the experimental sonar to detect enemy submarines, so that he could destroy them.
- That when his ship was struck with a torpedo and started to sink, he felt it would be unethical to save his own life when he was aware that many of his sailors would perish.

What emerges is:

- Success in war is the destruction of the enemy and at the same time ensuring the security of own forces.
- No military commander should be given a task without a fair chance of success.

This is a story not only of a war, or of a ship, but also of a man who went unflinchingly into battle against far superior odds. Captain Mahendra Nath Mulla was a colossus as far as human character is concerned—a leader who practised what he believed was right, to his very last breath. He carried out his duty to the best of his ability, knowing full well the difficulties of his task and the limitations of his resources. When faced with the option of saving his own life, he rejected the easier option, because it was not in his character to save his own life when he knew that many of his men were trapped in the sinking ship, and his last moments were spent helping others to get off the sinking ship. Personal acts of cold courage like this are rare to come by, and when they do, they shake the world by the immensity of their heroic content.

Postscript

There are many lessons to be learnt from this story, the most important being that in a future war, the armed forces are not denied the wherewithal to defend the nation. Although the Indian Navy performed outstandingly in the war at sea in 1971, there are lessons to be learnt in the manner in which the *Khukri* had to fight its battle against extraordinary disadvantages. Hopefully, this type of situation will never again be repeated.

The Beginning of the End

'If you must play, decide three things at the start: the rules of the game, the stakes and the quitting time.'

—Proverb

It was the middle of April 1971, and the genocide by Pakistan against the citizens of her eastern province was at its peak. The holocaust had caused a huge influx of refugees who came to seek shelter in India. By the third week of April, the number had crossed ten million. Prime Minister Indira Gandhi was deeply disturbed by this development on our border—a situation that continued to escalate. The Chief Ministers of the states of West Bengal, Orissa and Tripura had declared that their administrative resources had been strained to breaking point, and they pleaded with the Prime Minister that they could take no more. They also stated that along with the refugees, subversive Pakistani elements had entered India; they feared a law-and-order situation.

The Prime Minister visited the states, which had been engulfed with refugees, to assess the situation. What she saw shocked her beyond belief. The state of suffering humanity that continued to pour across the border tore at her heart. The carnage

The refugees coming across to India.

and savagery inflicted by the Pakistan Army on helpless men, women and children went way beyond anyone's imagination. She met some of the elders from the refugee camps and was horrified by the stories narrated by them. It was difficult to believe that human beings could treat fellow humans with such barbaric savagery. She listened aghast at accounts of young girls and women raped in front of their menfolk, of throats being slit and men being beaten to death in front of their families, of men being thrown alive into burning furnaces of factories and being fed alive to caged leopards.* Most of the men and women that she met had a glazed, blank look, as though they had lost all sense of reality and were walking through a bad dream.

A very disturbed Mrs Gandhi returned to Delhi. She appealed to Pakistan to stop the pogrom, citing the difficulties this humanitarian crisis was causing the people of East Pakistan and India. Her protests, however, fell on deaf ears. In fact, it appeared that Pakistan took mischievous delight in the discomfort that it was causing India. They asserted that this was an internal problem of Pakistan, and that India must keep away and not interfere. Indignant at this response, Prime Minister Indira Gandhi took up the matter with the United Nations but fared no better—the UN accepted the contention of Pakistan that it was its internal matter, and that the issue of refugees should be solved bilaterally between India and Pakistan. The Security Council, led by the United States of America, equated Pakistan the belligerent, with India the aggrieved.

Pakistan continued to receive support from the United States. Regarding the continuing genocide in East Pakistan, the

---

* Ian Cardozo (ed.), *In Quest of Freedom: Personal Accounts of Soldiers from India and Bangladesh* (New Delhi: Bloomsbury, 2016), pp. 12–59.

Western nations followed the lead of the USA, all of whom had ditched their sense of morality and killed their conscience on the altar of political expediency.

Lieutenant General J.F.R. Jacob, in his biography *An Odyssey in War and Peace*, says:

> The Americans were supportive of the Pakistani position regarding the Eastern Wing being an inseparable part of Pakistan. Dr. Henry Kissinger, the Secretary of State, was under an obligation to Pakistan for their arranging Nixon's visit to China as also making a rapprochement between China and the U.S. Nixon too favoured tilting towards Pakistan, comfortable with the Pakistani military regime and very uncomfortable with Mrs Indira Gandhi, who he intensely disliked. On 6 July he visited Delhi en route to Islamabad, achieving little in Delhi. The American and Chinese support for Pakistan grew, and to counter this, Mrs Gandhi turned to the Soviet Union. She sent feelers to Moscow regarding a Treaty of Friendship that had been mooted since 1969 and received a favourable Soviet response. A Treaty of Friendship was signed without compromising Indian sovereignty or our Non-Aligned policy and was almost tailor-made to suit our requirements. The core element of the Treaty states: 'In the event of either party being subject to an attack or threat thereof, the high contracting parties shall enter into mutual consultations in order to remove any threat and to make appropriate effective measures to ensure the peace and security of their countries.'*

* Lieutenant General J.F.R. Jacob, *An Odyssey of War and Peace* (New Delhi: Roli Books, 2011), pp. 93–94.

This was a masterstroke by Mrs Gandhi. It put the Chinese on the back foot and also the Americans.

Meanwhile, in India, pressure by the Opposition in Parliament, protests by the public and outcry by the media continued to build up against the Prime Minister for the failure of her government to take action against Pakistan. The public demanded immediate military action against Pakistan so that the refugees could return to their homes.

The Indian Prime Minister, however, had her own compulsions—political, social and moral—against hasty military action. The problem of the refugees was a crisis of gigantic proportions, and she believed that the humanitarian aspect had to be resolved first. This involved food, housing and medical attention that the refugees urgently needed. Most of them had crossed the border with nothing but the clothes they wore.

The act of invading a neighbouring country, for whatever reason, would be difficult to defend. Would the world accept the enormity of the refugee problem as a justified reason to warrant military action? The problem of the refugees was, however, spiralling out of control. Towards the end of April, Mrs Gandhi decided to ask the Army Chief, General Sam Manekshaw, to brief her on the military situation.

Brigadier Behram Panthaki and his wife, Zenobia, have described what happened at this meeting in their book *Field Marshal Sam Manekshaw: The Man and his Times*:

> . . . the Army Chief was invited to a cabinet meeting. The Prime Minister and her cabinet wanted the army to launch an immediate offensive against Pakistan. Sam stood his ground. The knee-jerk reaction of the government and the proposal

> emanating from the government was completely flawed. Spelling out facts that were germane to any military planning, he queried the impulse to jump the gun. The timing was not right. He needed time to mobilise formations to their operational locations and ensure adequate and uninterrupted logistical support. This would entail requisitioning trains, railway wagons and civilian aircraft. Crops were ready to be harvested in the Punjab and the diversion of railway stock would result in food shortages. To ensure uninterrupted reinforcements and supplies to forward locations, additional roads would have to be built by the Border Roads Organisation (BRO). Logistically any operation in summer spelt disaster with the entire delta region of West Bengal turning into a vast swamp with the monsoon rains. This would confine the movement of armoured vehicles to the roads and expose his plans to the enemy. Air support would be restricted because of poor visibility. Any entry into East Pakistan would be suicidal until the rivers had ebbed and the snows had blocked the Chinese from opening a third front along the northern border. The army was not adequately equipped. The Armoured Division had just eleven tanks in operational condition out of 189; requisitions for purchase were pending with the Ministry of Finance. Sam refused to be bulldozed into a misadventure.*

This is corroborated by S. Muthiah in his book *Born to Win: The Life of Lieutenant General Inderjit Singh Gill*. He says:

---

* *Sam Manekshaw: The Man and His Times* (New Delhi: Niyogi Books, 2014), pp. 109–111. Behram Panthaki, earlier on, was Sam Manekshaw's ADC.

> The Chief of Army Staff, Sam Manekshaw briefed the Cabinet on the situation and, despite the bureaucracy's snide whispered comments questioning the military's courage and efficiency, stuck to his guns saying that the Army would be ready to move only by late November, after the monsoon, and when it did move, he assured them, it would be victorious within weeks. He offered Prime Minister Indira Gandhi his resignation if she did not like his military plans, but she accepted them, and preparations began on the diplomatic, military and logistical fronts keeping the target date in mind.*

In his book, Behram Panthaki goes on to say:

> The Army Chief assured the Prime Minister that East Pakistan would capitulate within a month, but only if he was given a free hand, if the timing was of his choice and if he had only one political master to report to – the Prime Minister. The Prime Minister agreed to his terms. With that began the most brilliant plan in Indian military history. Preparation and coordination with departments of government and ministries commenced. The Army Chief and representatives of key ministries met weekly to track progress. For the first month the civil government continued to drag its feet which left Sam with no option but to convey his frustration to the Prime Minister; he was losing valuable time. The next meeting was held in the Ops Room of Army Headquarters. Sam summed up the situation: progress had been glacial. The Finance Ministry had yet to approve expenditures and release funds

---

* *Born to Win: The Life of Lieutenant General Inderjit Singh Gill* (New Delhi: Penguin Viking, 2008), p. 181.

to line ministries. The Army was awaiting approval from the Defence Ministry to make up deficiencies. The Railways had reneged on all deadlines; work on extending railheads up to the borders had not commenced nor had railway stock been released, holding up the movement of troops and material. A furious Prime Minister turned on her ministers.

Each of them was made to commit to a deadline and with that preparations for war began in earnest.

The cabinet meeting was followed by a briefing at the Operations Room at Army Headquarters which was attended by the Prime Minister, Mrs Gandhi who was accompanied by the Defence Minister Jagjivan Ram, Y.B. Chavan and the Defence Secretary K.B. Lall. A presentation was made to the Prime Minister based on a brief prepared at Headquarter Eastern Command. After the presentation, General Manekshaw asked for a postponement of operations till 15 November. Some retired generals publicly argued in favour of immediate action before Pakistan reinforced her Eastern Wing with additional forces. They argued that more time given to Pakistan would make any venture in that country all the more costly. It was rumoured that Defence Minister Jagjivan Ram backed by Finance Minister Y.B. Chavan had urged Mrs Gandhi to resort to armed action immediately, adding that if Manekshaw had any misgivings, he should be replaced.*

General Manekshaw, however, stuck to his position. He made it clear that the army was not in a fit situation to go to war. The present state of the army was due to the failure of the defence and finance ministries to give the army the wherewithal

* Major General Sukhwant Singh, *The Liberation of Bangladesh* (New Delhi: Vikas Publishing House Pvt. Ltd., 1981), p. 18.

it needed for war, and if immediate action was insisted upon, then his resignation would be on the Prime Minister's table.

Fortunately, the Prime Minister supported the Army Chief and accepted that intervention would have to take place at a time most suitable to India, allowing him to make his plans in the time frame that he had asked for. However, she was disappointed that immediate military action was not possible and that the return of the refugees would therefore be deferred.

Mrs Gandhi realized that something needed to be done in the meanwhile, to make things difficult for the Pakistan Army to operate in East Pakistan with impunity and continue their genocide; and that the answer to that lay in assisting the Mukti Bahini in their efforts to liberate their homeland.

The core of the Mukti Bahini consisted of military personnel of the East Bengal Rifles and the East Bengal Regiment, who had escaped from the Pakistan Army in West and East Pakistan. They were joined by young men eager to liberate their homeland. The military aim of the Mukti Bahini was to harass the Pakistan Army through guerrilla operations and to make it difficult for them to function by attacking and destroying bridges, supply dumps, rear administrative units and to disrupt their lines of communication. The Mukti Bahini, however, had to be trained in guerrilla warfare, especially the youth who had no military experience at all. The government permitted camps to be set up in India for the training of these cadres, acknowledging that only when they were properly trained could their operations be successful. The Mukti Bahini was split into platoon-, company- and battalion-sized groups, and allotted sectors and subsectors from where they were to operate. Initially, they operated through the Border Security Force sectors. Later on, they operated on their own but in liaison with the army formations under which they fell. The basic deployment that was made by Eastern Command put Major Zia in charge of the Chittagong sector, Khalid Musharraf for Comilla, Major Safiullah for Mymensingh, Wing Commander Bashar for Rangpur, Lieutenant Colonel Zaman for Rajshahi, Major Usman for Kushtia, Major Jalil for Khulna and Tiger Siddiqui for Tangail.*

Thereafter, Mrs Gandhi undertook a diplomatic offensive, during the third quarter of 1971. She visited the capitals of the major countries of the world to bring home to them the reality of continuing genocide in East Pakistan and the need to rein in the Pakistani military, who were going all out to destroy the democratic rights of the people of East Pakistan. Her efforts, however, met with a cynical response. Not one of them condemned Pakistan or acknowledged the genocide. The general attitude was that it was an internal matter of Pakistan.

The initial lack of a military response from India, the failure of the world to condemn the genocide and the move of additional Pakistani troops from West to East Pakistan only emboldened the Pakistan Army, making them more reckless and ruthless. Border incidents multiplied. This brought Pakistan and Indian paramilitary units in direct confrontation with each other.

As these clashes grew in number and intensity, Indian border posts manned by the BSF had to be reinforced by the Indian Army in October 1971.

By the end of October 1971, these border clashes had become more violent and had escalated to military operations that were accompanied by mortar and artillery fire by both sides.

The essence of this story centres on the operations of the Mukti Bahini in a subsector contiguous to the police station

* Lt Gen. J.F.R. Jacob, *An Odyssey in War and Peace*, p. 68.

at Boyra. In this sector, the Mukti Bahini had caused considerable damage by destroying bridges and disrupting the Pakistan Army's line of communications. Incensed by the audacity of the Mukti Bahini, the Pakistani Brigade Commander launched a joint operation with armour, artillery and air power to destroy the Mukti Bahini and the bases from which they were operating. These operations spilled across the border into India, causing considerable damage and casualties to the BSF and Indian Army personnel.

The offensive by the Pakistanis took place on 21 November. War had not been declared, and the use of this large a quantum of force, that too in a joint operation launched by the Pakistan Army and Air Force, called for a strong counterattack by the Indian forces. A fierce encounter took place with troops of 9 Indian Infantry Division. The Pakistanis withdrew after they suffered heavy casualties. Thirteen Chafee tanks were destroyed by 45 Cav, the Indian tank regiment, and three tanks, which were in running condition and abandoned by the Pakistanis, were driven off by personnel of the Indian tank regiment and the damaged tanks towed across to the Indian side of the border.

The next day, 22 November, a Monday, was bright and sunny, but the beauty of the day was marred by a succession of air attacks by Pak Sabre jets. These attacks appeared to be in retaliation to the damage the Indian forces had inflicted on Pakistani ground forces on 21 November. The attacks continued from 1000 hours onwards.

When the concerted assault on Indian Army positions by Pakistani ground and air elements was underway on 21 November, 350 Indian Infantry Brigade had asked for air cover, but their request was turned down by the Indian Air Force, probably because war had not been declared.

The officers and men of the Indian Army units on the ground who were bearing the brunt of the Pakistani air attacks were indignant at the denial of air support. The ground forces deployed near the Boyra salient consisted of Headquarters 350 Indian Infantry Brigade, which had 4 Sikh, 26 Madras and the 1st Jammu and Kashmir Rifles on its strength. It appeared to them that higher headquarters seemed blind to their predicament.

The absence of the IAF allowed the Pakistani Sabre jets to operate with ease. Their aircraft would climb leisurely to about 2000 feet, dive down to level off at about 500 feet before unleashing their bombs and armament on the hapless Indian troops below.

Finally, when it became clear that the Pakistanis were operating freely and without constraint against our troops on our side of the border, air support was sanctioned. Indian Gnats, which were located at Dum Dum airport near Calcutta, made an appearance. However, by the time they arrived, the Sabres had exited the area.

At around 1440 hours the same day, the pilots appeared to have anticipated a call. A set of four young pilots—Flt Lt Roy Andrew Massey, with Flying Officer Sunith Soares as his wingman, and Flt Lt Ganapathy and Flying Officer Don Lazarus at Number 3 and 4 positions—were ready and waiting. The Forward Air Controller (FAC) was Flt Lt Sharad Savur and the Fighter Controller was Flying Officer Bagchi.

An eyewitness account of what happened next is given by Brigadier Ajit Apte (retd), who at that time was the Gun Position Officer in 14 Field Regiment, which was in support of 350 Indian Infantry Brigade. He says:

> All was quiet on the Eastern Front. Sunith Soares and Don Lazarus were playing scrabble and the others were relaxing

when suddenly the klaxon* started blaring. Indian radar had picked up the intrusion of three enemy Sabres at 1440 hours and within minutes the Operational Readiness Platform at Dum Dum had scrambled four Gnats who were airborne and hurtling at tree top level towards Boyra.

The Gnats soon reached the International Border (IB) and Bagchi told Massey on the Air Defence Radio Channel: Enemy two o'clock. Four nautical miles.

Massey replied, 'Contact! I see them. Pulling up.'

Ganapathy and Don being on the right flank couldn't spot the enemy aircraft.

Soares spotted one enemy aircraft at three kilometres which was perched to commence a dive and called out 'Contact!'

The officers and soldiers of the army units on the ground came out of their defensive positions to watch the dogfight with growing excitement and interest.

Massey spotted an enemy Sabre and maneuvered to get behind it. The Sabre tried to evade, but Massey got within firing range and fired a small canon burst. It missed the target but he followed quickly with another burst, which slammed into the right wing of the Sabre and the aircraft spiraled out of control. Khalil Ahmed, the enemy pilot, ejected.

Massey, Soares, Ganapathy and Lazarus now latched on to the remaining Sabres. Ganapathy fired a burst at a Sabre and missed and the third Sabre got behind him at a distance of 200 yards; Don swerved and got behind him and his cannons slammed onto the Sabre, causing it to explode, with

---

* Klaxon: A loud hooter or horn used to give a warning signal of some sort.

the debris hitting Don's aircraft on its nose and drop tank. This pilot also ejected. He was Flt Lt Pervez Mehdi.

Ganapathy meanwhile fired accurately at the remaining Sabre and hit it on its right wing and set it aflame. The aircraft was badly damaged but it managed to straggle across the border, trailing smoke. This was probably Wg Cdr Chaudhury, the Pak mission leader from Pakistan's Air Force 14 Squadron.

As soon as the dogfight was over, the Gnats did a victory roll over the Brigade location and returned home.

Flt Lt Pervez Mehdi, who was the second Pak pilot to eject, parachuted into the field defences of 4 Sikh, where Captain HS Panag (who later rose to be the Army Commander of Northern Command) was the Adjutant of the battalion. He quickly got into a jeep and picked up Pervez Mehdi. Flg Offr Khalil Ahmed, the first pilot to eject, landed within the defences of 1st Jak Rifles. Both pilots were sent to 14 Field Regiment, which was 1500 metres to the rear and to a flank. They were properly treated, given a cup of tea and blindfolded and sent to Headquarter 350 Brigade. No one knew at that time that Flt Lt Pervez Mehdi would one day rise to be a future Chief of the Pakistan Air Force.

Massey, Ganapathy and Lazarus were awarded VrCs, and Flg Offr Bagchi was awarded with the VM for his effective control of the air battle. The next day, All India Radio and the newspapers announced the news of this air battle and the award of the nation's first three gallantry awards.*

---

* Extracts from an account given in a WhatsApp message. The account is by Brigadier Ajit Apte (retd), who was a Gun Position Officer of 14 Field Regiment and a witness to this dogfight that took place on 22 November 1971.

The Gnats hurtling towards Boyra.

The next day, far away in Islamabad, in West Pakistan, a different story was unfolding.

Agha Mohamed Yahya Khan, Commander-in-Chief of the Armed Forces and President of Pakistan, had heard about the debacle at Boyra and was in an ugly mood. The cause of his anger was a BBC broadcast he had heard on the evening of 22 November. He had immediately telephoned Lieutenant General Gul Hassan, his Chief of General Staff. On the directions of the President, General Hassan called for a meeting the next day. Officers holding key appointments in the Pakistan Army and Air Force were directed to attend.

The next day, the approach to the Army Chief's office on what is now Iftikhar Janjua road, Rawalpindi, was cordoned off by the military police to facilitate the smooth passage of the senior officers who were to attend the meeting. The air was filled with the wailing of vehicle sirens that announced the arrival of the members of Pakistan's military hierarchy.

The BBC broadcast of the previous evening had announced that the Pakistan Army had suffered heavy casualties, on 21 and 22 November 1971, in a clash with the Indian Army and Air Force at a place called Boyra. What infuriated Yahya Khan was that there was hardly any time lag between when he was briefed about the incident and the broadcast by the BBC, which gave more details of the battle than he had received at his briefing.

The BBC reported that the Pakistani forces had suffered the loss of three F-86 Sabre jets and thirteen Chaffee tanks in a battle with elements of the Indian Army and Air Force that had taken place on the border with East Pakistan on 21 and 22 November 1971. The BBC added that two of the Pakistan Sabre jets had fallen well within Indian territory, and that the pilots, who had ejected, had been captured.

The third Sabre jet, which was severely damaged, had managed to straggle across the border and had fallen within the territory of East Pakistan.

The destruction of the tanks and the fighter aircraft, and the capture of the two Pakistani Air Force pilots well within Indian territory, had given the Indian Army moral high ground even before the war had started. This infuriated General Yahya Khan. It proved conclusively that it was the Pakistani forces that were committing acts of aggression across the border, which was the opposite of what Pakistan was trying to tell the world.

The destroyed tanks had been recovered by the Indians, and the three that had been abandoned in good running condition were driven off and shown to foreign war correspondents. This, too, was reported by the BBC. The loss of these tanks and aircraft meant that these precious ground and air resources would not be available to Pakistan for a war with India, which appeared to be increasingly imminent.

The meeting at Army Headquarters was scheduled for 23 November 1971, 11 a.m.

The staff cars had begun to arrive 10 a.m. onwards. The first to arrive was the Director of Military Operations, and the last to arrive was Air Marshal Rahim Khan, the Chief of

Air Staff. In between, came the Principal Staff Officers and heads of some of the arms and services, the Corps Commanders and the Chief of the General Staff. The Corps Commanders of the corps located at Kharian, Lahore and Bahawalpur were in attendance. The line-up of the officers, including the Commanders of the 'Strike Corps' meant for offensive operations, indicated that the meeting was very much an 'Operation of War' conference. Some wondered whether the President was going to give them the date of the launch for the long-expected offensive against India. The President had been making statements like 'In ten days' time, I shall be off fighting a war', and 'I shall teach India a lesson that she will never forget'. In the beginning of November, Yahya Khan had told *Newsweek* magazine that war with India was imminent, and that the Chinese could be counted on to come to Pakistan's aid with arms and ammunition. He went a step further the following week and said, in an interview with Columbia Broadcasting System, that China would intervene if Pakistan was attacked by India. These statements by the Pakistani Army Chief made it clear that war was around the corner.

The dogfight.

When General Yahya Khan arrived at the meeting, at 11.15 a.m., he looked as though he had not slept at all the previous night. He was bear-like in appearance—not very tall, heavily built, with a florid complexion and a full head of hair, greying slightly at the sides.

The President was visibly angry. He responded to the 'Salaam Walekum' by the assembled officers, who stood up when he walked in, with a growl and that too very grudgingly. He followed it up with a dressing-down of all those present and also those who were absent. He made no pretense of telling them exactly what he thought of them in language that was colourful and typical of the man. He also expressed vividly what he thought of those responsible for the debacle of the battle at Boyra.

There was tension in the air, but all kept quiet.

His first question was, 'Who was the officer who planned the operations at Boyra, and who was the commander of the force who botched it up so badly?' The question hung in the air and remained unanswered. The silence was taut with suspense. No one knew what would follow. Success has many claimants—failure has none. More importantly, no one wanted to become a scapegoat for someone else's failure.

Yahya Khan glowered at the Director of Military Operations and growled, 'Give me a report on what actually happened within the next twenty-four hours. I learnt more about this damn fiasco from the BBC than from yesterday's briefing. No frills, no cover ups. Someone will have to pay for this. I will not accept failures of this kind.'

'Secondly,' he asked, 'how was it that the action which was fought the day before yesterday and yesterday was broadcast by the BBC yesterday evening with full details of our losses? I was briefed on the action only yesterday, and the story was told a few hours later by the BBC to the whole world!'

'Thirdly,' he continued, 'if, as it appears, the Indian Army is able to instantly communicate with the foreign press, what are you damn fellows doing to ensure similar media coverage?'

The Chief of the General Staff explained that the Indian Army had allowed foreign war correspondents to co-locate with front-line troops and to report as they thought fit. No restrictions were placed on them. They lived and marched with the troops. What he could not say openly was that the atrocities perpetrated by the Pakistan Army on the hapless people of East Pakistan had given them such a bad image worldwide that it was not possible to allow foreign reporters to accompany Pakistani troops. They had too much to hide.

Yahya Khan got the message. He was aware of the atrocities perpetrated by the Pakistan Army on the people of East Pakistan, and he knew that allowing foreign correspondents to move with Pakistani front-line troops was, therefore, out of question. He was, however, irritated at the advantage that the Indian Army had achieved in using foreign media to broadcast authentic front-line action but decided not to say anything more, because of his own complicity in the ravaging of East Pakistan.

For a brief moment, his thoughts went back to the evening of 25 March 1971, when he had left Dhaka secretly, accompanied to the airport only by Lieutenant General Tikka Khan, the newly appointed Military Governor and Martial Law Administrator of East Pakistan.

He had gone to East Pakistan ostensibly to apprise himself of the situation that had developed there as a result of the landslide victory of the Awami League, but actually to give final orders for administering a coup de grâce to the movement in East Pakistan for greater freedom and autonomy. He recalled his last words to Tikka Khan, uttered at 6.14 p.m., as he entered the military aircraft that was taking him back to Islamabad. He had turned around and said to the Military Governor, 'Now sort them out.'

Those four words spoken in English were a death sentence for the people of East Pakistan, who had voted against military rule. The killings that followed were pure genocide, and the massacres were to earn Tikka Khan the sobriquet of the 'Butcher of Bangladesh' in addition to the title that he had already notched up as the 'Butcher of Baluchistan'.

Coming back to the conversation at hand, he switched to the war that he said would soon take place. The Director of Military Operations, the Director Armoured Corps and the Air Chief felt relieved that explanations from them for the Boyra fiasco were not immediately demanded. The remainder waited for the orders they felt would come. If they were to go to war with India, then there was a lot of work that had yet to be done.

The President then took off on a tirade against India, which he said was interfering in the internal affairs of Pakistan and that he would teach the country a lesson she would never forget. The USA and China, he added, had guaranteed support to Pakistan, and the Middle East had always provided help and could be relied upon to come to their assistance once again. War with India, he said, was inevitable. He repeated that he did not therefore want precious resources to be frittered away on inconsequential skirmishes in an undeclared war between India and Pakistan in the eastern theatre.

It was these losses and their accurate reporting by the BBC that had infuriated the Pakistani President. Although it was clear from the escalation of attacks by Pakistani troops on Indian border posts that war was inevitable and close at hand, it was not clear as to when this would happen. But this incident probably hastened the Pakistani timetable for war. The conference now turned to a discussion of dates and timings and moves of formations on the Eastern and Western fronts, in which the Corps Commanders, the Director of Military Operations, the Quartermaster General and the Pakistani Air Chief had important parts to play.

It was on 23 November 1971, after the Pakistani debacle at Boyra, that Yahya Khan probably took the fatal decision to launch his offensive against India. After he had heard about the Boyra incident, he had called his Strike Corps Commanders and Principal Staff Officers to his headquarters in Rawalpindi. The composition of this Operational Conference and the time lag between this meeting and the launching of his offensive on 3 December 1971, are prime indicators that it was on this day that he finally decided on the date and time of his attack on India. It was after this meeting, on 23 November, that a state of emergency was declared in Pakistan.

Strangely, far away in New Delhi, at 11 a.m. on 23 November 1971, a similar meeting had been ordered by the Chiefs of Staff Committee. All the Commanders-in-Chief of the three services made presentations of their operational plans to their Chiefs of Staff. The Defence Minister and Defence Secretary were present. These presentations enabled each C-in-C to know what the others were planning and to tie up the loose ends.*

The return of the refugees to East Pakistan was the core issue. Their return, however, was contingent on the destruction of the

* Vice Admiral G.M. Hiranandani, *Transition to Triumph*, pp. 125–26.

Pakistani military machine in East Pakistan. War plans had been made and Indian forces deployed against Pakistani forces in East and West Pakistan, in anticipation of the Pakistani offensive. The Indian armed forces were close to finalizing their war plans. Both sides had finalized their D-Day. An unstated problem was: How could the Pakistani armed forces be destroyed if there was no war? What would the Indian armed forces do if Pakistan did not attack?

Ultimately, Yahya Khan resolved the issue by attacking Indian airfields on 3 December, at 5.45 p.m. Incensed and irritated by the guerrilla tactics of the Mukti Bahini and the incident at Boyra, Yahya Khan attacked India from the air and on the ground. He had, however, waited too long. Yahya Khan had hoped to destroy the Indian Air Force on the ground. But he was to be disappointed. India was ready and prepared. IAF aircraft had been protected and concealed, and India's counteroffensive over land, sea and air was launched the very next day. Pakistan was taken aback by the swiftness and precision of the Indian response. For India, the main criterion for the counteroffensive had to be speed because Yahya Khan had openly spoken of help from the USA, China and the Middle East. Sam Manekshaw had therefore decided that the war had to be decisively wrapped up well before outside help from these countries could arrive.

Pakistan attacked exactly ten days after the conference of 23 November. It would take about that much time for an offensive of such a magnitude to be launched by the three services from the moment the order was given. General Yahya Khan did not realize that this decision of his was going to cost Pakistan dearly and that it would result in the loss of half of Pakistan. In the words of Brigadier Siddiqi of Pakistan, 'This was a self-imposed war with India."* Yahya Khan's decision heralded the beginning of the 1971 war and the end of East Pakistan.

As the title of this story suggests, it was 'The Beginning of the End'!

Postscript

It was, in fact, the beginning of the end in many other ways as well! It was a new beginning for the people of East Pakistan who were freed from overwhelming, ruthless domination. It was also the end of an era which had bled the eastern wing of all her resources, without it getting anything back in return. It was also the beginning of the return to the rich traditions and culture of *Sonar Bangla*, and the end of forceful imposition of the Urdu language on the people of East Pakistan. Finally, it was the beginning of Bangladesh and the end of the 'two-nation theory'.

---

* Brigadier Abdul Rehman Siddiqi, *East Pakistan: The End Game: An Onlooker's Journal* (Karachi: Oxford University Press, 2004), p. 15.

The Race for Dhaka

'A good plan is like a road map; it shows you your final destination and usually the best way to get there.'

—Anonymous

The decision taken by General Yahya Khan to commence the war against India on or around 3 December 1971 came to be known to General Jacob at Headquarters Eastern Command on 1 December. His radio intercepting stations reported a message from West to East Pakistan regarding a warning to merchant shipping not to enter the Bay of Bengal and restricting civilian aircraft from flying near the Indian border. These intercepts indicated that Pakistan intended to attack India in the course of the next few days. General Jacob passed this information to the Indian Army, Navy and Air Force, who took action accordingly.* The credence of this information was reinforced when the Australian military attaché, called on General Inder Singh Gill, Director of Military Operations, Indian Army a few

* Lieutenant General J.F.R. Jacob, *An Odyssey in War and Peace* (New Delhi: Roli Books, 2011), p. 77.

days before the war, and stated that something was brewing in Pakistan, because all the women and children were being asked to leave in twenty-four hours, and it looked as if Pakistan was getting ready to move militarily. General Gill immediately informed General Manekshaw, who in turn informed Prime Minister Indira Gandhi.*

The overall aim of the three protagonists was not difficult to discern. India just wanted the genocide of the people of East Pakistan to stop, so that the refugees could go back to their homes. Pakistan, on the other hand, wanted to forever crush the democratic aspirations of East Pakistan, and their dreams of autonomy and self-rule. The aim of the Bangladesh government in exile was to free themselves forever from the oppressive rule of Pakistan.

The overall military strategy laid down by India was 'offence in the east; offensive defence in the south, west and the north'. The east meant East Pakistan; the south meant the desert region of Rajasthan; the west meant the plains of Punjab; and the north meant the plains and hills of Jammu and Kashmir, and the snow-clad mountains of Ladakh. The navy's strategy was to go on the offensive on both the western and eastern seaboards, and the air force decided that their best strategy was to destroy the air element of East Pakistan in the early stages of the war.

The focus of offensive operations was in the east because that was where the problem had started and that was where it needed to be finished. Time was critical, and in keeping with the principles of war of 'offensive action', 'concentration of force'

---

* S. Muthiah, *Born to Win: The Life of General Inder Singh Gill* (New Delhi: Penguin Viking, 2008), p. 186.

and 'maintenance of momentum', additional forces had to be allocated to Eastern Command to ensure quick success.

In line with the military strategy, preparations had begun well in advance. The Army Chief accepted the risk of diverting some of Army Headquarters reserves facing the north to provide the necessary resources to Eastern Command for the offensive. He sent two divisions to the east and ordered the raising of a new corps headquarters—Headquarters 2 Corps—for command and control of these divisions under the Eastern Army. The infantry divisions in Nagaland and Mizoram were extricated from their commitments and made available for operations in the east grouped under a headquarters loaned by 4 Corps. These divisions had no artillery, and this deficiency had to be made up by denuding other fronts. A regiment of medium armour and two regiments of light tanks were also diverted to Eastern Command. Bridging resources were built up to the extent that the Eastern Army could and did lay 10,000 feet of bridging—the largest bridging effort in military history.*

The divisions that had been moved from Western Command to the east meant that Army Commander Western Command was denuded of the forces he had planned to use for offensives on the Western Front. This was very disappointing, and he said as much to the Army Chief.

Eastern Command, however, would bear the brunt of the war, and a lot of preparation had to be done before war broke out. This meant that road communication to forward areas had to be improved, landing grounds constructed, ammunition of various categories moved up and dumps created, cables

---

* Major General D.K. Palit, *The Lightning Campaign* (New Delhi: Thomson Press, 1972), pp. 68–9.

laid to ensure an infallible communication system, bridging equipment and stores moved forward in anticipation of the need to cross river obstacles. Arrangements had to be made for evacuation of casualties and space requested in civil hospitals. Contingency plans had to cater for the use of rivercraft to move troops across rivers, road space demanded for the movement of convoys, railway trains requisitioned to move troops forward, and workshops moved to forward areas to repair transport and equipment. Liaison had also to be carried out with the state governments bordering East Pakistan, to warn them of the possible effects of the war and get the assistance that might be required from them.

The army realized that the major problems of the defence policy could not be dealt with purely on military terms, and that these had to be dovetailed with internal, external and financial policies. The Army Chief's close rapport with the Prime Minister helped. As Chairman of the Chiefs of Staff Committee, General Manekshaw pressed for the political involvement of the government in evolving a broad strategy and clear directive for the achievement of military aims. For this, he was able to secure the involvement of D.P. Dhar, Chairman of the Planning Committee of the Ministry of External Affairs. He reactivated the Joint Intelligence Committee and the Joint Planning Committee, and commenced work as a Combined Service Operational Headquarters, thus facilitating coordination and cooperation between the three services. On the civil side, a Secretaries Committee was set up to take executive decisions dealing with the preparation for war. The Committee consisted of Secretaries of defence, home, finance and foreign affairs. Other secretaries were co-opted as and when required, as also the Director Generals of the paramilitary forces and Civil Defence.

The apex level of coordination, however, remained with General Manekshaw and Dhar. The Prime Minister was kept informed, and the Public Affairs Committee was briefed when necessary. The Chief brooked no delay, whether in giving decisions or oiling the wheels of sluggish machinery to get things moving. He was 'on the spot', whether in the national capital or in the field.*

Yet there were differences of opinion between Eastern Command and Army Headquarters on the possible intervention of the Chinese and the capture of Dhaka. General Jacob, who had been monitoring the movement of Chinese Army formations, was convinced that the Chinese would not intervene, but Army Headquarters thought otherwise. With regard to the capture of Dhaka, Eastern Command was clear that Dhaka, the geopolitical and geostrategic heart of East Pakistan, was the primary and final objective. Army Headquarters, on the other hand, felt that in keeping with the political aim, the objectives should be the river line bordering the capital, and that Dhaka would automatically fall once the formations reached there. These differences between Eastern Command and Army Headquarters continued till the closing stages of the war.

The implications of Chinese and US intervention were that Indian forces in the north and the east could not be withdrawn from their locations till it was clear that the passes were closed due to the winter snows. It was decided that the answer to this problem was to complete the offensive in the east in the shortest possible time, before external forces could come into play.

General A.A.K. Niazi, the General Officer commanding all Pakistani forces in East Pakistan, had adopted the strategy of

* Major General Sukhwant Singh, *India's Wars Since Independence*, pp. 54–5.

what he called the 'Fortress Concept', i.e., a very strong belt of defences based on points which he called fortresses. He hoped the Indians would attack these strong defences, and he planned to defeat them by a process of attrition. This strategy ensured a strong outer crust, but there were hardly any reserves to cater for unforeseen situations. He demanded additional forces, and a massive airlift of troops took place from West Pakistan. These troops had to fly into East Pakistan via Sri Lanka, because the Indian government had stopped all flights by Pakistan across Indian territory.

Dhaka was the citadel and core of Pakistan's defences in East Pakistan, and it became increasingly clear that it was the pivot on which the whole concept of Niazi's survival depended. However, deliberate defence of Dhaka was not conceived of by the Pakistanis, and they hadn't nominated any force for its protection. Nor had India planned for its capture.

A plan for a paradrop on the outskirts of Dhaka had been made to facilitate its capture if and when the need arose. The plan was made by Air Vice Marshal Devasher, Brigadier Mathew Thomas, the Commander of the Para Brigade and General Jacob. The plan envisaged the paradrop to take place at Tangail, and a link-up with 101 Communication Zone coming from the north and the Mukti Bahini located in the area.

Tangail, in central East Pakistan, was chosen for the paradrop because it was the road junction where highways from Mymensingh and Jamalpur met the road to Dhaka. Its capture would prevent Pakistan from reinforcing its forces in the north and prevent withdrawal of the Pakistani forces stationed there.

Before Independence, India and Pakistan had been trained by the British to attack defensive positions where the enemy was strongest and to proceed further only after the enemy position was destroyed. This is what General Niazi hoped India would do. But Generals of the Indian Army realized that if they fell into this trap, they would get involved in a hard slogging match and do exactly what the Pakistani planners wanted, i.e., to impose delay till outside help arrived.

India therefore decided to exploit the gaps between the fortresses, bypass the strongholds and head for the interior areas. The Indian Army strategy was based on mobility and speed. All units and formations were imbued with the importance of the time factor and understood that irrespective of difficulties, it was essential that the offensive be successfully concluded before other countries or the UN could intervene. Every soldier was encouraged and motivated to improvise and move fast, and to wrap up the operations as quickly as possible.

The Army Chief, General Sam Manekshaw, had visited all front-line troops and, in his own inimitable way, told them he wanted a quick victory so that the citizens of East Pakistan could go back to their homes and the Indian Army to its barracks. This was a war where everyone in the armed forces, right from the top leaders to the soldiers on the ground, knew what was required of them—what was to be done, how it was to be done and by when it was to be done!

It also needs to be remembered that Sam Manekshaw and Yahya Khan were the senior-most generals in their respective armies. Prior to Partition, Sam and Yahya had worked in the same section in the Military Operations Directorate. Sam was the GSO1, and Yahya was his GSO2, serving directly under him.* Sam could therefore read Yahya like a book and anticipate his every move.

* GSO1 and GSO2: General Staff Officer Grade 1 and General Staff Officer Grade 2.

Meanwhile, General Niazi was strengthening all the communication centres and towns to prevent advancing forces from getting through to the interior areas. He consequently based his defences on the important communication centres of Jessore, Jhenida, Bogra, Rangpur, Jamalpur, Mymensingh, Sylhet, Bhairab Bazar, Comilla and Chittagong as theatre fortresses. He felt that the Indian attacking forces could be held by these strong defences based on river obstacles and deep minefields. He grouped the theatre fortresses in the various sectors so that they fell within the command and control of his divisions and brigades.

The basic flaw in this concept was that whereas the outer crust of his defence line was strong, it did not have depth, and he did not have reserves against enemy assaulting forces that got through the gaps between the fortresses.

The Indian concept of 'jugaad'* was very much in evidence! Bicycles and rickshaws were used to move battalion mortars and machine guns. Local boats and rafts made of bamboo and the trunks of banana plants were used to ferry ammunition and stores across rivers, and the people of East Pakistan helped the Indian Army in every possible way.

The Indian Army advanced into East Pakistan from three different directions. The success of bypassing strong points and heading for interior communication centres by the Indian Army was paying off well. Encouraged by the success of the innovative methods used by battalions to move fast across river obstacles, and the speed of the advancing Indian forces, the Indian Corps Commanders now began to set their eyes on Dhaka, as it became increasingly obvious that Dhaka needed to be the main

---

* Jugaad: the concept of improvisation and innovation.

focus of operations both militarily and politically. Dhaka was the centre of gravity of Pakistan's civil and military government in East Pakistan, and if Dhaka wobbled and fell, the Pakistani government in East Pakistan would collapse.

East Pakistan was surrounded by India on three sides. Accordingly, it was decided to launch the land and air offensives from three directions while the Indian Navy would blockade the fourth, which was open to the sea. It was also important that the Pakistan Air Force in East Pakistan was knocked out of the war as early as possible, to ensure air superiority.

Though the initial military plan had been the capture of all territory of East Pakistan up to the river lines, it now became necessary to keep Dhaka as the ultimate objective. Early capture of the river lines and the ferries would facilitate operations into Dhaka and its ultimate capture. Eastern Command was initially given the task of destroying Pakistani forces and occupying all important areas of East Pakistan. It tasked the corps and the communication zone accordingly. Orders were subsequently modified to liberate the whole of East Pakistan, and that included Dhaka. A flexible response to new opportunities was necessary, and the army responded magnificently.

The race for Dhaka had begun.

The Race for Dhaka

India's border with East Pakistan was approximately 4000 kilometres long. It was surrounded by the state of West Bengal to the west, Meghalaya to the north, the Cachar state of Assam and the state of Tripura to the east, and the Bay of Bengal to the south. To the south-east lay the Chittagong Hills, which had a common border with Burma. East Pakistan had three major rivers flowing through it—the Padma, the Jamuna and the Meghna. Before emptying into the Bay of Bengal, these rivers form vast deltas that reach far inland. With the exception of the Chittagong Hill Tracts and Sylhet, the countryside is low-lying and waterlogged, consisting as it does mostly of land intersected by numerous rivers and rivulets. A large part of the country is marshy due to the cultivation of rice and jute. The rivers flow from north to south, are very wide and become tidal in the lower reaches. Hills, lakes and marshland cover the southern region. The monsoon breaks with full force in the middle of May and lasts till mid-October. The heavy rains make the rivers into seas and the low-lying country into lakes.

India's Eastern Army, which had been tasked for offensive operations against East Pakistan, comprised 2 Corps in the South-Western Sector, 33 Corps in the North-Western Sector, 101 Communication Zone in the Northern Sector and 4 Corps in the Eastern Sector.

2 Corps

Commanded by Lieutenant General T.N. Raina, 2 Corps had on its orbat* two mountain divisions, a para brigade less a battalion, a regiment of armour (PT-76) and a squadron of T-55 tanks to capture Jhenida, Jessore and subsequently Hardinge Bridge, Goalundo Ghat, the Faridpur ferries and Khulna, and then move on to Dhaka.

This sector had excellent road and rail communications, and 2 Corps stood the best chance of making it first to Dhaka.

* Orbat: Order of battle. The formations and units allotted to a formation for a particular operation.

Several important objectives lay on its approach. Jessore, in fact, was next only in importance to Dhaka, especially as it had an airfield which, when captured, would facilitate IAF operations in the corps sector. The Ferry sites and river crossings, if speedily captured, would threaten Dhaka. Facing 2 Corps was a Pakistani infantry division commanded by Major General M.H. Ansari.

33 Corps

Commanded by Lieutenant General M.L. Thapan, 33 Corps had on its orbat a mountain division and a mountain brigade to cut the line Hilli-Gaibanda, and to capture Bogra and Rampur. The corps was operating in the north-western sector of East Pakistan, and its eastern limits were bounded by the Brahmaputra–Jamuna rivers. The 33 Corps sector was not considered of strategic value as it did not offer a quick route to Dhaka or other towns or cities whose capture would be of propaganda value.

This sector, however, contained the largest chunk of the Pakistani Army as well as the bulk of Pakistani armour. The key objectives of the corps were the theatre fortresses of Rangpur and Bogra, and the important communication centres of Hilli, Nawabganj and Dinajpur. General Officer Commanding 16 Pakistan Division had deployed his forces well ahead of the fortresses and the communication centres to deny them to the advancing Indian forces. These forces were to fall back if pressed hard by the Indians.

4 Corps

Commanded by Lieutenant General Sagat Singh, 4 Corps had on its orbat three mountain divisions. Its area of operations was east of the Meghna River, which was a natural line of defence to the Dhaka area, encompassing the Sylhet sector in the north-east to Chandpur in the east and the Chittagong Hill Tracts to the south. In addition to the mountain divisions, it had armoured elements, an independent brigade and several East Bengal Infantry battalions. The three divisions were tasked with the capture of the Sylhet, Comilla and Chandpur sectors, respectively.

To be sure, 4 Corps had a critical advantage over the other sectors in that it held all helicopter assets for heliborne operations. The Hunters operating from Kumbhigram and the MiGs operating from Guwahati could provide it with close air support.

101 Communication Zone

Commanded by Major General Gurbaksh Sing Gill and later on by Major General Nagra (after General Gill got wounded), 101 Communication Zone had on its orbat 95 Infantry Brigade and FJ Sector. It was tasked to capture Jamalpur, Mymensingh and subsequently Tangail. It had the closest approach to Dhaka.

50 Independent Para Brigade

The Para Brigade consisted of a brigade less a battalion. It was commanded by Brigadier Mathew Thomas. A paradrop was to take place at Tangail independently of the Para Brigade.

Conduct of Operations

On the 2 Corps front, General Raina sent his infantry divisions in two thrusts to liberate areas west of the Madhumati River.

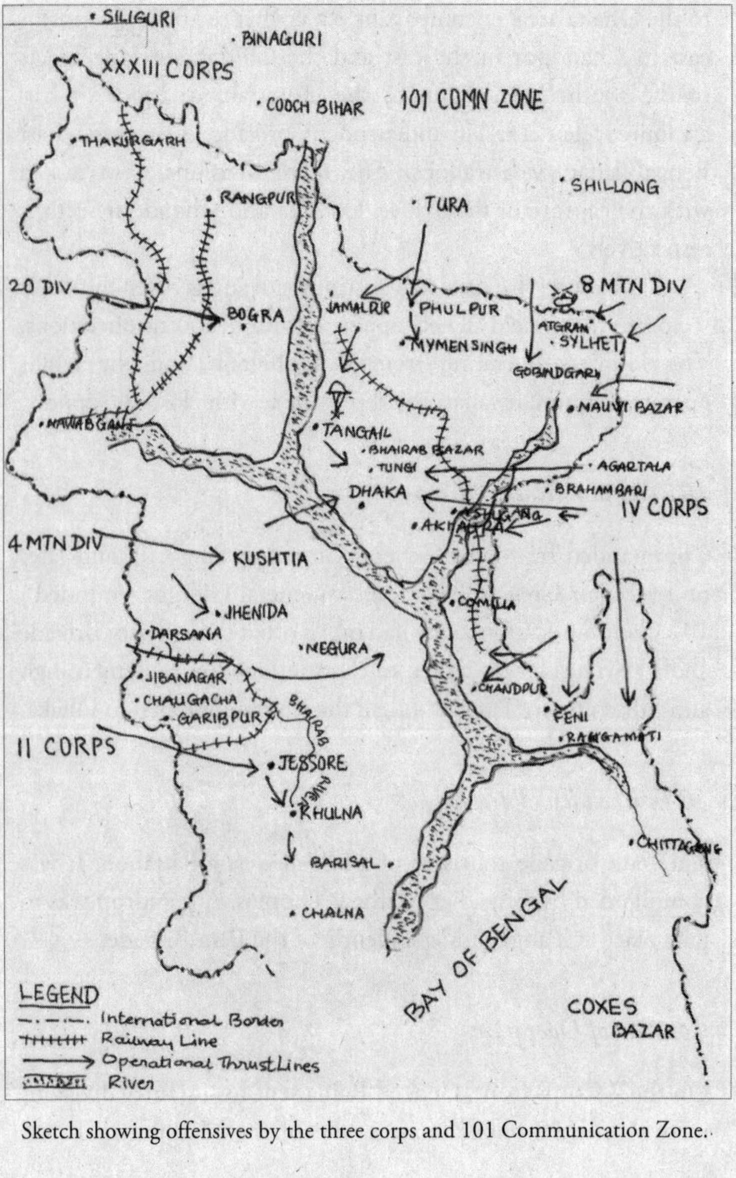

Sketch showing offensives by the three corps and 101 Communication Zone.

Niazi's strongholds were contained while fast-moving columns bypassed them and raced towards key areas in the interior. The two divisional thrusts broke up into several columns heading for Jhenida, Jessore, Khulna and Barisal—to cut the Khulna–Jessore–Khustia rail line and prevent the lateral move of the enemy. Raina considered Jessore to be the key to this sector.

The brigades in all the sectors moved on foot across paddy fields, streams, rivers and marshland, carrying all their gear. Every form of local transport was used, including cycles, cycle rickshaws, bullock carts, village boats and rafts, and the locals were only too eager to help the Indian Army to go cross-country into battle. By 7 December, the rail link was cut and Jhenida captured. On the same day, Jessore, considered to be a very strong fortress, was vacated by the enemy without a fight.

Jessore was held by an infantry brigade group supported by tanks and artillery—a force of over 5000 men. Yet, when the time came to fight, the enemy just melted away. In less than twenty-four hours, Indian forces took an objective they had estimated would take a week of bitter fighting. By 12 December, Khustia and Hardinge Bridge were taken after severe fighting.

Meanwhile, Gnats and Hunters from Kalaikunda and Sukhois from Panagarh attacked Pakistani troops trying to use ferries to withdraw across the Padma. By 14 December, 2 Corps were on the outskirts of Dhaka. The fall of Jessore without a fight had facilitated the speed by which 2 Corps reached the periphery of the capital of East Pakistan.

On the 33 Corps front, Rangpur and Bogra were fortresses and Hilli, Dinajpur and Nawabganj important communication centres. Major General Nazar Hussain Shah deployed his forces well ahead of the fortresses to deny axes of advance to the Indians.

These forces were to fall back to the fortresses when forced to yield ground. Strong concrete bunkers were constructed along the routes of ingress. Hilli, in particular, was very strongly held. At some places, whole railway coaches had been dug into the ground to serve as pillboxes. The enemy in this sector resisted to the last. Hilli was invested on 6 December, and every bunker had to be virtually destroyed before it could be captured. Indian troops suffered heavy casualties. The Bogra defences, on the other hand, were contacted on 13 December and captured by the next day after heavy fighting.

By 14 December, Bogra was cleared and the Brigade, commanded by Bakshi Joginder Singh, was earmarked for operations in the Western Sector. So it marched out of the east to the Western Front. The remaining elements of 20 Indian Infantry Division headed for Rangpur and, on the of night 14–15 December, arrived on the outskirts of Dhaka.

Under Lieutenant General Sagat Singh, 4 Corps was the strongest corps of India's Eastern Army. It had the longest stretch of border as its operational front. Its task was to liberate all territory of East Pakistan up to the Meghna River. General Sagat felt that if he could close up to the Meghna in the area of Daudkhandi–Chandpur, he could pose a threat to Dhaka. At the same time, he had to ensure that enemy forces in the area of the Sylhet–Maulvi Bazar sector and the Feni–Chittagong sector did not interfere with his operations.

He accordingly launched General K.V.K. Rao towards Sylhet to capture Maulvi Bazar, the Sherpur Ferries and, if possible, Sylhet. General Ben Gonsalves was tasked to capture Akhaura, Daudkhandi and Chittagong. Major General R.D. Hira was made responsible for operations in the Chandpur sector and for the clearance of the enemy from the Lalmai Hills.

Constantly hovering over the battle areas in his helicopter, Sagat learnt that an enemy brigade was withdrawing from the Sylhet sector for the defence of Dhaka. He concluded that this was 202 Pakistan Infantry Brigade, which was holding Sylhet, and he tasked the 4th Battalion of the 5th Gorkha Rifles (FF) to capture Sylhet in the Indian Army's first heliborne operation. This battalion had already fought two fierce battles at Atgram and Gazipur, and had suffered heavy casualties. It was, in fact, less than half its original strength.

Unknown to General Sagat Singh, the brigade that was to withdraw to Dhaka was not 202 Pakistani Brigade that was holding Sylhet; it was Pakistan's 313 Brigade at Maulvi Bazar. This brigade, instead of withdrawing to Dhaka, moved to Sylhet. So, by the time the Gorkha Battalion landed in Sylhet on the evening of 7 December, it was faced with an enemy strength of two brigades and the Sylhet Garrison in the disadvantageous ratio of 1:20. The battalion, however, hung on to Sylhet for nine days and nights in an epic defensive operation that kept the strength of nearly a division's worth of enemy troops away from the main battle for Dhaka, allowing the corps to operate across the Meghna without interference.

Gangasagar was taken on 4 December and Akhaura on 5 December after heavy fighting (Lance Naik Albert Ekka was awarded the Param Vir Chakra for his courage at the battle of Gangasagar). On 9 December, Sagat moved 4 Guards and 10 Bihar by his small helicopter force across the Meghna after two spans of the bridge across the Meghna had been destroyed. By 12 December, Sagat had lined up a divisional-sized force to assault Dhaka from different directions. Later, the whole of 311 Indian Infantry Brigade concentrated at Narsinghdi for the main attack on Dhaka, which was planned for the night 14–15

December. Medium guns mounted on rafts for the investment of Dhaka were towed across the Meghna by motor launches.

By its sudden and spectacular heliborne crossing of the Meghna, 4 Corps surprised everyone. Commanders at all levels showed courage, innovation and initiative. The exemplary drive and boldness of General Sagat Singh brought 4 Corps to the gates of Dhaka on 14 December, in record time.

Events followed one after another that put General A.A.K. Niazi on the back foot and made him apprehensive of his ability to hold the Indians who were converging on to Dhaka. Among these offensive actions was the paradrop at Tangail.

Foreign correspondents had noticed Indian paratroopers at Dumdum airport in their distinctive camouflage jackets, maroon berets, cap badges and insignia, which make this elite group of soldiers recognizable all over the world. War correspondents sought clarification from Eastern Command as to whether this force was the Indian Parachute Brigade. The Chief of Staff of Eastern Command, Major General Jacob, deliberately gave no clarification. All he said was, 'We have no comments. You can come to your own conclusions.'

The foreign correspondents came to the conclusion that if Headquarters Eastern Command was not clearly indicating the strength of the paratroopers, their strength must therefore be on the higher side. They therefore came to the wrong conclusion that the force was a para brigade. The force, in fact, was only a para battalion.

On the afternoon of 11 December, the 2nd Battalion of the Parachute Regiment was dropped on the outskirts of Dhaka. Based on the mistaken assumption that the paratroopers were in brigade-strength, the CBS network reported that an Indian para brigade had been dropped around Dhaka. So, once again, an exaggerated strength of Indian forces was reported by reliable news agencies, causing panic and consternation in the ranks of the Pakistani higher command. The Pakistani military high command in Dhaka felt greatly intimidated to see the sky covered by the parachutes of hundreds of paratroopers literally dropping out of the sky on the outskirts of their garrison.

Earlier, in the fighting around Sylhet, the BBC had mistakenly broadcast that a Gorkha Brigade had landed at Sylhet, whereas it was an under-strength Gorkha Battalion. So, genuine mistakes by foreign correspondents pushed the Pakistanis to believe that they were being attacked by forces larger than they were actually facing. This shaped their perception on the unfolding events of the war and had a profound effect on their decision-making.

By 13 December 1971, Indian forces had begun closing in on Dhaka, bypassing the Pakistani brigades and divisions which were left holding on to their defensive positions. Meanwhile, Sam Manekshaw, the Indian Army Chief, made three broadcasts advising the Pakistani forces to surrender or to accept destruction.

In his broadcast of 14 December, the Indian Army Chief warned Major General Rao Farman Ali, who was commanding the Dhaka garrison, of the futility of protracting the conflict. The Indian Army Chief reiterated his guarantee of complete protection and just treatment under the Geneva Conventions. In his final warning, General Manekshaw said:

> I have appealed to you twice already. But there has been no response from you so far. I wish to repeat that further resistance is senseless and will mean death to many poor soldiers under your command quite unnecessarily. I reiterate

> my guarantee of complete protection and just treatment under the Geneva Conventions to military and quasi-military personnel who surrender to my forces. Neither need you have any apprehension with regard to the forces of Bangladesh as they are all under a joint operation command and the Government of Bangladesh has issued instructions for the compliance of the provisions of the Geneva Conventions.
>
> My forces are now closing in around Dhaka and your garrisons there are within range of my artillery. I have issued instructions to my troops to afford complete protection to foreign nationals and all ethnic minorities. It should be the duty of all commanders to prevent useless shedding of innocent blood and I am therefore appealing to you once again to cooperate with me in discharging this humane responsibility.
>
> Should you, however, decide to continue to offer resistance, may I strongly urge that you ensure that all civilians and foreign nationals are removed to safe distance from the area of conflict. For the sake of your own men, I hope you will not compel me to reduce your garrison by the use of force.

On14, 15 and 16 December, events took place that were critical to the fall of Dhaka.

By the night of 14–15 December, the advance elements of the three corps of the Eastern Army and 101 Communication Zone, which had converged on the outskirts of Dhaka, were stopped from continuing their offensive operations. Poised as they were on the outskirts of the capital of East Pakistan, the formations were straining at the leash for their entry into the city, but their move forward was stopped by Headquarters

Eastern Command on orders from Army Headquarters, New Delhi. Entry by our troops into Dhaka would have resulted in bloody street fighting and would have resulted in heavy civilian casualties which the Government of India wanted to avoid. A unilateral ceasefire was ordered by the Indian Army Chief from 7 p.m. on 15 December to 9 a.m. on 16 December, to give the Pakistani military and political hierarchy time to make up their minds to surrender or continue the war.

The race for Dhaka was terminated just before India's offensive formations could cross the finish line!

In the meanwhile, in the Security Council of the UN, resolution after resolution backed by the Americans and their allies was being passed to order a ceasefire. But the Soviets were able to veto these resolutions till it became quite impossible for them to exercise their veto any longer, and they urged Delhi to wind up the war quickly.

On the evening of 14 December, it was learnt that the nuclear-powered aircraft carrier USS *Enterprise*, of the American Seventh Fleet, accompanied by a fleet of eleven warships consisting of a mix of destroyers, missile frigates, amphibious assault ships and a helicopter carrier, had crossed the Straits of Malacca on the night 13–14 December and were on their way to the Bay of Bengal. The fleet had been ordered by President Nixon to come to the rescue of Pakistan, his beleaguered ally.

On the morning of 14 December, while Rao Farman Ali and his advisers were still dithering on a possible response to General Manekshaw's call for surrender, the Army Chief walked from his office to Military Operations Directorate, known as 'the Cage', and swung into the office of Major Vijay Oberoi, the then GSO2 of the section dealing with East Pakistan.

This section had a direct 'hotline' with Headquarters Eastern Command, Calcutta.

Major Oberoi was surprised to see the Chief walk into his office, just like that! The Chief, however, in his own inimitable style, put Oberoi at ease and asked him to put him through to the Chief of Staff Eastern Command. Vijay picked up the phone, and there was an immediate response from the other end.

'Hi, Vijay,' said a voice from Eastern Command. 'What is it now?'

Vijay said, 'Can you please get General Jacob on the line? The Chief would like to speak with him.' There was a response from the officer which Vijay did not want the Chief to hear—but he did.

The Chief smiled and said, 'Give me the phone . . . Sam here, can I speak with the Chief of Staff immediately please?'

After a minute, the Chief of Staff Eastern Command was on the line. 'Jakes here, sir.'

'What is their response to my ultimatum?'

'Nothing yet.'

'Do you think a few artillery rounds in the vicinity of Abdullah's* headquarters would speed things up a bit?'

'Yes, I do. I was thinking of doing something on those lines myself.'

'Okay. Go ahead. Place a few rounds as close as possible to his headquarters and repeat the salvo every ten minutes. Let's hope they understand we mean business.'

'Wilco,† sir. Is that all? Anything else?'

---

* Abdullah: General A.A.K. Niazi, General Officer Commanding-in-Chief in command of all Pakistani forces in East Pakistan.

† 'Wilco' is army slang for 'will comply with your orders'.

'No. Just keep Inder* informed.'

Although the race for Dhaka was terminated on the city's outskirts by Army Headquarters, Major General Nagra, GOC, 101 Communication Zone, accompanied by Brigadier Kler, Commander, 95 Infantry Brigade, and Brigadier Sant Singh reached the area of Mirpur Bridge on the outskirts of Dhaka, being held by 2 Para which had been paradropped on the outskirts of Dhaka on 11 December. Nagra sent a message to Niazi through his ADC and two officers of 2 Para. The message read as follows:

> My dear Abdullah, I am here. The game is up. I suggest you give yourself up to me, and I will look after you.†

Nagra had been posted some years earlier as the Indian Military Attache to Pakistan and knew Niazi personally.

So, was there a race after all for the capture of Dhaka?

The answer is 'Yes'. GOC 4 Corps, by his statements and actions, certainly indicated that he wanted to be the first into Dhaka and used heliborne forces to reach there on 14 December. As 2 Corps was best placed to reach Dhaka early, it justified this expectation, helped perhaps by the fact that Jessore fell without a fight. Closest to Dhaka from the north was 101 Communication Zone. It aimed to reach Dhaka first but arrived on the same day as the other formations. It was, however, the first to enter Dhaka. Furthest away was 33 Corps, and it had the bulk of Pakistani opposition facing it. So there was no question

---

* Inder: Major General Inder Gill, Director, Military Operations, Army Headquarters.

† Major General Sukhwant Singh, *The Liberation of Bangladesh* (New Delhi: Vikas Publishing House Pvt Ltd, 1981), p. 213.

of its participating in any race. Yet it reached the outskirts of Dhaka around the same time as the others.

It must be remembered, however, that in addition to the race by the offensive formations to reach Dhaka first, the real race for Dhaka was a race against time!

It was imperative for the Indian Army to reach Dhaka soonest, so as to wrap up the war before the Americans, the Chinese or the United Nations could intervene. In this race against time, the Russians were extremely helpful. They exercised their power of the veto time and again in the UN, preventing the Americans, the Chinese and the Pakistanis, who were desperately trying to stop the war through their calls for a ceasefire. The veto by the Russians and the amazing speed with which the Indian armed forces wrapped up the war on the Eastern Front got India the time it critically needed to terminate the war on its own terms.

Although India's Eastern Army was euphoric about the speed with which the formations had reached the outskirts of Dhaka, there was an element of disappointment with the directive that prevented them from continuing the war. Commanders wanted to capture objectives in Dhaka that were well within their reach, but Delhi had decided to call a halt to further operations, and the formations had to fall in line.

The offensive formations of the Indian Army were stopped from entering the city, on orders from Delhi to prevent unnecessary bloodshed—but the threat of further fighting shook the Pakistani government in East Pakistan.

Dhaka trembled, toppled and fell.

By the time USS *Enterprise* and the rest of the American Seventh Fleet could reach the Bay of Bengal, East Pakistan had been liberated and Bangladesh was born.

The arrival of the Seventh Fleet in the Bay of Bengal triggered a response from the Soviets, who directed a taskforce which was already operating in the Indian Ocean to move towards the American Fleet, should it be required to do so. A nuclear-powered submarine was part of this force. Seeing that the situation in East Pakistan had gone beyond redemption, the Seventh Fleet hung around for a few days and returned from where it had come.

The world now sat up and took notice. They were taken aback by the speed with which the Indian armed forces had defeated an entrenched enemy. The world, including the United States of America and the United Kingdom, had no option but to express grudging admiration for the manner in which the war was conducted and wrapped up in record time.

The speed of operations and the winding up of the war by the Indian Army in East Pakistan in just thirteen days was compared by some Western authors to the blitzkrieg conducted by Germany over Western Europe during World War II. The part played by the IAF in knocking out the Pakistan Air Force in East Pakistan was a major contributary factor in this victory, because by destroying the PAF in East Pakistan during the early stages of the war, the Indian Army and Navy were able to carry out their operations without hindrance.

The Indian soldier came in for his share of praise for his conduct in the war. The Indian government's permission to allow foreign war correspondents to accompany our front-line troops in the offensives gave the world unbiased reportage on the war and the ethical way in which the war had been conducted by India.

It is worth listening to what Sydney Schanberg of the *New York Times* had to say about the conduct of the soldiers of the Indian Army: 12

> I don't like sitting around praising armies. I don't like armies because armies mean war – and I don't like wars. But this (the Indian Army) was something . . . They were great all the way. There was never a black mark . . . I lived with the officers and I walked, rode with the jawans – and they were all great. Sure, some of them were scared at first – they wouldn't be human if they weren't. But I never saw a man flinch because he was scared. There is a tremendous spirit (in the Indian Army) and it did one good to experience it . . . I have seen our boys in Viet Nam – and this army was different. Their (the Indian Army's) arms and equipment weren't as good – but what they had, they used with effect . . . and could they improvise! I saw recoilless guns carried on shoulders, big guns pushed across marshes like ox-carts by jawans, villagers, officers; everybody was in it together . . . And they were the most perfect gentlemen – I have never seen them do a wrong thing – not even when they saw how bestial the enemy had been.*

There were other reasons why the Pakistan Army in the east was defeated so decisively and quickly. As the *Sunday Telegraph* of 19 December put it, 'India won above all, because of a sense of vision, a carefully defined and maintained sense of purpose with which the leadership, inspired, by Mrs. Indira Gandhi had imbued the nation.'†

The 1971 war also revealed the competence of the leadership in the armed forces, and among them, Lieutenant General Sagat Singh proved to be one of the finest strategic and tactical Commanders that the war produced. His aggressiveness,

---

* *The Indian Army: A Brief History*, p. 157.

† Major General D.K. Palit, *The Lightning Campaign*, p. 16.

ability to quickly read the battle situation, propensity to take risks, belief in the competence of his subordinate Commanders and the soldiers gained for him the reputation of being a soldier's General. He was on the top of every battle situation that presented itself. He could read the mind of the enemy Commander and anticipate what he would do and take action, giving no respite to his opponent. He showed imagination and innovation in his heliborne operations in the capture of Sylhet and his crossing of the Meghna, by surprising the enemy and leaving him flat-footed.

Sagat was fortunate in having colleagues like Group Captain Chandan Singh and Battalion Commanders like Lieutenant Colonel Harolikar, who matched his energy, commitment and resolve. The guts, perseverance and determination of the helicopter pilots also played a big part in the success of these operations. A conversation with his Army Commander, General J.S. Aurora, with regard to the crossing of the Meghna, indicates General Sagat's firm resolve to let nothing stop him from being the first to reach Dhaka. He is reported to have said:

> 'Jaggi, I am a Corps Commander, I am expected to exploit an opportunity. If an opportunity presents itself to cross the Meghna, and gives you an aim plus, I will take it. I am giving you the West Bank and beyond; you should be happy.'*

---

* Conversation between Lieutenant General Sagat Singh, GOC, 4 Corps, and Lieutenant General Jagjit Singh Aurora, Army Commander, Eastern Command. From *A Talent for War: The Military Biography of Lieutenant General Sagat Singh* by Randhir Sinh (New Delhi, Vij Books, 2013), p. 81–3.

The 'race for Dhaka' can in some ways be compared to the 'race for Berlin' during World War II. In that war, it was a race between the Allied Forces—the British, the Americans and the Russians—to reach Berlin first. Berlin, too, was never captured. Berlin fell!

But there was a difference, and the difference was that the fall of Berlin was precipitated by a lot of street fighting. The Allies at the close of the war were racing forward for the conquest of territory and spheres of influence for their respective countries. India, however, was fighting for the liberation of East Pakistan and the creation of Bangladesh, and not for the conquest of territory. Fighting on the streets of Dhaka was to be avoided, to prevent unnecessary bloodshed and ensure that lives of the citizens of Dhaka were not jeopardized.

It also needs to be remembered that one of the causes of the success of Indian operations was the fact that it was faced with a rabble of officers and soldiers—as an enemy—not a disciplined army!

The wanton killings, rape of women and children, lack of respect for ethics and accepted rules for the conduct of war in East Pakistan by depraved soldiers of the Pakistan Army, led by its debauched officers, broke the bond of trust between their officers and men. Lack of self-respect of every individual of that army permeated right from General Niazi down to the last soldier. How could such an army fight? Yes, in some battles, the Pakistani soldiers, who were well led, did fight well, but overall, it was a debased, dissolute and immoral army that had lost the will to fight.

After the war, Sam Manekshaw, the Indian Army Chief, was asked to comment on the war. In his inimitable and humorous way, he said: 'Many years ago, before Independence and the

Partition of India, Yahya and I served together at Military Operations Branch, Army Headquarters, New Delhi. I had a motorbike which Yahya wanted. I gave it to him for Rs 1000. He said he would pay me later. He never did. However, nearly twenty-five years later, he paid me back with half his country!'

Postscript

1. The account of this story terminates here. The sequel, which elaborates on the final days of the war and the surrender by General Niazi and all Pakistani forces in East Pakistan, falls into the pages of the next story, 'The Last Straw'.
2. This narrative gives the reader some idea of how the war was conducted. I have deliberately not gone into detailed descriptions of the conduct of operations, as the reader would get bogged down with military detail. What has been described is the barest minimum. Those who are interested in specifics may refer to the bibliography, which gives a list of books by military authors from both India and Pakistan that offer detailed descriptions of the operations and also views from the 'other side of the hill'.

The Last Straw

'It was the last straw that broke the camel's back.'

—Proverb

Although the race for Dhaka was dramatic, there was more drama to follow. This time, it was the Indian Air Force and General J.F.R. Jacob who would hold centre stage during the final days of the war.

Whereas India was looking for the surrender of all Pakistani forces on the Eastern Front, Pakistan was doing its level best, both in the United Nations and through its diplomatic channels, to ensure a ceasefire and not a surrender.

Time was at a premium. The United States of America and her acolytes were pushing the UN for a closure of the war and for a ceasefire. However, there was not a single reference, either by the UN or in the many US motions, to the genocide perpetrated by Pakistan on the hapless citizens of its eastern wing or on the political aspirations of an independent Bangladesh, let alone the manner in which these could be fulfilled. The resolutions moved by France, UK and the non-permanent members of the Security Council conformed to the contents of the US motions.

The Russians were doing their best to exercise their veto to let the Indian Army conclude the war to its advantage, but they were also urging India to finish the war as quickly as possible, because they were running out of reasons to continue exercising their veto.

Meanwhile, a taskforce of the American Seventh Fleet from the Pacific was on its way to aid Pakistan—America's beleaguered ally. The American nuclear aircraft carrier, USS *Enterprise*, and its support ships had crossed the Straits of Malacca on the night of 13–14 December and would soon be entering the Bay of Bengal. The Indian Navy did not know what to make of it, and what would happen when the two navies faced each other in Indian territorial waters.

There was also concern at Army Headquarters New Delhi, as to the status of the towns and fortresses that had been bypassed by the Indian attacking formations. If it was going to be a ceasefire, then technically, those areas that had not been captured would be considered as islands of Pakistani territory, and that would cause major problems for India and Bangladesh. This made it all the more important to force the Government of East Pakistan to surrender. A ceasefire was just not acceptable.

Time was running out on all fronts, and something had to be done to ensure the capitulation of East Pakistan and the early surrender of all its forces.

In the course of the war, 14 December was an important day. It was the day when elements of the Indian Army formations were approaching the outskirts of Dhaka; it was the day when the Indian Army Chief gave time to the East Pakistani military and political hierarchy to surrender or accept the consequences; and it was the day that the Seventh Fleet of the United States Navy had entered the Bay of Bengal.

The USS *Enterprise* and ships of the Seventh Fleet.

It was also the day when something happened that would set in motion a series of events that would have far reaching effects on the closure of the war.

On the morning of 14 December 1971, the telephone operator at the Intercontinental Hotel in Dhaka answered an urgent call by a representative of the East Pakistan government. The caller asked for John Kelly, the representative of the UN High Commission for Refugees, who was taking sanctuary in the hotel, which now functioned as a Red Cross-designated neutral zone. The caller put Kelly through to Dr A.M. Malik, the Governor of East Pakistan. Malik asked Kelly and his colleague Peter Wheeler to visit him at Governor's House, to attend a meeting with his cabinet and tender advice. The invitation had also been extended to Sven Lampell, the representative of the International Committee of the Red Cross (ICRC).

These radio telephonic conversations were intercepted by an Indian Air Force wireless interception unit operating in unison with similar units of the Indian Army's Eastern Command. The conversations were encrypted, and on decoding it was learnt that the list of those who would also attend the meeting included the Martial Law Administrator and the Air Officer Commanding, Pakistan Air Force Dhaka, among others. Lieutenant Colonel

P.C. Bhalla, officer in charge of Signal Intelligence at Eastern Command Calcutta, brought the intercept to Major General Jacob at 0930 hours. General Jacob immediately phoned Air Vice Marshal Devasher, Senior Air Staff Officer at Eastern Air Command in Shillong. Both felt that a disruption of the meeting would help push the Governor to accept the call for surrender. Governor Malik was the highest decision-making person in East Pakistan and could take decisions on future courses of action to prolong or to terminate the war by insisting on a ceasefire or accepting a surrender. An airstrike on the Conference Room where the meeting was to be held would help to move the decision in India's favour, by paralysing the decision-making process.

The communication from the office of the Governor indicated that the meeting would be held at the conference room of Governor's House. The message not only indicated the room but also the time. The scheduled time for the meeting was twelve o'clock on the afternoon of 14 December 1971.

It was concluded by the Indian high command that if Indian fighter aircraft could target the conference room with a few rockets, a few minutes before the scheduled time of the conference, it would push the cabinet of the Governor of East Pakistan to decide that surrender was a preferable option, as their very lives were at stake. A ceasefire was of no use to a dead Governor and dead members of the cabinet. Fear was the key to this plan!

Air Headquarters instructed Eastern Air Command barely an hour before the meeting was to take place, to take immediate action. Eastern Air Command quickly sent orders out to its squadrons at Guwahati and Hashimara for an airstrike.

Time was running out and the minutes went ticking by—pilots had to be briefed, aircraft fuelled and armed, and then pilots had to fly all the way to Dhaka, which was nearly twenty minutes' flying time away. The window of opportunity was small and was getting smaller by the minute.

Group Captain Wollen at Guwahati was told that the meeting would take place at the Circuit House. The pilots at Guwahati were not familiar with individual buildings in Dhaka. How would the pilots know which was the Circuit House in the mass of buildings in an extremely populous town? And how could they know the exact location of the room where the meeting was to be held? A frantic search for a map was initiated, but all that could be found was a Burma Shell tourist map of Dhaka, which gave the pilots some very basic information.

Wollen rushed to the Operations Room to find Wing Commander B.K. Bishnoi and a group of pilots, who had just returned from a close support mission, having a cup of tea. He quickly briefed them on the mission and the need to hit the target by 11.20 a.m. Indian Standard Time and 11.50 East Pakistan Time. The time was 10.55 a.m. IST. Bishnoi was sceptical. Flying time to Dhaka was a little more than twenty minutes, and he had no clue where the Circuit House was. Briefing Bishnoi from the Burma Shell tourist map, Wollen indicated the Circuit House, which was located north of the Race Course in a densely populated area.

The strike would be led by Bishnoi with Flight Lieutenant Chandrashekar as his wingman. Flight Lieutenant G. Bala and Flight Lieutenant Hemu Sardesai would follow. All four MiG-21s were armed with rockets. Bishnoi and Chandrashekar ran towards their fighter aircraft, which had already been refuelled and rearmed in accordance with standing orders and battle drills. Bishnoi tucked the map in his side pocket. They had barely strapped in and started their engines when Bishnoi noticed an officer from his squadron running towards his aircraft waving a piece of paper, which was handed over to him.

Bishnoi looked at the paper. On it were a few hastily scribbled words: 'NOT CIRCUIT HOUSE—GOVERNOR'S HOUSE!' Bishnoi acknowledged the message, but it was too late to inform the other three pilots. Bishnoi decided to maintain radio silence for fear of his communication being intercepted. He decided to fly to Dhaka, read the map en route and locate the Governor's House once he was over Dhaka.

Equipped with this scanty information, Bishnoi and his wingman took off for Dhaka on their critical mission, followed by Bala and Sardesai.

Meanwhile, 150 miles to the west, at Hashimara, Wing Commander S.K. Kaul was similarly briefed for the same mission. However, he was correctly informed that the target was Governor's House. No one knew the location of Governor's House, but here too a Burma Shell tourist map was produced. Kaul and his wingman, Flying Officer Harish Masand, would go in with only front guns. Another pair of aircraft, armed with T-10 rockets and flown by Squadron Leader A.A. Bose, with Flight Lieutenant K.B. Menon as wingman, would follow. Wing Commander Kaul's first question was: 'Where is Governor's House?' As in the case of Bishnoi, the only available map was the Burma Shell tourist map! This is what Kaul said:

> It was a one-inch map. I couldn't make head or tail of it. It showed a cluster of buildings. From where it was produced or how it came there, how it was found in the underground operations room of Hashimara, which had no town or anything, is a mystery! It was a road map of Burmah Shell of Dacca town, which you can buy from a railway station.

> How it appeared there I don't know, don't ask me. But it was there!

Meanwhile, Bishnoi, who had taken off first, took the map out of his pocket and looked at it again when he was a few minutes away from the capital. As he and his wingman pulled up over Dhaka, he radioed Chandrashekar, Bala and Sardesai that the target was Governor's House and not the Circuit House. Sardesai acknowledged the change in target and said that he could see Governor's House. It was the only prominent building close to the Dhaka railway station: a magnificent old building, in a lush green compound, similar to the Raj Bhavans found in India; and that the house and the surrounding lawns and gardens stood out starkly against the sprawl of shops and houses around it. Governor's House was located close to the Dhaka cricket stadium, which was a prominent landmark.

Down below on the ground, it was nearing midday at Governor's House. The pilots could see a few cars parked outside the house belonging probably to the Governor and officials of the East Pakistani government. The Governor, A.M. Malik, John Kelly, the UN representative, and his colleague Peter Wheeler had already arrived ahead of the others. Malik took Kelly and Wheeler to a room adjoining the conference room to ask about the situation. Dr Malik, frightened, asked Kelly, 'Should we give up now, do you think?' Kelly did not want to commit on behalf of the United Nations and hedged. However, Kelly warned him that he and his cabinet would be in grave danger when the war was brought to a close, and that it would be safer for him, his officials and his family to seek refuge at the Intercontinental Hotel, the designated neutral zone.

While they were talking, Bishnoi and his wingman in their MiG-21s had arrived over the target area. Bishnoi noticed the dome of Governor's House and reasoned that the conference room would be the largest room in the building and that it would be immediately below the dome. He accordingly briefed his wingman, and the aircraft that were following, as to what he was going to do and specified the room as the target. In the first pass, Bishnoi and his wingman each fired a salvo of sixteen rockets and went around and fired their remaining rockets in the second pass. Inside the building there was pandemonium. Kelly exited the building. This is what he says in his book *Three Days in Dacca 1971*:

> During the first part of the attack, Muzzaffar Hussain, then Chief Secretary, emerged looking very pale and we exchanged salutations. As the strike continued, I ran to a trench twenty yards away which was already full of soldiers and lay on top of them. General Rao Farman Ali ran past, also looking for shelter, and said to me as he passed, 'Why are the Indians doing this to us?' Under the circumstances it did not seem a suitable occasion to engage in a discussion and I let General Farman carry on to find his own shelter. The sound of the attacks was deafening. All this time I kept a running commentary of the attack over the walkie-talkie to Paul Mark-Henri at the UN location.*

Bishnoi and his wingman, Chandrashekar, had fired 128 rockets into Governor's House. After they finished, the

* John Kelly, *Three Days in Dacca 1971*, Bangladesh Documents, 8 March 1972, pp. 649–55; and P.V.S. Jagan Mohan and Samir Chopra, *Eagles over Bangladesh* (Noida: HarperCollins, 2013), pp. 326–36.

MiG-21s attacking Governor's House.

building was covered with smoke. As soon as they exited and pulled out, Bala and Sardesai entered the arena in their MiG-21s and made four passes, firing four rockets each from their pods. Their multiple passes attracted some feeble ground fire. As the pilots exited from the area, Sardesai noticed that the Intercontinental Hotel rooftops were teeming with onlookers, resembling spectators watching a cricket match. In fact, the thundering crescendo of the jets had residents hanging out of their windows to view the spectacle of fighter aircraft flying well below the tops of their buildings in a drama they thought they would never witness again. Little did they realize that there was more to follow.

In the meanwhile, Sven Lampell, the ICRC representative, arrived at Governor's House. He was late for the meeting and was approaching Governor's House when the air attack started. He stopped his car to watch the raid and entered after the 'All Clear'. His account of what he saw is worth noting. He said:

> Nobody was guarding the main entrance. We walked in without any hindrance and entered the room where the Governor was sitting along with his cabinet colleagues. These were the people who were once radiant in their pride and authority, and who pulled all sorts of bureaucratic strings to interfere in our day-to-day activities. It was hard to believe that these people were the same breed as the poor and miserable ones we were trying to help. The men sitting around the table looked pale, exhausted, broken and uncertain. They had not heard anything from President Yahya after their last message about a possible negotiation. They could not wait anymore; they wanted to take refuge in a 'neutral zone'. Their lives were in our hands. Fate was indeed having the last laugh. I felt like an actor standing on the stage of a Greek tragedy.*

The council room of Governor's House was a mess, and every window of the building had been shattered. Kelly and his colleague returned to their UN office and briefed Marc-Henri about what had happened. Gavin Young, the *London Observer* correspondent, suggested that he and Kelly return to Governor's House to review the situation. Gavin felt that if the aircraft planned to return, they would take time to get to base, refuel,

* P.V.S. Jagan Mohan and Samir Chopra, *Eagles over Bangladesh*, pp. 333–34.

re-arm and return, and so it would be safe for another hour or so to be in the vicinity of Governor's House. They got into a jeep and drove to Governor's House.

By the time Kelly and Gavin Young arrived at Governor's House, which was still smoking from the air attack, the Governor and his staff had moved into a bunker on the building's grounds. When the bunker was being made, the Governor had felt that there would never be a need for him to take shelter there. He now realized how wrong he was. Kelly resumed the conversation with the Governor that had been interrupted by the air attack. Malik was still undecided about resigning. Kelly once again reminded him about the danger that they were in when their discussion was once again interrupted by the clatter of yet another raid by the IAF.

Kelly found himself once again running for cover. This time it was Kaul and Masand in their Hunters. Wing Commander Kaul and Flying Officer Harish Masand pulled up before their target. They did an improvised glide from 6000 feet, located Governor's House, which was still smoking, and attacked it. There was plenty of anti-aircraft fire from guns that had awoken to the fact that the city was being attacked by the Indian Air Force, but their fire was ineffectual. Kaul and Masand used their front guns and were able to assess the damage they were causing to the building more clearly than they would have been able to if they had been using rockets. After a couple of passes, both the Hunters exited the target area, flying past the Dhaka Intercontinental Hotel, where Masand also noticed that a huge crowd of spectators had gathered on the terrace and were watching the attacks with great interest.

Kaul and Masand were followed by Squadron Leader A.A. Bose and Flight Lieutenant K.B. Menon. Menon, during his interview with P.V.S. Jagan Mohan, said that there was heavy anti-aircraft fire and the sky was covered by black puffs. Based on the information radioed to them by Kaul and Masand, they easily identified Governor's House, and they too attacked the target. After expending their rockets, the duo headed home.

The Hunter attacks were the last straw for Governor Malik. Gavin Young sent out a story that was broadcast around the world. This is what it said:

> The jets made a shattering row. The ground crashed and heaved outside. 'We are refugees now, too,' choked Mr. Malik. There seemed nothing to say to that. Kelly looked at me, silently saying 'What led me to come back here?' Then Malik produced a shaking pen and a sheet of office paper. The ministers mumbled, held on together. Between one crash and the next, Kelly and I looked at the paper and saw that it was addressed to President Yahya Khan and that Malik had at last resigned. Then, the raid still seething round us, Malik, a devout Muslim, took off his shoes and socks, carefully washed his feet in a small washroom opening into the bunker, spread a white handkerchief over his head, and knelt down in a corner of the bunker and said his prayers. That was the end of Governor's House. That was the end of the last Government—of East Pakistan.*

* Ibid., p. 336.

Soon after, Malik and his colleagues fled to the Intercontinental Hotel. They had had enough. The IAF attack was an act of intimidation that struck a visible blow to East Pakistan's civil government—a government that was a willing partner to the genocide perpetrated by the army of West Pakistan. That regime had now been rendered a toothless shadow of its former self and had packed up like a house of cards.

India's former Foreign Secretary, J.N. Dixit, has this to say about this incident in his book *Liberation and Beyond*:

> Indian Air Force jets carried out a precision rocket attack on this room a few minutes before the meeting was due to begin. No other part of the building was damaged. I saw this room after the surrender on December 16. The rockets hit and extensively damaged only this room and its conference table. My Bangladeshi friends told me later that this air operation specially unnerved the East Pakistani rulers and perhaps hastened a quick response to the call for unconditional surrender.*

The army of East Pakistan was, however, still holding out against the demand for surrender. It had about 30,000 troops within the city of Dhaka and could easily hold out for at least another week. But it would be a bloody battle of fighting in the streets of Dhaka, which was something that the Indian government wished to avoid because in such a scenario, civil casualties would have been high.

* J.N. Dixit, *Liberation and Beyond* (Delhi: Konark Publishers Pvt Ltd, 1999), p. 101.

In the meantime, a signal had been received from General Yahya Khan addressed to Malik and General Niazi. The signal noted that 'they had fought heroic battles against overwhelming odds' but had 'reached a stage where further resistance is no longer humanly possible nor serves any useful purpose'. Accordingly, Yahya Khan urged Niazi and Malik 'to take necessary steps to stop the fighting and preserve the lives of all personnel'. The signal made no mention whether cessation of hostilities would be through a ceasefire or a surrender!

This was the option that Niazi was hoping for. He wanted space to negotiate for a ceasefire, and a withdrawal and safe passage of Pakistani forces and civilians under the auspices of the UN. On the evening of 14 December, he, along with Major General Rao Farman Ali, went to the office of the US Consul General in Dhaka to meet Herbert Spivak, the Consul General. Niazi requested Spivak to negotiate the terms for a ceasefire with the Indian forces. Both Niazi and Farman Ali avoided the term 'surrender'. Spivak told Niazi that he could only assist in passing his message and that he had no authority to negotiate on his behalf.

Niazi and Farman Ali drafted a message to the Indian Army Chief, Sam Manekshaw, calling for a ceasefire. Spivak, instead of sending the message to the American embassy in New Delhi, sent it to Washington, thereby causing a delay of a day. Insistence of a ceasefire by Niazi instead of a surrender was an invitation for more air attacks on Pakistan Army installations in and around Dhaka.

Late on the afternoon of 15 December, Niazi received a response to the request for a ceasefire through a broadcast on All India Radio by General Manekshaw. He had received Niazi's request to end the fighting at 2.30 p.m. from the American embassy. In the broadcast, Manekshaw reiterated that it had to be a surrender and not a ceasefire, and that he would ensure the safety of those who laid down their arms. He declared that the Indian Army and Air Force would cease operations from 5 p.m. to 9 a.m. the next day, to allow them time to decide on his ultimatum, and gave the radio frequencies to be used by Pakistani Eastern Command to contact him.

Notwithstanding the demand by General Manekshaw for a surrender and Governor Malik's acceptance of surrender, Niazi was still insisting on a ceasefire and not a surrender. A few minutes before the ceasefire was to expire at 9 a.m. on 16 December, a message was received from Pakistan Army HQ for an extension of the ceasefire and for an officer to be sent from Delhi to Dhaka to finalize the laying down of arms.

At 9.15 a.m., General Manekshaw called the Indian Army's Eastern Command HQ at Fort William and instructed General Jacob, the Chief of Staff, to fly out to Dhaka and meet General Niazi to finalize the terms of surrender. General Manekshaw instructed Eastern Command to ensure that the surrender took place the same day in the afternoon. A draft 'Instrument of Surrender' had been prepared; General Jacob was to fly to Dhaka in an IAF helicopter along with this draft.

General Jacob, Air Commodore Purushotam from Advance Air Headquarters Eastern Air Command, and Colonel M.S. Khara of the Intelligence Corps left in a Chetak helicopter. The team changed helicopters at Jessore and took off again for Dhaka.

The city of Dhaka was in a volatile state and close to chaos. No Indian troops had been allowed to enter the city on orders from Delhi and Calcutta—although now the presence of Indian troops was necessary. It had been reasoned earlier that if the troops entered the city, fighting might break out again. No one knew what had been decided—ceasefire or surrender. Anything could happen if the combatants faced each other again within the city. Niazi was still holding out. In this state of confusion, the Mukti Bahini had entered the city. Prominent among them was 'Tiger Siddiqui', with about 20,000 of his troops all thirsting for revenge.

General Jacob's helicopter was tracked by Pakistani anti-aircraft guns till it landed. On landing, Jacob was met by his East Pakistani counterpart, Brigadier Baqar Siddiqui. Also present was the UN representative at Dhaka, who offered his good offices to negotiate with the Pakistanis, but General Jacob had no intention of involving the United Nations, as he could see no role for them in the current situation. The foreign press corps was also present. On the way to Niazi's headquarters, Jacob's jeep was stopped by the Mukti Bahini. General Jacob and his team were unarmed. About that day, he said:

> They were in a very belligerent mood and ready to go on the rampage. Representatives of the international press were with them. I explained to them that the war was over and the surrender of the Pakistani Army would take place on the Race Course. They started shouting and wanted to take over the Pakistan Eastern Command Headquarters and to mete out retribution to Niazi and his staff. Heated words were exchanged. I made it clear that there would have to be a bloodless transfer of power to the Bangladesh government whose members would be arriving in Dacca shortly to take over charge. I asked the Mukti Bahini to ensure that law and order was maintained and that there were no reprisals. Since there was a ceasefire in force and

> the Pakistani High Command had agreed to surrender, the provisions of the Geneva Conventions would have to be respected. They shouted slogans and threatened to act unilaterally. I told them that we would ensure that the provisions of the Geneva Conventions would be honoured. The foreign press reported instead that I had threatened to shoot them. They then let us pass and we reached the Headquarters at 1500 hrs.*

General Jacob was received by General Niazi in his office. Along with him were Major General Rao Farman Ali, Major General Jamshed, Rear Admiral Sharif, the Naval Chief, Air Commodore Imam, the Air Force Commander and Brigadier Baqar Siddiqui. Major General G.C. Nagra, General Officer Commanding 101 Communication Zone of the Indian Army, was also there. He was closer to the capital than the other formations which had been stopped on the outskirts of the city. A day after the temporary ceasefire came into effect, Nagra had contacted one of the Pakistani outposts and sent a message to Niazi saying: 'My dear Abdullah. I am here. The game is up. I suggest you give yourself up to me and I will look after you.' Niazi, who was expecting General Jacob, was at a loss as to what to make of it; he was not aware if Nagra had any role in the surrender negotiations.

Nagra had no orders to enter Dhaka and had acted on his own. It was, however, fortunate that he was in Dhaka, as there were no Indian troops in the city at that time and fighting was going on between the Pakistan Army and the Mukti Bahini. Jacob called Nagra outside and told him to move sufficient

---

* Ibid, p. 140.

troops into Dhaka in order to establish law and order, and to be prepared to organize the surrender ceremony. He explained to Nagra that it would have to be a public surrender in full view of the people of Dhaka who had suffered so terribly at the hands of the Pakistan Army. He was also told to organize a guard of honour by the Parachute Regiment, who had by this time started trickling into Dhaka, and also by a Pakistani unit. The world over, surrender ceremonies after a war are organized with due time for preparation—but on this occasion the situation was fluid, resources were scant and only a few hours given to organize the surrender and a guard of honour. Nagra was told to have a table and two chairs for the signing of the surrender document. He was also told to ensure the protection of the Intercontinental Hotel, where the United Nations personnel, the Red Cross, members of the East Pakistan government and foreign residents had taken shelter; to leave a small escort and a radio detachment to permit him to carry out his functions; and to receive the Army Commander, who was flying in from Calcutta.

General Jacob then returned to Niazi's office and informed him that sporadic fighting was still taking place and that he should issue instructions to his troops to cease fighting.

It is best to report what followed in the words of General Jacob. In his book *An Odyssey in War and Peace*, he says:

> I re-entered the building. The draft Instrument of Surrender was read out. Niazi, with tears rolling down his cheeks, said: 'Who said I'm surrendering? You have only come to discuss a ceasefire and withdrawal as proposed by me.' The Service Chiefs present also voiced their objections. Rao Farman Ali objected surrendering to a 'Joint Command'. Time was running out so

I called Niazi aside. I told him that if he did not surrender, I could not take the responsibility for their families and ethnic minorities but if he did, I would ensure their protection. I asked him to reconsider, again reminding him that if he did not surrender, I would not be responsible for the safety of their families. I then added that I would give him 30 minutes to reconsider and if he did not, I would order resumption of hostilities and the bombing of Dacca. I then walked out to be met by the press. I was extremely worried. Niazi had 26,400 troops in Dacca. We had about 3,000 some 30 miles out. I was in a quandary as to what to do in the event of his refusing. Aurora and his entourage were to land in an hour or two and the ceasefire was to expire shortly. I had nothing in hand. The Pakistan Commission of Enquiry report later stated, 'there was General Jacob pacing outside calmly puffing his pipe'. Far from it. I was extremely worried and tense. I spoke to the Pakistani sentry and asked him about his family. He burst into tears saying that I as an Indian Officer was speaking to him while his own officers did not. After 30 minutes I walked in to be met with a deathly silence, my draft surrender document was lying on the table. I asked Niazi if he accepted this document, to which he did not reply. I repeated the enquiry thrice. He still did not respond. I then held up the document, holding it high, and said 'I take it as accepted'. Tears rolled down Niazi's cheeks, and there were glares from those present. I then called Niazi aside and then told him that I had arranged for the signing to take place at the Race Course in public. He objected strongly. I then told him that he would have to surrender his sword. He said that he did not have a sword but he would surrender his revolver. I then told him he would have to provide a guard of honour . . . Niazi said there was no one to command it.

> I pointed to his ADC and said that he should command it. I permitted them to retain their weapons for their protection until such time as we could disarm them.*

At around 1500 hours, Jacob asked Niazi to accompany him to the airport. Since Nagra had not left a jeep for Jacob, he went in Niazi's staff car, with his pilot jeep leading the way. Niazi's car was like a red rag to a bull. The Mukti Bahini tried to prevent the car from moving forward. Some of them threw themselves on to the bonnet of the car. It was fortunate that Colonel Khara, a Sikh, was also in the car. He stuck his head out to indicate that they were Indians, that Niazi was a prisoner and that they should not impede them in bringing the surrender to its logical conclusion. The cavalcade reached the airport with great difficulty. En route, they came across a jeep with two Indian paratroopers who appeared to be lost. This was a stroke of luck, as Jacob now had at least two Indian soldiers to give them protection. Other than the two paratroopers, there were no Indian troops in sight.

General Jacob told Colonel Khara to get hold of some Indian troops and, if possible, some tanks. Jacob knew that 4 Corps was trying to swim some tanks across the Meghna on the evening of 15 December. Khara went off to see what he could find while he sat with Niazi in his staff car. Jacob and Niazi were now alone except for the two Indian paratroopers. At this precarious moment, a truck arrived at the other side of the runway with armed Mukti Bahini soldiers. General Jacob describes the situation as under:

---

* Lt Gen. J.F.R. Jacob, *An Odyssey in War and Peace* (New Delhi: Roli Books, Lotus Collection, 2011), pp. 124–25.

> A man wearing our olive-green uniform, wearing the badges of rank of a Major General, approached us followed by two armed men. I placed the man as 'Tiger' Siddiqui, and sensed trouble . . . I felt they had come to kill Niazi. I had to ensure that Niazi lived to sign the Instrument of Surrender and asked the two paratroopers to protect Niazi. I walked towards Siddiqui. I told the two paratroopers to cover Niazi and to point their rifles at Siddiqui. I politely asked Siddiqui to leave the airfield. He did not respond. I repeated this request. He still did not respond. I then shouted to him, to get the truckload of fighters off the airfield and heaved a sigh of relief when they finally left.*

A little while later, Khara returned with a PT-76.† General Aurora and his entourage, which included Lieutenant General Sagat Singh and Vice Admiral Krishnan, arrived in a fleet of five Mi-4 and four Alloutte helicopters at 1630 hours. Generals Jacob and Niazi received them, and they all proceeded to the Race Course ground for the surrender ceremony. After General Aurora and General Niazi inspected the combined guard of honour, they proceeded to the table that had been placed for the signing ceremony. The surrender documents that had been brought with General Aurora were placed before them. Niazi glanced at them curiously and signed, followed by General Aurora. Niazi then undid his epaulette and removed his .38 revolver with attached lanyard and handed it over to General Aurora. There were tears in his eyes. By this time it had got dark, and the crowd at the Race Course started shouting anti-Niazi and anti- Pakistan

---

* Ibid., p. 125.

† PT-76 is a light tank.

slogans and abuses. General Jacob was concerned about Niazi's safety, so the senior officers of the Indian armed forces formed a cordon around Niazi and escorted him to the Indian Army jeep. General Jacob then briefed General Sagat Singh regarding the disarming of all Pakistani soldiers, the maintenance of law and order and the movement of prisoners of war to India.

As the war was proceeding inexorably towards the defeat of the Pakistan Army in East Pakistan, the Security Council met on 16 December. Zulfikar Ali Bhutto, who was leading the Pakistan delegation, was strong in his condemnation of India. However, Sardar Swaran Singh sometime during the debate was able to inform the Security Council that Pakistani forces in East Pakistan had surrendered and that India had declared a unilateral ceasefire on the Western Front, to commence from 8 p.m., 17 December. Zulfikar Ali Bhutto, who was sitting three to four yards away from Sardar Swaran Singh, was infuriated. He tore up the Council documents, accused India of violence and aggression, stated that the Security Council could not play any useful role in the vital interest of member countries, and stormed out of the meeting. His tantrums did not help the Pakistani cause in any way; in fact, it reduced whatever little sympathy members of the Council had for that renegade country. The announcement of Pakistan's surrender, however, brought to an end any further resolutions demanding a ceasefire.

There are many factors that forced Niazi and the High Command in East Pakistan to finally accept that they had no option but to surrender. First was the realization that Niazi's strategy of fortresses to defend East Pakistan had failed. Second was the fact that the Indian Army had enveloped Dhaka from all dimensions—land, sea and air. The Indian Army had encircled Dhaka; the Indian Air Force were dominating the skies and were pulverizing the city; and the Indian Navy had blocked the escape route via the sea. The paradrop in Tangail, on the outskirts of Dhaka, only served to enhance their feeling of isolation. Third, was the fact that neither the Americans not the Chinese had come to Niazi's aid as promised, and that even his Army Chief and President had failed to come to his rescue. Last, but not least, was the fact that if Niazi failed to surrender, he, his staff and the remnants of his forces would be destroyed by the Indian Army or, worse still, left to the mercy of the Mukti Bahini and the citizens of Bangladesh.

The ceremony at the Race Course had an unreal finality about it. This was the end of a war that had brought so much agony to a people who suffered only because they had exercised their democratic rights for better self-governance. The 1971 war in the east had come to an end, but the raucous crowds could not believe that their oppressors had finally been given the boot. The perpetrators were there in front of them, and nothing would please them better than to deliver to them the same treatment that they had suffered for so many months at their hands. What they could not understand was why the Indian armed forces, who had intervened to save them, were now protecting these war criminals. They would realize only later that had they been allowed to lynch these Pakistani marauders, their action would stain forever the birth of 'Sonar Bangla'. But they found it difficult to believe that they were finally free from these accursed oppressors, and that from now onwards they had the opportunity to have a new beginning and start a new life.

The Pakistani officers and soldiers were escorted away by soldiers of the Indian Army, who by this time had arrived in sufficient numbers. The Pakistanis must have felt a sense of shame that they were led away like cattle by the very soldiers that they had been trying so desperately to kill. However, they must have also felt a sense of relief that these very soldiers were now all that stood between them and the crowds who were baying for their blood.

The picture of the surrender has made history and hangs on a wall of the library of the United Service Institution, New Delhi, along with a copy of the surrender document. On another wall is displayed the huge map on which General Jacob had planned his operations. The map extends from ceiling to floor, and on it are marked the Pakistani and Indian formations, with arrows depicting the thrust lines of the advancing formations of the Indian Army and the locations of units of both sides. When I saw the map for the first time, and the symbols depicting our formations, I looked for Sylhet, where I had fought, and wondered whether future generations would ever understand what those symbols on that map mean, or know the meaning of war or comprehend the agony of death and destruction which is what war is all about. Many of my comrades in arms had died on the battlefields spread across that map. Only those who have lived with death will understand the value and meaning of life. The final ecstasy of victory was robbed by the tragedy of the ultimate sacrifice made by thousands of brave Indian soldiers and their courageous officers. The epitaph at the Kohima War Memorial conveys this sentiment aptly. It says, 'When you go back, tell them of us and say, for your tomorrow, we gave our today.'

Looking back, one cannot but help recall that the surrender that symbolized that victory was facilitated by two events. First, the attack on Governor's House on 14 December by Indian Air Force pilots who, at a moment's notice and an extremely short window of space and time, forced the collapse of the civil government of East Pakistan. Second, the ability of General Jacob, who entered a volatile city of Dhaka armed only with a draft surrender document, and used psychological pressure to force a stubborn and recalcitrant Niazi to understand that he was in an extremely dangerous situation and had no option but to surrender, rather than be held responsible for the defeat and destruction of his troops and himself. As General Jacob said: 'It was a very close thing.'

It was in fact these last two events that constituted the 'last straw' that finally broke the back of the civil and military government of East Pakistan. The rest is history.

Postscript

In all wars and in every battle, there comes a moment when the situation can go either way. It devolves on a Commander to grasp an opportunity to tilt the balance in his favour. In the case of the fall of the civil government of East Pakistan in Dhaka, the opportunity was the intercepted signal that gave away the location and time of the meeting at Governor's House. Although the time available was minimal, Indian military leaders exploited the opportunity; the air force accepted the challenge, and targeted the conference room. This was enough to intimidate the Governor and his colleagues to call for an unconditional surrender.

In the case of the military, it was the intuition of Major General Jacob, his understanding of the mental make-up of Niazi, Rao Farman Ali and the other military leaders that confronted him—to make Niazi and the military hierarchy understand that they had no option but to give up. Please see

'Hunt for the *Vikrant*' in this book, to understand why a study of your opponent in any field of endeavour is critically important.

Both these actions used psychology as a weapon of war to unnerve the opposition and to force them to surrender. It was this last straw that enforced a surrender and ensured the avoidance of a bloody finale to the war.

Afterword

'If you must play, decide three things at the start: the rules of the game, the stakes and the quitting time.'

—Proverb

Through the stories in this book, I have attempted to give the reader some understanding of what happened on the ground, in the air and at sea during the Indo–Pak war of 1971. India's strategy and conduct of the war was exceptional. At the highest level, the synergy between the armed forces, the politicians and bureaucrats outshone past record, thereby ensuring a strategy that fully met India's political and military aims.

In the east, Pakistan's strategy of strong defences on river obstacles fortified by dense minefields was based on the outworn belief that the Indian Army would assault these well-fortified defences and get bogged down in a war of attrition, giving the United States of America, China and the countries of the Middle East time to come to Pakistan's aid.

Indian tacticians saw through Pakistan's intention and countered her plan by bypassing these defences and thrusting through the gaps. The Pakistan Army was outwitted and outmanoeuvred—and it collapsed. The war was won by India in a span of just thirteen days.

This victory was a result of meticulous planning and hard training. During the conduct of the war, word went out to the troops that the war needed to be wrapped up before the Americans and the Chinese could intervene. The troops improvised and innovated to move speedily over marshy ground and river obstacles. Jugaad was the order of the day, and RCL guns and mortars were moved on bullock carts and cycle rickshaws, and rivers were crossed on improvised rafts made from bamboo and trunks of banana trees.

In the north, west and south, the strategy was 'offensive defence', and we did pretty well with large areas captured in the northern areas of Ladakh, Jammu and Kashmir and the Rajasthan–Sind deserts. In the Punjab there was some amount of 'give and take', but overall we had the upper hand.

Every individual in uniform rallied to the call for speed in operations and more importantly, their vigour was accompanied by ethical behaviour. War correspondents had converged on to the war zone from most of the Western countries, and the decision by the Indian government to allow foreign war correspondents to accompany the troops was a good one. In consequence, the world got unbiased reportage on the war and grudgingly accepted that the Indian Army had been and was ethical in its fighting on ground, in the air and at sea.

Before the start of the war, Sam Manekshaw, the Army Chief, made it quite clear that the excesses of war would not be tolerated. After the war, even though the atrocities perpetrated by the Pakistan Army exceeded imagination, the Indian Army went beyond the Geneva Conventions to ensure that the 93,000 Pakistani prisoners were treated fairly. Indian troops were made to vacate their barracks and moved into tents so that the Pakistani prisoners were suitably housed.

In remembering the successes of the 1971 war, we need to remember the sacrifice by the servicemen and citizens of both Bangladesh and India. In this war, 3843 Indian servicemen were killed and 9851 wounded*—some of them disabled for life. Lights in the homes of the dead and disabled went out when reports about their loved ones reached them through that dreaded telegram that starts with the words, 'Regret to inform you that . . .', creating sadness beyond words.

The war concluded with the liberation of East Pakistan and the birth of Bangladesh. It also resulted in the dismemberment of Pakistan, with the loss of its eastern wing and the capture of 93,000 Pakistani prisoners of war—the largest number since World War II!

Reacting to pressure from her own people who were demanding an explanation for this abysmal defeat, Pakistan went through the motion of instituting a Commission of Inquiry to find out what had happened and why. The Hamoodur Commission, among its other findings, revealed and condemned the atrocities committed by the Pakistan Army, but they had to withdraw this report on orders from the military junta and to replace it with a watered-down version that displayed a dramatic disregard of what really happened. As a result, unlike the Nuremburg trials after World War II, no Pakistani person—military or civil—was taken to the International Court of Justice and punished for the war crimes they had committed.

As a matter of reflection, one wonders what would have happened had Prime Minister Indira Gandhi delayed the

* War Book in the Library of the United Service Institution, New Delhi.

ceasefire in the west for a couple of more days. The psychological pressure on Pakistan would have been colossal. Pakistan had her back to the wall, and even they must have wondered why we left them off the hook!

Unfortunately, the Army Chief General Manekshaw had no say in the negotiations at Shimla, where critical decisions were to be taken. What was won by the military on the battlefield was lost by politicians and bureaucrats at the negotiating table. The synergy—between the armed forces, politicians and bureaucrats—which had helped us win the war evaporated soon after the war, and the politicians and bureaucrat reverted to type by excluding the military from the negotiating table—a development that is unheard of in any country after any war. The result is there for all to see. We had the upper hand with 93,000 prisoners of war with us, and the Pakistani people were ranting for their return. We failed to use this opportunity to solve outstanding issues. Not only that, we failed to even ensure the return of fifty-four Indian service personnel who are still languishing today in Pakistani jails, if not already tortured to death.

General Jacob, in his book *Surrender at Dacca: Birth of a Nation*, has this to say about the Shimla Conference: 'It has been reported that Bhutto had agreed that the Cease Fire Line or the Line of Control be the basis for delimitation of the international boundary, but insisted that this not be committed to writing for it would jeopardise his political future. In this context, it may be appropriate to recall a famous Sam Goldwynism: "A verbal contract is not worth the paper it is written on."'

It has been fifty years since that outstanding victory. The question is, have we learnt the lessons of history? Are the armed forces well equipped to fight a two-front war against China and Pakistan? These are questions that need to be asked and answered as war clouds once again gather on our borders.

—Ian Cardozo

'When you go back, tell them of us and say,
For your tomorrow, we gave our today.'
—Epitaph to the war dead at the
Kohima War Cemetery

Acknowledgements

There are many reasons why the 1971 Indo–Pak war resulted in one of the quickest victories in modern military history. One of them being that the victory happened because the synergy between the armed forces, politicians and bureaucrats was perfect. The Service Chiefs thereafter provided the leadership, and the soldiers, sailors and airmen did the rest. This needs to be acknowledged.

In recognition of the principle of cooperation, I take this opportunity to thank all those who have helped me to bring to life stories of events that took place half a century ago.

Their names, in no particular order, are given below.

Brigadier Arun Harolikar, MVC
Colonel Yeshwant Rawat
Major General A.J.S. Sandhu, VSM
Brigadier V.H.M. Prasad, VSM
Air Vice Marshal B.K. Bishnoi, VrC
Lieutenant General J.F.R. Jacob, PVSM
Lieutenant General Satish Nambiar, PVSM, AVSM, VrC
Commander Arun Saigal, IN
Major General Gopal Gurung

Brigadier Kulvender Singh, AVSM
Lieutenant Colonel Quazi Sajjad Ali Zahir, Swadhinata Padak, Bir Protik
Lieutenant Colonel K.S. Puntambekar
Vice Admiral Mihir K. Roy, PVSM, AVSM
Lieutenant General Vijay Oberoi, PVSM, AVSM, VSM
Squadron Leader Rana Chhina, MBE
Commander Vijay Jerath, VrC
Commander Vinayak Agashe
Admiral S.M. Nanda, Padma Vibhushan, PVSM, AVSM, NM
Admiral (Podgy) Kulkarni, PVSM, AVSM, VSM
Colonel Abu Taher, Bir Uttam
Major S. Kipgen, SM
Major J.V. Raju
Air Vice Marshal B.K. Bishnoi, VrC
Brigadier Kuldip S. Chandpuri, MVC
Major General Suresh Gupta, VrC
Lieutenant General Anil Nandal, PVSM, AVSM
Lieutenant Colonel D.B.S. Mian, SM
Lieutenant Colonel Amolak Sharma
Colonel Sheel Puri, VrC, VSM
Manish Bawa
Colonel Sunith Cardozo
Colonel M.M.P. Kala
Lieutenant Colonel B.S. Verma
1/5 Gorkha Rifles (FF)
4/5 Gorkha Rifles (FF)
1 Maratha Light Infantry
Centre for Armed Forces Historical Research
United Service Institution of India

In addition to the names given above, I would like to also acknowledge the special contribution to these stories by the persons as listed below.

Admiral S.M. Nanda, Padma Vibhushan, PVSM, AVSM, for elaborating the facts given in his book *The Man Who Bombed Karachi* during an interview at the Claridges hotel—facts that have embellished the stories 'Mission Karachi' and 'The Hunt for the *Vikrant*'.

Lieutenant General J.F.R. Jacob, PVSM, for additions to the events described in his books *Surrender at Dacca* and *An Odyssey in War and Peace* during frequent interactions at the USI, New Delhi, that have added spice to the stories 'The Hunt for the *Vikrant*', 'The Beginning of the End,' 'The Race for Dhaka' and 'The Last Straw'.

Vice Admiral Mihir K. Roy, for his encouraging support and for facilitating my introduction to those who led the attack on Karachi, and to the experts on submarine and anti-submarine warfare, all of whom contributed to the stories 'The Hunt for the *Vikrant*', 'Mission Karachi' and 'The Sinking of the *Khukri*: A Captain's Dilemma'.

Ameeta Mulla Vattal, for her inputs into the life of her father, Captain Mahendra Nath Mulla, MVC, and the values he believed in and lived by, in the story of the 'The Sinking of the *Khukri*: A Captain's Dilemma.'

Brigadier Kuldip S. Chandpuri, MVC, for elaborating on what happened at Longewala during the Indo–Pak war of 1971 during an interview at Panchkula in 2015; glimpses of his courage and that of his men can be seen in the story 'Long Shot at Longewala'.

Air Marshal M.S. Bawa, PVSM, AVSM, VM, for his 'Occasional Paper No. IV' on 'The Air Battle of Longewala', which gives an account of how the air battle at Longewala was fought and the fabulous outcome that was achieved by the Indian Air Force.

Major General Suresh Gupta, VrC, for interminable discussions on what really happened during the battle of Sejhra during the 1971 Indo–Pak war on the Western Front, as described in the story 'The Gates of Rattoke'. The story highlights that it is not only physical courage that wins battles—moral courage is equally important.

Brigadier Arun Bhimrao Harolikar, MVC, for his written account, interjections and clarifications as Commanding Officer of the 4th Battalion, 5th Gorkha Rifles (FF), and also other officers of the battalion on what really happened at the battles of Atgram, Gazipur and Sylhet during the 1971 war as described in the stories 'The Beeb's Best Broadcast' and 'The Race for Dhaka'.

Air Vice Marshal B.K. Bishnoi, VrC, for the narration of an incident that hastened the surrender of the Pak Army at Dhaka in the story 'The Last Straw'.

The Pakistani book of naval anecdotes, titled *Bubbles of Water*, which I read a long time ago. The book was with the Maritime History Society, Mumbai. It is one of the anecdotes from this book, combined with a corresponding account from *Transition to Triumph: History of the Indian Navy 1965–1975*, that forms the basis of the story 'Touch of Luck'.

Lieutenant General Satish Nambiar, PVSM, AVSM, VrC, for his personal narration of the battle of Jamalpur, which forms the background to the story 'A Bullet for Breakfast'.

Lieutenant Colonel K.S. Puntambekar, whose written account of his experience of the battle of Jamalpur helped in fleshing out 'A Bullet for Breakfast'.

The family of Colonel Abu Taher, whom I had the good fortune to meet at the Dhaka airport, filled me in on the story of this incredible and indomitable officer of the Bangladesh Army, narrated in 'And Then There Was One'.

Maman Kipgen, for her book *A Life in Service: The Biography of Major S. Kipgen, SM* on her husband, Major S. Kipgen, an outstanding officer of the Indian Army who was killed by terrorists in Manipur; they gunned him down in front of his wife and children. His story forms part of 'And Then There Was One'.

Commander Vijay Jerath, VrC, for numerous conversations on the Indian naval attack on Karachi during the 1971 war, and his book *25 Missile Squadron: An Untold Story*, which formed the basis of the story 'Mission Karachi'.

The underwater aspects of warfare, mentioned in 'The Hunt for the *Vikrant*', 'A Touch of Luck', 'Mission Karachi' and 'The Sinking of INS *Khukri*: A Captain's Dilemma', have been gleaned from *Transition to Triumph: The History of the Indian Navy 1965–1971*, and from oral descriptions from submarine Commanders of the Indian Navy about what happens in war under the sea.

The details of 'The Last Straw', which gives the story of the last days of Dhaka before the surrender, have been gleaned from the book *Eagles over Bangladesh* by P.V.S. Jagan Mohan and Samir Chopra; and from *Surrender at Dhaka: Birth of a Nation* and *An Odyssey of War and Peace* by Lieutenant General J.F.R. Jacob. Whereas I had the opportunity to discuss the details with General Jacob, I have never had the good fortune to meet Jagan Mohan and Samir Chopra, whose accounts of the air aspects of the battle of Sylhet and the raid on Governor's House in Dhaka have made my accounts of these events come alive.

I would like to specially thank Major General A.J.S. Sandhu, better known as 'Abdo', for his intervention as a military historian. His comments and suggestions helped greatly to put the stories in the correct historical perspective. And Brigadier Madhav Prasad, who is a close friend, for reading each story and for his encouraging words.

I would most specially like to thank Meghna Girish for taking the trouble to edit each story and for giving me valuable suggestions to make each story 'special'. She owns this book as much as I do.

My grateful thanks to Rachna Bisht Rawat for introducing me to Gurveen Chadha, the commissioning editor at Penguin Random House India. Gurveen shepherded me in the writing of this book, guiding me all along. Thank you, Gurveen. Thanks also to Vineet Gill, my editor, for his meticulous editing of the stories and for his patience.

Most of all, I wish to thank Priscilla, my wife, who in the evening of our lives allowed me to spend long hours researching and writing these stories at the cost of time spent together.

Bibliography

Brigadier Arun Bhimrao Harolikar, MVC, *Manuscript Narrative of the Saga of the 4th Battalion, the 5th Gorkha Rifles (FF) in the 1971 War*, unpublished

The Hamoodur Rehman Commission of Inquiry into the 1971 War, revised edition as declassified by the Government of Pakistan, Vanguard Books, Lahore, Pakistan

Major General D.K. Palit, VrC, *Lightning Campaign*, Palit and Dutt, Delhi, 1972

Lieutenant General J.F.R. Jacob, PVSM, *Surrender at Dacca: Birth of a Nation,* Manohar, New Delhi, 2006

Lieutenant General J.F.R. Jacob, PVSM, *An Odyssey in War and Peace,* Roli Books, New Delhi, 2011

Vice Admiral G.M. Hiranandani, PVSM, AVSM, VM, *Transition to Triumph: History of the Indian Navy 1965–1971*, Naval Headquarters, New Delhi, in association with Lancers Publishers, New Delhi, 1999

Admiral S.M. Nanda, Padma Vibhushan, PVSM, AVSM, *The Man Who Bombed Karachi,* HarperCollins, New Delhi, 2004

Air Marshal P.C. Lal, DFC, Padma Vibhushan, Padma Bhushan, *My Years with the IAF,* Lancer International, New Delhi, 1986

Vice Admiral S.N. Kohli, PVSM, AVSM, *We Dared,* Lancer International, New Delhi, 1989

P.V.S. Jagan Mohan and Samir Chopra, *Eagles over Bangladesh: The Indian Air Force in the 1971 Liberation War,* HarperCollins India, Noida, Uttar Pradesh, 2013

J.N. Dixit, *Liberation and Beyond: Indo–Bangladesh Relations*, Konark Publishers Pvt Ltd, Delhi, 1999

Bubbles of Water, PN Book Club, NES Directorate, NHQ, Islamabad, Pakistan, 2001

Arjun Subramaniam, *India's Wars: A Military History 1947–1971*, HarperCollins, Noida, 2016

Air Marshal M.S. Bawa, PVSM, AVSM, VM, *Air Battle of Longewala,* Occasional Paper No. IV, Armed Forces Historical Research, United Service Institution of India, New Delhi, 2016

Major General Fazal Muqeem Khan, *Pakistan's Crisis in Leadership*, Alpha & Alpha Publishers, New Delhi, 1984

Lieutenant General K.P. Candeth, Padma Bhushan, PVSM, *The Western Front: The Indo–Pakistan War 1971*, Allied Publishers Pvt Ltd, New Delhi, 1984

S. Muthiah, *Born to Dare: The Life of Lt Gen. Inderjit Singh Gill*, Penguin Books India, New Delhi, 2008

Major General Ian Cardozo, AVSM, SM (ed), *The Indian Army: A Brief History*, Centre for Armed Forces Historical Research, USI, New Delhi, 2006

Commander Vijay Jerath, VrC, *25 Missile Boat Squadron: An Untold Story*, Prakash Books India Pvt Ltd, New Delhi, 2013

Major General Sukhwant Singh, *India's Wars Since Independence: The Liberation of Bangladesh*, Vikas Publishing House Pvt Ltd, New Delhi, 1981

Siddiq Salik, *Witness to Surrender: Onlooker's Journal 1969–1971,* Oxford University Press, Karachi, 1977

Brigadier Abdul Rahman Siddiqi, *East Pakistan: The End Game: An Onlooker's Journal*, Oxford University Press, Karachi, 2004

Major General Ian Cardozo, AVSM, SM, *The Sinking of INS Khukri*, Roli Books Pvt Ltd, New Delhi, 2006

Gary J. Bass, *The Blood Telegram,* Random House India, Noida, 2013

Sagat Shaunik (ed), *Untold Battlefield Tales*, Fauji Foundation, Navi Mumbai, 2019

Major General Shaukat Riza, *The Pakistan Army: 1966–71*, Book Club, Lahore, Pakistan, 1990

Sentinels of the Sea: The Pakistan Navy 1947–1997, PN Book Club, Public Relations Directorate, Naval Headquarters, Islamabad, 1997

Major General Ian Cardozo, AVSM, SM, *First Five Gorkha Rifles: An Illustrated History,* the Khukri Connection, New Delhi, 2008

A Life in Service: The Biography of Major S. Kipgen, SM, by his wife Maman, and published by members of his family, Imphal, Manipur, 1998

'Indian Navy's Submarine Arm Turns 50', *Shub Yatra* (the in-flight magazine of Air India), vol. 5, issue 11, December 2017